Microsoft®
Windows

ILLUSTRATED

Introductory

Microsoft®
Windows® 8

ILLUSTRATED Introductory

Steve Johnson

CENGAGE
Learning·

Australia • Brazil • Japan • Korea • Mexico • Singapore • Spain • United Kingdom • United States

Microsoft® Windows® 8—Illustrated Introductory
Steve Johnson

Executive Editor: Marjorie Hunt

Associate Acquisitions Editor: Amanda Lyons

Senior Product Manager: Christina Kling-Garrett

Product Manager: Kim Klasner

Editorial Assistant: Brandelynn Perry

Brand Manager: Elinor Gregory

Developmental Editor: Janice Jutras

Senior Content Project Manager: Cathie DiMassa

Copyeditor: Karen Annett

Proofreader: Harry Johnson

Indexer: Sharon Hilgenberg

QA Manuscript Reviewers: Serge Palladino, Susan
    Pedicini, Danielle Shaw, Jeff Schwartz

Cover Designer: GEX Publishing Services

Cover Artist: GEX Publishing Services

Composition: GEX Publishing Services

For product information and technology assistance, contact us at
Cengage Learning Customer & Sales Support, 1-800-354-9706

For permission to use material from this text or product, submit all requests online at **www.cengage.com/permissions**
Further permissions questions can be emailed to
permissionrequest@cengage.com

Library of Congress Control Number: 2013935450
ISBN-13: 978-1-285-17022-0
ISBN-10: 1-285-17022-9

Cengage Learning
200 First Stamford Place, 4th Floor
Stamford, CT 06902
USA

Cengage Learning is a leading provider of customized learning solutions with office locations around the globe, including Singapore, the United Kingdom, Australia, Mexico, Brazil, and Japan. Locate your local office at:
www.cengage.com/global

Cengage Learning products are represented in Canada by Nelson Education, Ltd.

For your course and learning solutions, visit **www.cengage.com**

Purchase any of our products at your local college store or at our preferred online store **www.cengagebrain.com**

Printed in the United States of America
1 2 3 4 5 6 7 19 18 17 16 15 14 13

Brief Contents

Contents

Preface

Welcome to *Microsoft Windows 8—Illustrated Introductory*. This book has a unique design: Each skill is presented on two facing pages, with steps on the left and screens on the right. The layout makes it easy to learn a skill without having to read a lot of text and flip pages to see an illustration.

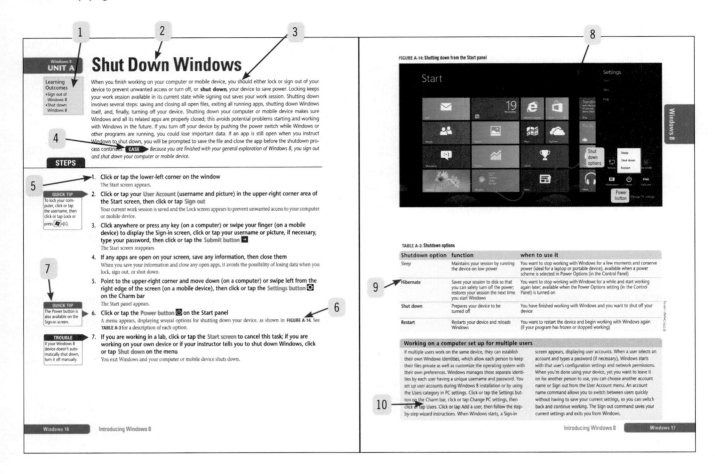

1 New! Learning Outcomes box lists measurable learning goals for which a student is accountable in that lesson.

2 Each two-page lesson focuses on a single skill.

3 Introduction briefly explains why the lesson skill is important.

4 A case scenario motivates the steps and puts learning in context.

5 Step-by-step instructions and brief explanations guide students through each hands-on lesson activity.

6 New! Figure references are now in red bold to help students refer back and forth between the steps and screenshots.

7 Tips and troubleshooting advice, right where you need it—next to the step itself.

8 New! Larger screenshots with green callouts keep students on track as they complete steps.

9 Tables provide summaries of helpful information such as button references or keyboard shortcuts.

10 Clues to Use yellow boxes provide useful information related to the lesson skill.

This book is an ideal learning tool for a wide range of learners—the "rookies" will find the clean design easy to follow and focused with only essential information presented, and the "hotshots" will appreciate being able to move quickly through the lessons to find the information they need without reading a lot of text. The design also makes this a great reference after the course is over! See the illustration on the left to learn more about the pedagogical and design elements of a typical lesson.

What's New in this Edition

- **Coverage** — This book helps students learn how to use Microsoft Windows 8 including step-by-step instructions on navigating the user interface, working with Windows 8 apps, managing files and folders, using security tools, and managing devices.

- **New! Learning Outcomes** — Each lesson displays a green Learning Outcomes box that lists skills-based or knowledge-based learning goals for which students are accountable. Each Learning Outcome maps to a variety of learning activities and assessments. (See the *New! Learning Outcomes* section on page xii for more information.)

- **New! Updated Design** — This edition features many new design improvements to engage students — including larger lesson screenshots with green callouts placed on top, and a refreshed Unit Opener page.

- **New! Independent Challenge 4: Explore** — This new case-based assessment activity allows students to explore new skills and use creativity to solve a problem or create a project.

Assignments

This book includes a wide variety of high quality assignments you can use for practice and assessment. Assignments include:

- **Concepts Review** — Multiple choice, matching, and screen identification questions.
- **Skills Review** — Step-by-step, hands-on review of every skill covered in the unit.
- **Independent Challenges 1-3** — Case projects requiring critical thinking and application of the unit skills. The Independent Challenges increase in difficulty. The first one in each unit provides the most hand-holding; the subsequent ones provide less guidance and require more critical thinking and independent problem solving.
- **Independent Challenge 4: Explore** — Case projects that let students explore new skills that are related to the core skills covered in the unit and are often more open ended, allowing students to use creativity to complete the assignment.
- **Visual Workshop** — Critical thinking exercises that require students to create a project by looking at a completed solution; they must apply the skills they've learned in the unit and use critical thinking skills to create the project from scratch.

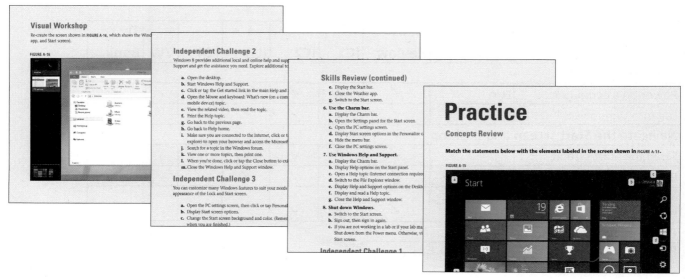

New! Learning Outcomes

Every 2-page lesson in this book now contains a green **Learning Outcomes box** that states the learning goals for that lesson.

- **What is a learning outcome?** A learning outcome states what a student is expected to know or be able to do after completing a lesson. Each learning outcome is skills-based or knowledge-based and is *measurable*. Learning outcomes map to learning activities and assessments.

- **How do students benefit from learning outcomes?** Learning outcomes tell students exactly what skills and knowledge they are *accountable* for learning in that lesson. This helps students study more efficiently and effectively and makes them more active learners.

- **How do instructors benefit from learning outcomes?** Learning outcomes provide clear, measurable, skills-based learning goals that map to various high-quality learning activities and assessments. A **Learning Outcomes Map**, available for each unit in this book, maps every learning outcome to the learning activities and assessments shown below.

Learning Outcomes Map to These Learning Activities:

Book lessons: Step-by-step tutorial on one skill presented in a two-page learning format.

Learning Outcomes Map to These Assessments:

1. **End-of-Unit Exercises: Concepts Review** (screen identification, matching, multiple choice); **Skills Review** (hands-on review of each lesson); **Independent Challenges** (hands-on, case-based review of specific skills); **Visual Workshop** (activity that requires student to build a project by looking at a picture of the final solution).
2. **Exam View Test Banks:** Objective-based questions you can use for online or paper testing.

Learning Outcomes Map

A **Learning Outcomes Map**, contained in the Instructor Resources, provides a listing of learning activities and assessments for each learning outcome in the book.

Learning Outcomes Grid

> **KEY:**
>
> **IC**=Independent Challenge
>
> **VW**=Visual Workshop

	Concepts Review	Skills Review	IC1	IC2	IC3	IC4	VW	Test Bank
Start Windows 8								
Power on a computer	N/A	✓	✓	✓	✓	✓	✓	✓
Log into Windows 8	N/A	✓	✓	✓	✓	✓	✓	✓
Navigate the Start screen and desktop								
Scroll the Start screen		✓	✓	✓		✓		✓
Display the Charms bar		✓	✓	✓	✓	✓	✓	✓
Switch between Start screen and desktop		✓	✓	✓		✓		✓
Point, click and drag								
Point to, select								

Instructor Resources

This book comes with a wide array of high-quality technology-based, teaching tools to help you teach and to help students learn. The following teaching tools are available for download at our Instructor Companion Site. Simply search for this text at *login.cengage.com*. An instructor login is required.

- **New! Learning Outcomes Map** — A detailed grid for each unit (in Excel format) shows the learning activities and assessments that map to each learning outcome in that unit.

- **Instructor's Manual** — Available as an electronic file, the Instructor's Manual includes lecture notes with teaching tips for each unit.

- **Sample Syllabus** — Prepare and customize your course easily using this sample course outline.

- **PowerPoint Presentations** — Each unit has a corresponding PowerPoint presentation covering the skills and topics in that unit that you can use in lectures, distribute to your students, or customize to suit your course.

- **Figure Files** — The figures in the text are provided on the Instructor Resources site to help you illustrate key topics or concepts. You can use these to create your own slide shows or learning tools.

- **Solution Files** — Solution Files are files that contain the finished project that students create or modify in the lessons or end-of-unit material.

- **Solutions Document** — This document outlines the solutions for the end-of-unit Concepts Review, Skills Review, Independent Challenges and Visual Workshops. An Annotated Solution File and Grading Rubric accompany each file and can be used together for efficient grading.

- **ExamView Test Banks** — ExamView is a powerful testing software package that allows you to create and administer printed, computer (LAN-based), and Internet exams. Our ExamView test banks include questions that correspond to the skills and concepts covered in this text, enabling students to generate detailed study guides that include page references for further review. The computer-based and Internet testing components allow students to take exams at their computers, and also save you time by grading each exam automatically.

Key Facts About Using This Book

Data Files are needed: To complete many of the lessons and end-of-unit assignments, students need to start from partially completed Data Files, which help students learn more efficiently. By starting out with a Data File, students can focus on performing specific tasks without having to create a file from scratch. All Data Files are available as part of the Instructor Resources. Students can also download Data Files themselves for free at cengagebrain.com. (For detailed instructions, go to www.cengage.com/ct/studentdownload.)

System requirements: This book was developed using Microsoft Windows 8.

Screen resolution: This book was written and tested on computers with monitors set at a resolution of 1366 x 768. If your screen shows more or less information than the figures in this book, your monitor is probably set at a higher or lower resolution. If you don't see something on your screen, you might have to scroll down or up to see the object identified in the figure.

Tell Us What You Think!

We want to hear from you! Please email your questions, comments, and suggestions to the Illustrated Series team at: **illustratedseries@cengage.com**

Acknowledgements

Author Acknowledgements

The task of creating any book requires the talents of many hard-working people pulling together to meet impossible deadlines and untold stress. I would like to thank the entire team responsible for making this book possible. I would like to especially thank Janice Jutras for making this book easier to read, understand, and follow. I would also like to thank the manuscript reviewers for their helpful feedback during the writing process, and the product manager, Christina Kling-Garrett, for keeping this project on track. And, most importantly, I would like to thank my wife Holly, and three children, JP, Brett, and Hannah, for their support and encouragement during the project.

–Steve Johnson

COURSECASTS Learning on the Go. Always Available...Always Relevant.

Our fast-paced world is driven by technology. You know because you are an active participant—always on the go, always keeping up with technological trends, and always learning new ways to embrace technology to power your life. Let CourseCasts, hosted by Ken Baldauf of Florida State University, be your guide into weekly updates in this ever-changing space. These timely, relevant podcasts are produced weekly and are available for download at http://coursecasts.course.com or directly from iTunes (search by CourseCasts). CourseCasts are a perfect solution to getting students (and even instructors) to learn on the go!

Other Illustrated Titles

Microsoft® Office 2013 -
Illustrated Fundamentals
**Marjorie Hunt/Barbara Clemens
(9781285418292)**

Microsoft® Access® 2013 -
Illustrated Complete
Lisa Friedrichsen (9781285093277)

Microsoft® Office 2013 -
Illustrated Introductory, First
Course
**Beskeen/Cram/Duffy/
Friedrichsen/Reding
(9781285088457)**

Microsoft® Excel® 2013 -
Illustrated Complete
**Elizabeth Eisner Reding/Lynn
Wermers (9781285093192)**

Microsoft® Office 2013 -
Illustrated Second Course
**Beskeen/Cram/Duffy/
Friedrichsen/Wermers
(9781285082257)**

Microsoft® PowerPoint® 2013 -
Illustrated Introductory
**David W. Beskeen
(9781285082592)**

Microsoft® Office 2013 -
Illustrated Third Course
**Cram/Friedrichsen/Wermers
(9781285082462)**

Microsoft® Word 2013 -
Illustrated Complete
**Jennifer Duffy/Carol Cram
(9781285093116)**

Introducing Windows 8

CASE You just purchased a new computer or mobile device with Windows 8 running on it. You want to explore the capabilities of Windows 8 and learn how to use it to work with your applications and files.

Unit Objectives

After completing this unit, you will be able to:

- Start Windows
- Use Windows on devices
- Use the Start screen
- Use the desktop

- Use the Start bar
- Use the Charm bar
- Use Windows Help and Support
- Shut down Windows

Files You Will Need

No files needed.

©Itana/Shutterstock

Start Windows

Learning
Outcomes
• Power on a
  Windows device
• Close the lock
  screen
• Sign-in to
  Windows 8

Microsoft Windows 8 is an **operating system**, software that controls the operation of your computer or mobile device and the applications you run on it. **Applications** ("**apps**" for short), also known as **programs**, help you accomplish specific tasks, such as sending and receiving electronic mail, browsing the Internet, and managing files. When you first start Windows 8, you see a **Lock screen**, a full screen image with the time, date, and notification icons (with app status), or the **Sign-in screen**, a secure way to identify yourself on your device. With a simple drag of a mouse or movement of your finger, you can dismiss the Lock screen to display the Sign-in screen. After you sign in, you see the **Start screen**, as shown in FIGURE A-1. When you work with Windows 8, you will notice **tiles** and **icons**, which are small pictures intended to provide information or meaningful symbols for the items they represent. When you click a mouse or tap a finger on a tile, icon, or thumbnail, a window (thus the name of the operating system) opens on your screen that can contain an app, the contents of a file, or other usable data. A **file** is a collection of information that has a unique name, distinguishing it from other files. This use of tiles, icons, thumbnails, and windows is called a **graphical user interface** (**GUI**, pronounced "gooey"), meaning that you interact ("interface") with your device through the use of graphics. **CASE** ▶ *Windows 8 automatically starts when you turn on your computer or mobile device. If your device is not on, you turn it on now.*

STEPS

1. **Turn on your computer or mobile device and wait for Windows to start**

   Windows automatically starts and displays a Lock screen, the Sign-in screen, or the Start screen. If the Lock screen appears, continue to Step 2; if the Sign-in screen appears, continue to Step 3; if the Start screen appears, skip to the next lesson, "Using Windows on Different Devices."

2. **If a Lock screen appears, click anywhere on the Lock screen or press any key (on a computer) or move your finger sideways from the edge (on a mobile device)**

   The Sign-in screen opens in your window. This is where you select your username or picture and enter a password to identify yourself on your computer or mobile device. A password prevents other users from accessing your device without proper authorization. You enter the default password, which is text-based, in the Password box. You can also create a picture-based password where you specify a sequence of gestures on a picture or a PIN (Personal Identification Number)-based password. You enter a four-digit code to use this type of password, as if you were using a bank ATM. If multiple password options are available, Sign-in options will appear under the Password box, where you can switch between the different password methods. If you share your device with other users, multiple usernames will appear at the Sign-in screen.

3. **On the Sign-in screen, click or tap your username or picture, if necessary, then type your password**

   Windows passwords are **case sensitive**, which means that Windows makes a distinction between upper- and lowercase letters and nonalphabetic characters (numbers and symbols). Notice that bullets appear as you type your password, rather than letters or numbers. This prevents other people from seeing your password as you type. If you sign in with a Microsoft account, such as hotmail.com or live.com, your device is connected to the cloud, which allows you to share information with others.

4. **On the Sign-in screen, click or tap the** Submit button →

   The Windows 8 Start screen appears on your device, as shown in FIGURE A-1.

FIGURE A-1: Windows 8 Start screen

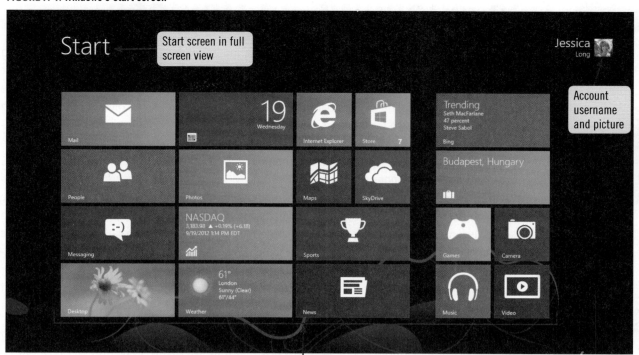

Start screen in full screen view

Account username and picture

App tiles; your tiles may differ

Using and changing a password

You can set up your computer or mobile device to require users to sign in with a username and password. You specify a username and password when you install Windows 8, or an instructor or technical support person assigns you a username and password on a device owned by the school or business. If you own your own device and you want to change your password, or if you don't have one and want to set one up, point to the upper- or lower-right corner (on a computer) or swipe left from the right side of the screen (on a mobile device) to show the Charm bar, click or tap Settings, click or tap Change PC settings, and then click or tap Users. To change your password, click or tap Change your password, enter your old password, enter a new password twice, click or tap Next, and then click or tap Finish. In addition to the default text-based password, you can also create a picture password and a four-digit PIN code. To create a picture password,

click or tap Create a picture password, type your password, click or tap OK, click or tap Choose picture to select an image file, click or tap Use this picture, draw a combination of three circles, straight lines, and taps on the picture, repeat them again to confirm, then click or tap Finish. The size, position, and direction of your gestures become the picture password. To create a PIN, click or tap Create a PIN, type your password, click or tap OK, enter your PIN twice, then click or tap Finish. After you create a picture or PIN password, you can change or remove it. To close the Change PC settings window, point to the top of the screen (cursor changes to a hand), then drag or swipe down to the bottom of the screen. Never write down your password or let someone look over your shoulder as you sign in to your device. Always be sure to sign out or shut down if you are going to leave your device unattended or if you are finished.

Use Windows on Devices

Learning Outcomes
• Point to an item
• Select and dese-
  lect an item
• Scroll through
  content

The user interface for Windows 8 is designed to work on computer desktops and mobile devices, including smartphones and tablets. You can control Windows by using a pointing device or gestures with your finger. A **pointing device** is hardware connected to or built in to the computer you use to position the **pointer**, the small symbol on the screen that indicates the pointer's position. The most common pointing devices are a **mouse**, as shown in **FIGURE A-2**, for desktop computers and a **touch pad** for laptop or note-book computers. When you move the mouse across a flat surface (such as a desk or a mouse pad), or place your finger on the touch pad and drag it across, the pointer on the screen moves in the same direction. The shape of the pointer changes to indicate different activities. **TABLE A-1** shows some common mouse pointer shapes. Once you move the pointer to a desired position on the screen, you use the buttons on the mouse or touch pad to access the computer's functions and to "tell" your computer what you want it to do. For a mobile device or computer touch screen, all you need is your finger to make gestures. A **gesture** is the movement of one or more fingers on a touch screen. For example, dragging your finger with a flick-ing motion at the end of the movement is called **swiping**. **FIGURE A-3** shows commonly used gestures for a mobile device. **CASE** ▶ *You practice using the mouse (or another pointing device) or gestures on the Start screen to become familiar with these navigational skills.*

STEPS

1. **If you are using a mobile device, skip to Step 3. If you are using a computer, place your hand on the mouse, locate the pointer ⬚ on the Start screen, then move the mouse**
   As you move the mouse, the mouse pointer moves correspondingly.

2. **Move the mouse to position the pointer over the Desktop tile on the Start screen**
   Positioning the mouse pointer over an item on the screen is called **pointing**. When you point to an item, Windows often displays a **ScreenTip**, identifying the item or displaying status information.

3. **Locate the Weather tile on the Start screen, point to it, then press and release the left mouse button (on a computer) or touch and remove your finger (on a mobile device)**
   The Weather app opens in full screen view. The act of pressing a mouse button once and releasing it is called **clicking**, also known as single-clicking, and the act of touching and removing your finger is called **tapping**. The act of clicking or tapping an item, such as a tile or icon, indicates that you have selected it. To perform an operation on a tile or icon, such as opening or moving it, you must first select it. In some instances, such as working with the desktop, you need to click the mouse button twice in a row, known as **double-clicking** or tap twice, known as **double-tapping**, to open a window, program, or file.

4. **With your pointer on the screen, click the right mouse button (on a computer) or point your finger to the top or bottom edge of the screen, then swipe down or up (on a mobile device)**
   The App bar appears, as shown in **FIGURE A-4**. Clicking the right mouse button is known as right-clicking. **Right-clicking** an item displays a menu. When a step tells you to "click," it means to click the left mouse button. If you are supposed to click the right mouse button, the step will instruct you to "right-click." If you press and hold/flick your finger on a mobile device, it does the same thing as right-clicking an item.

5. **Click or tap anywhere outside the App bar to cancel the operation**

6. **Move the mouse (on a computer) to show the scroll bar, point to the white scroll box, press and hold down the left mouse button, move to the right, release the mouse button or touch the left side of the screen (on a mobile device), then swipe your finger to the right**
   The screen scrolls to the right. **Scroll bars** allow you to display more window content by dragging or swiping left or right or up and down. Holding down the left mouse or your finger and moving is known as **dragging**.

7. **Scroll back to the left to display the initial Weather screen**

FIGURE A-2: Typical mouse features

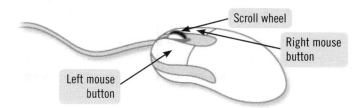

Scroll wheel

Right mouse button

Left mouse button

FIGURE A-3: Typical gestures

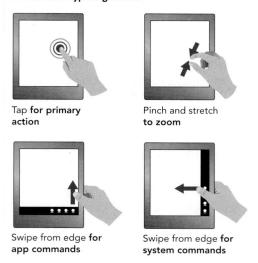

Tap **for primary action**

Pinch and stretch **to zoom**

Swipe from edge **for app commands**

Swipe from edge **for system commands**

FIGURE A-4: App bar

Home Places World weather

Weather app in full screen view

App bar for the Weather app

59°
Clear
Feels Like 61°

WED 19
61°/44°
Partly Cloudy

THU 20
63°/49°
Partly Cloudy

FRI 21
61°/41°
Showers/Clear

SAT 22
63°/51°
Partly Cloudy

SUN 23
64°/50°
Partly Cloudy

Change to Celsius

Refresh

TABLE A-1: Common mouse pointer shapes

shape	used to
▷	Select items, choose commands, start programs, and work with programs
I	Position the mouse pointer for editing or inserting text; called the insertion point or cursor
○	Indicate Windows is busy processing a command
↘, ↗, ↔, ↕	Position the mouse pointer on the edge of a window to change its size
◦	Position the mouse pointer to select and open mobile and Web-based content

Use the Start Screen

Learning Outcomes
- Display the Start screen
- Switch between screens
- Zoom in and out of the Start screen

The key to getting started with Windows 8 is learning how to use the **Start screen**. The Start screen provides a central place to access apps, utilities, and device settings. When you start Windows 8 and sign in, the Start screen appears, displaying app tiles in groups with information. Tiles allow you to view status information for the specific app or open the app to work with it. Windows 8 comes with an array of standard apps, such as Messaging, Mail, People, Music, Calendar, Weather, Photos, and Games, and you can download more from the Windows Store app. The key to using the Start screen is to understand how to use corners and edges. Pointing to a corner on a computer or swiping an edge on a mobile device displays a bar, icon, button, or thumbnail that you can use to perform operations. When you point to the upper- or lower-right corner or swipe in from the right edge, the **Charm bar** appears, displaying Search, Share, Start, Devices, and Settings options. When the Charm bar is visible, Windows also displays the date, time, and system or app notification icons on the left-side of the screen. When you move the pointer on the Start screen, the **Zoom button** appears that allows you to change the screen size to display items smaller or larger for better viewing. When you point to the upper- or lower-left corner or swipe in from the left edge, the **Start bar** appears. The Start bar, which contains thumbnails of currently opened apps, allows you to switch between open apps or the Start screen. You learn more about using the Start bar later in this unit. **TABLE A-2** lists the Start Screen features that are installed with Windows 8, and describes how to access them using either a computer or mobile device. **CASE** ▷ *To become familiar with the Start screen, you view it, display Start screen options, then practice moving around the screen.*

STEPS

1. **Point to the upper-right corner and move down (on a computer) or swipe left from the right edge of the screen (on a mobile device)**
   The Charm bar appears, as shown in **FIGURE A-5**, displaying Search, Share, Start, Devices, and Settings options along the right edge of the screen and the date, time, and system or app notification icons near the left corner.

2. **Click or tap the Start button 🪟 on the Charm bar**
   The Start screen appears in full screen view. The Weather app is still open behind the Start screen, and remains open until you close it. This allows you to quickly switch between open apps.

3. **Point to the lower-left corner (on a computer) or swipe right from the left edge of the screen (on a mobile device)**
   A thumbnail of the Weather app displays in the lower-left corner of the Start bar on the Start screen, as shown in **FIGURE A-6**.

4. **Click or tap the Weather app thumbnail**
   The Weather app appears. Clicking the lower-left corner of the screen or swiping right from the left edge switches between the Start screen and the most recently used app.

5. **Point to the lower-left corner (on a computer) or swipe right from the left edge of the screen (on a mobile device) to display a thumbnail of the Start screen, then click or tap the Start screen thumbnail**
   The Start screen reappears.

6. **Move the pointer to display the Zoom button, then click the Zoom button ➖ or pinch in (on a mobile device)**
   The Start screen zooms out to display more items on the screen but in a smaller size.

7. **Click a blank area of the Start screen (on a computer) or pinch out (on a mobile device)**
   The Start screen zooms in to display less on the screen but in a larger size.

FIGURE A-5: Charm bar

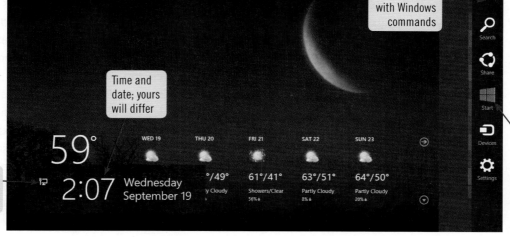

Charm bar with Windows commands

Time and date; yours will differ

Notification icons; yours might differ

Start button on the Charm bar

FIGURE A-6: Start bar on the Start screen

Start screen

Weather app thumbnail

TABLE A-2: Start screen features

feature	description	computer access	mobile device access
Tile	Displays program-specific information or opens the program	Click to open the program	Tap to open the program
User Account	Identifies the current user and opens a menu, where you can change account picture, lock, or sign out	Click to display a menu with options	Tap to display a menu with options
Charm bar	Provides options to search for programs and information, share information with others, switch to the Start screen, work with devices, or change device settings	Point to the upper- or lower-right corner	Swipe in from the right edge
Zoom	Changes the screen view size to display items smaller or larger for better viewing	Point to the lower-right corner, then click the Zoom button	Pinch gesture in or out; touch two fingers, then move toward or away from each other
Start bar	Switches to an open app or the Start screen	Point to the upper- or lower-left corner, move up or down to display the Start bar, then click a thumbnail	Swipe in from the left edge, then tap a thumbnail

Use the Desktop

Learning Outcomes
• Display the desktop
• Open the File Explorer window
• Resize a desktop window

In Windows 8, the desktop works more like an app that you start and close, yet it functions the same as previous versions with one main exception: It doesn't include the Start button (now replaced by the Start screen). The **desktop** is a graphical background on screen that represents a desk. It contains windows, icons, files, and apps, which you can use to access, store, organize, modify, and share information. The icon in the upper-left corner of the desktop is called the **Recycle bin**, which stores files until you empty, or delete, them. The horizontal bar at the bottom of the desktop is called the **taskbar**; it allows you to start apps and switch among currently running apps. At the left end of the taskbar are **pinned items**, which you can use to quickly start desktop apps or files; Windows 8 includes the Internet Explorer or File Explorer apps by default. At the right end of the taskbar is the **notification area** (also known as the system tray), which displays the app-related icons, network, volume, time and date, and the Show desktop button (the blank button next to the time and date. You can view the desktop by starting File Explorer from the Start screen. File Explorer allows you to navigate to different locations on your system and manage files. **CASE** *You view the desktop, start File Explorer, and open and switch between windows.*

STEPS

QUICK TIP
To display the desktop, press the Windows key [⊞]+[D]; to temporarily view the desktop, press the Windows key [⊞]+[,] (comma).

1. **With the Start screen still in view, click or tap the Desktop tile**
   The Desktop screen opens, displaying the Recycle bin and the taskbar.

2. **Click or tap the File Explorer button 📁 on the taskbar**
   The File Explorer window opens, as shown in **FIGURE A-7**. The File Explorer window is **active**, which means that any actions you perform take place in this window. The taskbar button for the active window (in this case, the File Explorer button) is highlighted. By default, the pinned items on the taskbar include Internet Explorer and File Explorer. Pinned items remain on the taskbar until you remove them.

QUICK TIP
In the desktop, you can also click or tap Settings on the Charm bar to open the Control Panel.

3. **In the File Explorer window, click or tap Computer in the Navigation pane**
   The File Explorer window includes a customizable Quick Access toolbar, a **Ribbon** with a set of tabs along the top that provide access to commands, an **Address bar** below the Ribbon to navigate and search for files, and a **Navigation pane** to display folder and disk locations. The hard drives, devices with removable storage, and any network locations appear in the view.

4. **Click or tap the Open Control Panel button 🖥 on the Computer tab**
   The Control Panel window opens, displaying settings that specify how your system looks and performs.

5. **Click or tap the Back button ⊖ on the Address bar**
   The File Explorer window reappears. Each window is surrounded by a border that you can drag to resize or move the window and has three buttons that enable you to control the size of the window or to close it.

QUICK TIP
To switch between maximizing and restoring the size of a window, double-click or double-tap the bar at the top of a window.

6. **Click or tap the Maximize button ☐ in the upper-right corner of the window, then click or tap the Restore Down button ❐ in the upper-right corner of the window**
   When you **maximize** a window, it fills the entire screen. When a window is maximized, the Maximize button is replaced by the Restore Down button. The **Restore Down button** returns a window to its previous size, and appears only when a window is maximized.

7. **Click or tap the Minimize button ➖ in the upper-right corner of the window**
   The File Explorer window no longer appears on the desktop. When you **minimize** a window, you do not close it but merely reduce it to a button on the taskbar so that you can work more easily in other windows.

QUICK TIP
To close an open window, click or tap the Close button [✕].

8. **Point to the File Explorer button 📁 on the taskbar, then point to the thumbnail**
   When you point to a minimized button on the taskbar, the desktop displays a live thumbnail. When you point to the live thumbnail, the window temporarily appears on the desktop.

9. **Click or tap the File Explorer thumbnail to display the File Explorer window**

FIGURE A-7: Desktop and File Explorer windows

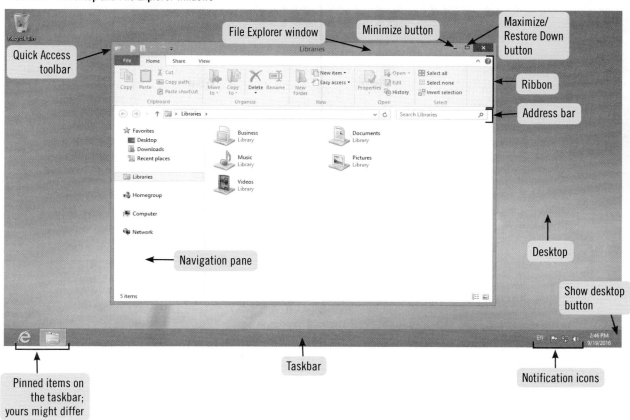

Working with the taskbar

The taskbar allows you to start apps and switch among currently running programs and open windows. When you start a program or open a window from the desktop, a corresponding button appears on the taskbar. If the taskbar becomes too crowded with buttons for open windows, then buttons associated with the same program automatically group together into a single button to conserve space. The taskbar allows you to pin programs or files to it for easy one-click access. To pin a program to the taskbar, right-click or tap-hold a program icon, then click or tap Pin this program to taskbar. To unpin a program from the taskbar, right-click or tap-hold a program icon on the taskbar, then click or tap UnPin this program from taskbar. After you pin a program to the taskbar or open a program, you can display a jump list of recently opened files for the program by right-clicking or tap-holding the taskbar button. The taskbar also provides you with several options for arranging open windows. If you want to show all open windows stacked side by side or overlapped (known as

cascading), you can right-click or tap-hold the taskbar, then click or tap the option you want. If you prefer using a mouse, you can drag a window to the side of the screen (where the mouse touches the edge) to resize it for side-by-side comparison. The taskbar is locked by default so it cannot be accidentally resized or moved. To unlock the taskbar, right-click or tap-hold a blank area on the taskbar, then click or tap Lock the taskbar on the shortcut menu to deselect the option. You can move the taskbar by dragging it to any edge (right, left, top, or bottom) of the desktop. You can also change the size of the taskbar in the same way you resize a window by dragging its edge. In addition to buttons, you can also show or hide toolbars on the taskbar. Right-click or tap-hold a blank area of the taskbar, point to Toolbars, then select a toolbar. To create a new toolbar with items from a folder, right-click or tap-hold a blank area of the taskbar, point to Toolbars, click or tap New Toolbar, select the folder you want to use, then click or tap Select Folder.

Use the Start Bar

As you learned earlier in this unit, the Start bar allows you to switch between or close currently open apps and the Start screen. When using Windows 8, the Start bar is not visibly noticeable on the screen. You access the Start bar by pointing to the upper- or lower-left corner on a computer or swiping in from the left edge on a mobile device. When you point to the upper- or lower-left corner, a thumbnail appears. If you have more than two apps open and move down from the upper-left corner or up from the lower-left corner, the Start bar appears with thumbnails for all open apps or the Start screen. Instead of pointing to a left corner, you can also click (on a computer) or swipe right from the left edge (on a mobile device) to quickly navigate between apps. When you click the lower-left corner on a computer, Windows switches between the most recently used app and the Start screen. When you click the upper-left corner on a computer, Window switches between all open apps. **CASE** ➤ *You use the Start bar to navigate between open apps and the Start screen.*

STEPS

1. **With the File Explorer window still open, point to the lower-left corner**

   A thumbnail for the Start screen appears, as shown in **FIGURE A-8**.

2. **Click or tap the lower-left corner of the screen**

   The Start screen appears.

3. **Point to the upper-left corner of the screen**

   A thumbnail for the desktop with the File Explorer window appears.

4. **Click or tap the upper-left corner of the screen**

   The desktop with the File Explorer window appears.

5. **Click or tap the upper-left corner again, then click or tap one more time**

   The Weather app window appears first, and then the File Explorer window appears. Notice that the Start screen doesn't appear; only open apps appear when using the upper-left corner to switch between apps.

6. **Point to the upper-left corner, then move the mouse down**

   The full-length Start bar appears with thumbnails for each open app or Start screen, except the active one on the screen (in this case, the desktop with the File Explorer window). See **FIGURE A-9**. If less than two apps are open, the full-length Start bar doesn't appear, only the Start screen thumbnail in the lower-left corner or an app thumbnail in the upper-left corner appears. If no apps are open, no thumbnails appear.

7. **Right-click the Weather thumbnail, then click Close (on a computer) or press and drag the Weather thumbnail to the bottom of the screen (on a mobile device)**

   The Weather app closes and the File Explorer window remains active on the screen.

8. **Click or tap the lower-left corner**

   The Start screen reappears.

FIGURE A-8: Desktop and File Explorer windows

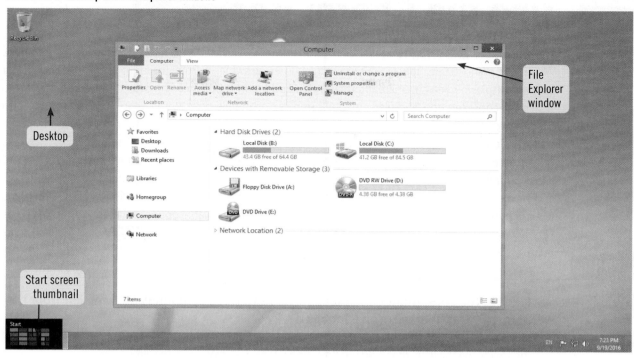

FIGURE A-9: Start bar with thumbnails

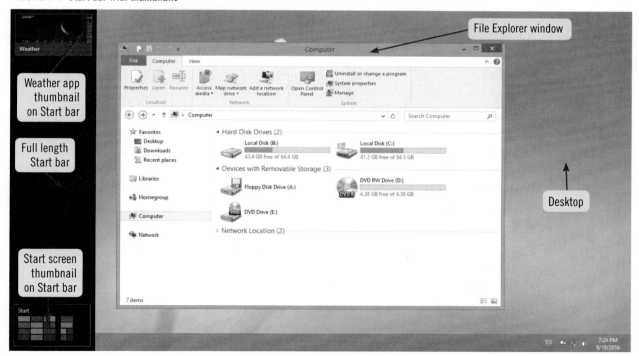

Use the Charm Bar

The Charm bar allows you to access Search, Share, Start, Devices, and Setting options for Windows 8. When you point to the upper- or lower-right corner or swipe in from the right edge, the Charm bar appears, displaying Search, Share, Start, Devices, and Settings buttons. The Search button allows you to search for apps, settings, and files on your computer or mobile device. The Share button allows you to share an app or information between other users on different devices The Start button displays the Start screen. The Devices button allows you to work with and send information or files to devices, such as a printer or television. The Settings button allows you to access Help information and display, set, or personalize computer or mobile device settings, including networks, volume, display, notifications, language, and power, for Windows 8. The Settings button also allows you to set app-specific options. When you select a button on the Charm bar, a panel appears, displaying available options. The options on the panel vary depending on the active window, such as the Start screen or an app. **CASE** *You use the Charm bar to display settings for the Start screen on a computer or mobile device.*

STEPS

1. **Point to the upper-right corner and move down (on a computer) or swipe left from the right edge of the screen (on a mobile device)**

   The Charm bar appears, displaying Search, Share, Start, Devices, and Settings options along the right edge of the screen and the date, time, and system or app notification icons near the left corner.

2. **Click or tap the Settings button ⚙ on the Charm bar**

   The Settings panel appears with options at the top related to the Start screen and options at the bottom related to your Windows 8 computer or mobile device, as shown in **FIGURE A-10**.

3. **Click or tap Tiles on the Start panel**

   The Tiles panel appears, showing Tile specific options at the top. You can drag the slider to show administrative tools on the Start screen or click or tap the Clear button to remove personal information from Start screen tiles.

4. **Click or tap the Back button ⊙ in the Tiles panel**

   The Start panel reappears.

5. **At the bottom of the Start panel, click or tap Change PC settings**

   The PC settings screen opens in full screen view, as shown in **FIGURE A-11**, displaying categories and options to customize your Windows 8 computer or mobile device. When you select a category on the left side of the screen, related options appear on the right. The Personalize category at the top of the list is selected by default; it allows you to set options for the Lock screen, Start screen, or Account picture.

6. **Click or tap Start screen**

   Start screen options appear that allow you to change the Start screen background and color.

7. **Point to the top of the screen (cursor changes to a hand), then drag (on a computer) or swipe (on a mobile device) to the bottom of the screen**

   The PC settings screen closes and the Start screen appears.

FIGURE A-10: Start panel

Start screen specific options

Windows options

Click or tap to access additional PC settings

FIGURE A-11: PC settings screen

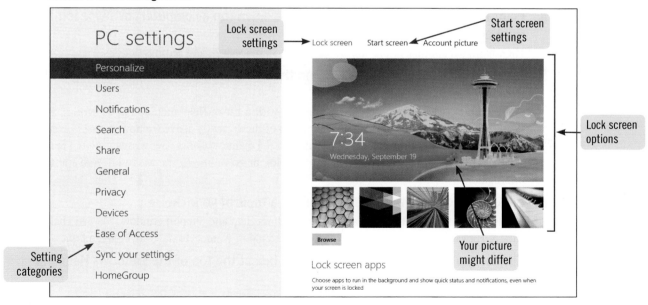

Lock screen settings

Start screen settings

Lock screen options

Your picture might differ

Setting categories

Use Windows Help and Support

If you have a question about how to do something in Windows 8, you can usually find the answer using Windows **Help and Support**. This feature is a complete resource of information, training, and support designed to help you learn and use Windows 8. Help and Support is organized like a book with a table of contents to make finding information easier, with the added benefit of links to the Internet and a search feature. If you have an Internet connection, you can get online help from a support professional at Microsoft or from other users on the Windows **newsgroup** (an electronic forum where people share information), or invite a friend with Windows to chat with you, view your screen, and work on your system to provide remote support. **CASE** ▶ *You access the Help and Support feature to learn more about a Windows 8 topic.*

STEPS

1. **Point to the upper-right corner and move down (on a computer) or swipe left from the right edge of the screen (on a mobile device)**

   The Charm bar appears, displaying Search, Share, Start, Devices, and Settings options.

2. **Click or tap the Settings button ⊖ on the Charm bar, then click or tap Help on the Start panel**

   The Help panel appears, as shown in **FIGURE A-12**, displaying links to online Help topics. When you select a link, your Web browser (in this case, the Internet Explorer app) opens, displaying a Microsoft Web site with related Help information. Instead of accessing the Web for help, you can also get local help from the desktop.

3. **Click the upper-left corner (on a computer) or swipe right from the left edge (on a mobile device)**

   The desktop screen with the File Explorer window appears.

4. **Point to the upper-right corner and move down (on a computer) or swipe left from the right edge of the screen (on a mobile device)**

   The Charm bar appears, displaying Search, Share, Start, Devices, and Settings options.

5. **Click or tap the Settings button ⊖ on the Charm bar, then click or tap Help on the Desktop panel**

   The Windows Help and Support window opens with a list of Help and Support categories, as shown in **FIGURE A-13**. Help windows always appear on top of the currently active window so that you can see Help topics while you work. You can find answers from the main categories (Get started, Internet & networking, or Security, privacy, & accounts), search for topics, or go online to the Microsoft Web site to get more information.

6. **Click or tap Get started, then click or tap a topic of your choice**

   The Help topic information appears in the Windows Help and Support window. You can click or tap the Back or Forward button in the Windows Help and Support window to navigate between topics.

7. **Click or tap Help home under the Search box at the top of the Windows Help and Support window**

   The main Windows Help and Support window reappears.

8. **Click or tap the Close button ❌ in the upper-right corner of the Windows Help and Support window**

   The Windows Help and Support window closes.

FIGURE A-12: Help panel

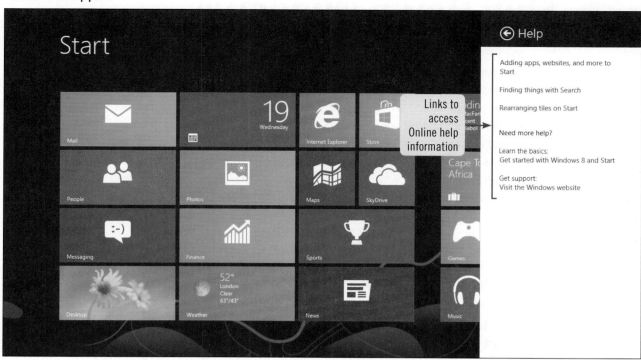

FIGURE A-13: Windows Help and Support window

Shut Down Windows

When you finish working on your computer or mobile device, you should either lock or sign out of your device to prevent unwanted access or turn off, or **shut down**, your device to save power. Locking keeps your work session available in its current state while signing out saves your work session. Shutting down involves several steps: saving and closing all open files, exiting all running apps, shutting down Windows itself, and, finally, turning off your device. Shutting down your computer or mobile device makes sure Windows and all its related apps are properly closed; this avoids potential problems starting and working with Windows in the future. If you turn off your device by pushing the power switch while Windows or other programs are running, you could lose important data. If an app is still open when you instruct Windows to shut down, you will be prompted to save the file and close the app before the shutdown process continues. **CASE** ▸ *Because you are finished with your general exploration of Windows 8, you sign out and shut down your computer or mobile device.*

STEPS

1. **Click or tap the lower-left corner on the window**
   The Start screen appears.

2. **Click or tap your User Account (username and picture) in the upper-right corner area of the Start screen, then click or tap Sign out**
   Your current work session is saved and the Lock screen appears to prevent unwanted access to your computer or mobile device.

3. **Click anywhere or press any key (on a computer) or swipe your finger (on a mobile device) to display the Sign-in screen, click or tap your username or picture, if necessary, type your password, then click or tap the Submit button →**
   The Start screen reappears.

4. **If any apps are open on your screen, save any information, then close them**
   When you save your information and close any open apps, it avoids the possibility of losing data when you lock, sign out, or shut down.

5. **Point to the upper-right corner and move down (on a computer) or swipe left from the right edge of the screen (on a mobile device), then click or tap the Settings button ⚙ on the Charm bar**
   The Start panel appears.

6. **Click or tap the Power button ⏻ on the Start panel**
   A menu appears, displaying several options for shutting down your device, as shown in **FIGURE A-14**. See **TABLE A-3** for a description of each option.

7. **If you are working in a lab, click or tap the Start screen to cancel this task; if you are working on your own device or if your instructor tells you to shut down Windows, click or tap Shut down on the menu**
   You exit Windows and your computer or mobile device shuts down.

FIGURE A-14: Shutting down from the Start panel

TABLE A-3: Shutdown options

Shutdown option	function	when to use it
Sleep	Maintains your session by running the device on low power	You want to stop working with Windows for a few moments and conserve power (ideal for a laptop or portable device); available when a power scheme is selected in Power Options (in the Control Panel)
Hibernate	Saves your session to disk so that you can safety turn off the power; restores your session the next time you start Windows	You want to stop working with Windows for a while and start working again later; available when the Power Options setting (in the Control Panel) is turned on
Shut down	Prepares your device to be turned off	You have finished working with Windows and you want to shut off your device
Restart	Restarts your device and reloads Windows	You want to restart the device and begin working with Windows again (if your program has frozen or stopped working)

© 2014 Cengage Learning

Working on a computer set up for multiple users

If multiple users work on the same device, they can establish their own Windows identities, which allow each person to keep their files private as well as customize the operating system with their own preferences. Windows manages these separate identities by each user having a unique username and password. You set up user accounts during Windows 8 installation or by using the Users category in PC settings. Click or tap the Settings button on the Charm bar, click or tap Change PC settings, then click or tap Users. Click or tap Add a user, then follow the step-by-step wizard instructions. When Windows starts, a Sign-in screen appears, displaying user accounts. When a user selects an account and types a password (if necessary), Windows starts with that user's configuration settings and network permissions. When you're done using your device, yet you want to leave it on for another person to use, you can choose another account name or Sign out from the User Account menu. An account name command allows you to switch between users quickly without having to save your current settings, so you can switch back and continue working. The Sign out command saves your current settings and exits you from Windows.

Practice

Concepts Review

Match the statements below with the elements labeled in the screen shown in FIGURE A-15.

FIGURE A-15

1. Which element enables you to open the desktop?
2. Which element enables you to display the Charm bar?
3. Which element enables you to zoom out the Start screen?
4. Which element enables you to open an app?
5. Which element enables you to switch between the Start screen and the most recent app?
6. Which element enables you to switch between open apps?
7. Which element enables you to switch users?
8. Which element enables you to shut down your device?

Match each term with the statement that describes it.

9. **Start bar**
10. **Start screen**
11. **Charm bar**
12. **Sign-in screen**
13. **File Explorer**
14. **Desktop**

a. The element you use to start an app
b. The element you use to switch between apps
c. The element you use to work with Search, Share, Start, Devices, and Settings options
d. The element you use to identify yourself on your device
e. The element you use to manage files
f. The element you use to work with files and apps

Select the best answers from the following lists of choices.

15. **Which screen displays a full screen image with the time, date, and notification icons?**
    a. Lock
    b. Sign-in
    c. Start
    d. Desktop

16. **Which item is *not* a pointing device?**
    a. Mouse
    b. Gesture
    c. Touch pad
    d. Stylus pen

17. **Which action displays a ScreenTip?**
    a. Dragging
    b. Swiping
    c. Pointing
    d. Clicking

18. **Which type of bar enables you to display the additional contents of a window?**
    a. Start
    b. Charm
    c. Scroll
    d. Commands

19. **The key to using the Start screen lies in understanding the use of:**
    a. Mouse and gestures.
    b. Corners and edges.
    c. The Start bar.
    d. The Charm bar.

20. **Which Start screen corner displays the Zoom button?**
    a. Upper-left
    b. Upper-right
    c. Lower-left
    d. Lower-right

21. **Which screen corner switches to the Start screen?**
    a. Upper-left
    b. Upper-right
    c. Lower-left
    d. Lower-right

22. **Which screen corner switches to open apps?**
    a. Upper-left
    b. Upper-right
    c. Lower-left
    d. Lower-right

23. **Which element is *not* on the taskbar?**
    a. Pinned items
    b. Recycle bin
    c. Notification area
    d. Show desktop button

24. **The Maximize button is used to:**
    a. Scroll slowly through a window.
    b. Reduce a window to a button on the taskbar.
    c. Return a window to its original size.
    d. Expand a window to fill the entire screen.

25. **The Minimize button is used to:**
    a. Scroll slowly through a window.
    b. Reduce a window to a button on the taskbar.
    c. Return a window to its original size.
    d. Expand a window to fill the entire screen.

26. **Which element is *not* on the Charm bar?**
    a. Search
    b. Start
    c. Share
    d. Shut down

27. **Which item allows you to access Windows Help?**
    a. Start bar
    b. Charm bar
    c. Desktop
    d. File Explorer

28. **Which shutdown option is *not* on the Power menu?**
    a. Sleep
    b. Shut down
    c. Lock
    d. Restart

29. Which shutdown option powers off your device and reloads Windows?

    a. Sleep   **c.** Lock

    b. Shut down   **d.** Restart

30. Which item allows you to access shutdown options?

    a. Start screen   **c.** Lock screen

    b. Sign-in screen   **d.** Desktop

Skills Review

1. Start Windows.

    a. Start Windows and sign in, if necessary.

    b. Identify and write down as many Start screen items as you can, without referring to the lesson.

    c. Compare your results with FIGURE A-1.

2. Use Windows on devices.

    a. Move the mouse (on a computer) and watch how the mouse pointer moves across the screen.

    b. Point at a tile (on a computer) on the Start screen.

    c. Click or tap the Weather tile once.

    d. Right-click any part of the screen except a corner (on a computer) or swipe down from the top edge (on a mobile device).

    e. Click or tap anywhere outside the commands to close the App bar.

    f. Drag or swipe to scroll right through the Weather app.

3. Use the Start screen.

    a. Open the Charm bar.

    b. Switch to the Start screen.

    c. Display the Weather app thumbnail.

    d. Switch to the Weather app.

    e. Display the Start screen thumbnail.

    f. Switch to the Start screen.

    g. Zoom out and in.

4. Use the desktop.

    a. Open the desktop.

    b. Display desktop items in the File Explorer window.

    c. Open the Control panel.

    d. Return to the File Explorer window. (*Hint*: Go back.)

    e. Maximize the File Explorer window, then restore it.

    f. Minimize the File Explorer window.

    g. Display the live thumbnail for the File Explorer window.

    h. Open the File Explorer window.

5. Use the Start bar.

    a. Display the Start screen thumbnail.

    b. Switch to the Start screen.

    c. Display the File Explorer window thumbnail.

    d. Switch to the File Explorer window.

Skills Review (continued)

    e. Display the Start bar.

    f. Close the Weather app.

    g. Switch to the Start screen.

6. Use the Charm bar.

    a. Display the Charm bar.

    b. Open the Settings panel for the Start screen.

    c. Open the PC settings screen.

    d. Display Start screen options in the Personalize category.

    e. Hide the menu bar.

    f. Close the PC settings screen.

7. Use Windows Help and Support.

    a. Display the Charm bar.

    b. Display Help options on the Start panel.

    c. Open a Help topic (Internet connection required), then close your browser.

    d. Switch to the File Explorer window.

    e. Display Help and Support options on the Desktop panel.

    f. Display and read a Help topic.

    g. Close the Help and Support window.

8. Shut down Windows.

    a. Switch to the Start screen.

    b. Sign out, then sign in again.

    c. If you are not working in a lab or if your lab manager approves of shutting down the computer, click or tap Shut down from the Power menu. Otherwise, view the Power options and then click or tap a blank area of the Start screen.

Independent Challenge 1

You are a student in a Windows 8 course and want to find out what's new in Windows 8. From the Start screen, use the Help panel to access the latest online information about Windows 8.

    a. Display the Start screen, display the Charm bar, open the Settings panel for the Start screen, then display Help options for the Start screen.

    b. Make sure you are connected to the Internet, click or tap the Get started with Windows 8 and Start link on the Help panel.

    c. Read the Windows 8 Web page to learn more about what's new in Windows 8.

    d. Click or tap links to topics or videos of interest related to Windows 8.

    e. Close your Web browser.

Windows 8

Independent Challenge 2

Windows 8 provides additional local and online help and support. From the desktop, you can open Windows Help and Support and get the assistance you need. Explore additional topics available in Help and Support.

a. Open the desktop.

b. Start Windows Help and Support.

c. Click or tap the Get started link in the main Help and Support window (Help home).

d. Open the Mouse and keyboard: What's new (on a computer) topic or the Touch swipe, tap, and beyond (on a mobile device) topic.

e. View the related video, then read the topic.

f. Print the Help topic.

g. Go back to the previous page.

h. Go back to Help home.

i. Make sure you are connected to the Internet, click or tap the Microsoft Answers Web site link (under More to explore) to open your browser and access the Microsoft Answers Web site.

j. Search for a topic in the Windows forum.

k. View one or more topics, then print one.

l. When you're done, click or tap the Close button to exit your browser.

m. Close the Windows Help and Support window.

Independent Challenge 3

You can customize many Windows features to suit your needs and preferences. One way you do this is to change the appearance of the Lock and Start screen.

a. Open the PC settings screen, then click or tap Personalize, if necessary.

b. Display Start screen options.

c. Change the Start screen background and color. (Remember what you've changed so that you can restore the settings when you are finished.)

d. Display Lock screen options.

e. Change the picture for the Lock screen. Either use one provided or browse for one. (Remember what you've changed so that you can restore the settings when you are finished.)

f. Close the PC settings screen.

g. Display the Start screen and view your background changes.

h. Lock your device to view your screen changes.

i. Sign in to your device.

j. Open the PC settings screen, restore the original settings to your device, then close the screen.

Independent Challenge 4: Explore

Many people move through different time zones as they travel, either on vacation or business. It is usually a good idea to set up your computer to reflect local time. You can do this in the Control Panel window from the desktop.

a. Open the desktop, then open the Control Panel window.

b. Click or tap the Clock, Language, and Region link, then click or tap Change the time zone.

c. On the Date and Time tab in the Date and Time dialog box, click or tap Change time zone.

d. In the Time Zone Settings dialog box, click or tap the Time zone list arrow.

e. Note the current time zone on your computer, then scroll through the list of time zones.

f. Select a time zone for a location you have visited (or would like to visit) from the list (scroll if necessary). Note that a line is added below the Current date and time in the dialog box telling you what the date and time will be after you apply the new time zone setting.

g. Click or tap OK, then note the changed time in the notification area.

h. Restore the original time zone setting, then close the Date and Time dialog box.

i. Close the Control Panel window, then close the desktop.

Visual Workshop

Re-create the screen shown in **FIGURE A-16**, which shows the Windows 8 desktop with the Start bar (PC Settings, Weather app, and Start screen).

FIGURE A-16

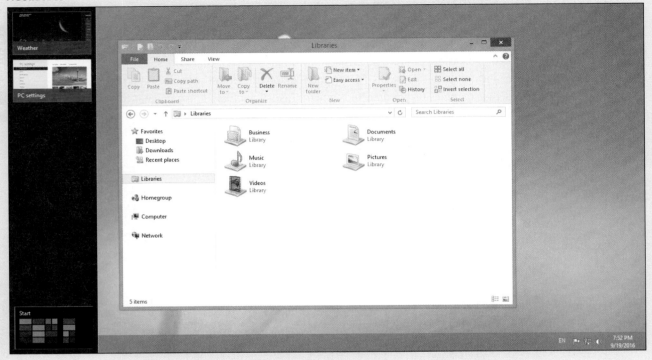

Working with Windows Apps

CASE Now that you are familiar with Windows 8, you want to learn how to use apps, specifically how to install new ones from the online Windows Store, and how to organize them on the Start screen.

Unit Objectives

After completing this unit, you will be able to:

- Display apps
- Search for apps
- Start and close apps
- Work with multiple apps
- Install apps from the Windows Store
- Uninstall apps
- Customize apps on the Start screen
- Group apps on the Start screen

Files You Will Need

No files needed.

Display Apps

Learning Outcomes
• Display all apps on a device
• Display apps by category

When you display the Start screen on Windows 8, you will notice tiles and icons, which you can use to get quick status information for apps or open them in full screen view. An **app** (short for application), also known as a program, is software you use to accomplish specific tasks, such as viewing the Internet with the Internet Explorer app or communicating with others with the Messaging app. The apps available on the Start screen are not all the apps installed on your computer or mobile device. Windows 8 comes with additional built-in Windows Accessories and System tools that, although not as feature rich as many apps sold separately, are extremely useful for completing basic tasks. For those who are familiar with Windows 7, you'll recognize them. They include Paint, WordPad, Windows Media Player, Sticky Notes, Calculator, Character Map, and Command Prompt to name a few. You can display all the available apps on your device by accessing the Apps screen from the Start screen. **CASE** *You display all the apps on your computer or mobile device to see what is available for you to use.*

STEPS

1. **If necessary, start Windows 8, then sign in with your username and password**
   The Start screen appears.

2. **Right-click a blank area of the screen (on a computer) or swipe up from the bottom edge of the screen (on a mobile device)**
   The App bar appears.

3. **Click or tap the All apps button ⊞ on the App bar**
   The Apps screen appears in full screen view, as shown in **FIGURE B-1**, displaying all the available apps and Windows 8 system–related tools installed on your device.

4. **Point to the lower-right corner, then click the Zoom button ▬ (on a computer) or pinch in (on a mobile device)**
   The Apps screen zooms out to display categories with alphabetical and Windows labels, as shown in **FIGURE B-2**. When you have a large number of apps installed on your device, Windows organizes them by categories to make it easier to find the apps you want to use.

5. **Click or tap the Windows Accessories tile on the Apps screen**
   The Apps screen zooms in to display the apps organized under the Windows Accessories category.

6. **Point to the lower-left corner (on a computer) or swipe right from the left edge of the screen (on a mobile device), then click or tap the Start screen thumbnail**
   The Start screen reappears.

FIGURE B-1: Apps screen

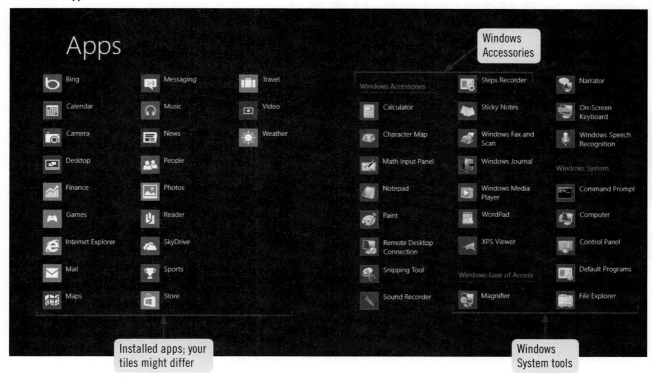

Installed apps; your tiles might differ

Windows Accessories

Windows System tools

FIGURE B-2: Apps screen with categories

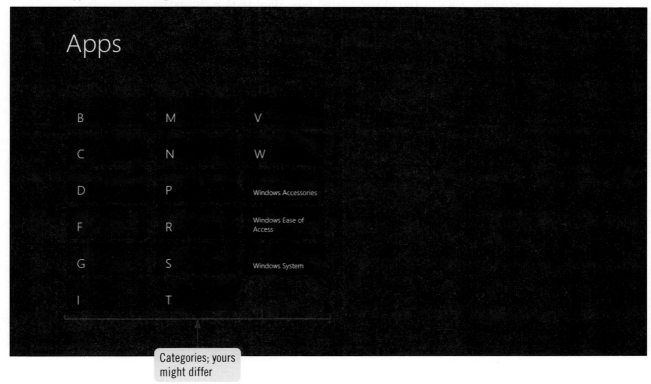

Categories; yours might differ

Search for Apps

The simplest way to look for a specific app is to scroll through the Start screen. However, when you have a lot of apps installed on your device, this method can be too time consuming. A more direct way to search for a specific app is through the Search panel, which you can access from the Charm bar, or simply typing text from the Start screen. The Search panel is a centralized place to search for apps, settings, and files in Windows 8. Its features include a Search box where you can enter the name of the item you want to find; the Apps, Settings, or Files search categories where you can narrow down a search; and a list of apps where you can designate a specific place to perform a search. As you type the search criteria in the Search box, Windows narrows down and displays the search results for the specified category. The Search panel also displays the number of matches found for each category. **CASE** *To become familiar with the search capabilities of Windows 8, you perform a typical search for apps on your computer or mobile device.*

STEPS

1. **Point to the upper-right corner and move down (on a computer) or swipe left from the right edge of the screen (on a mobile device)**

   The Charm bar appears, displaying Search, Share, Start, Devices, and Settings options along the right edge of the screen and the date, time, and system or app notification icons near the left corner.

QUICK TIP

To quickly start a search from the Start screen, you can simply start typing. To open the Search panel, press ⊞+[Q].

2. **Click or tap the Search button 🔍 on the Charm bar**

   The Search panel appears on the right side of the screen with a Search box at the top and categories—Apps, Settings, and Files—below it. The Apps category is selected by default along with the Apps screen, as shown in **FIGURE B-3**. Below the categories is a list of apps you can select to direct the search to take place within the app.

3. **If necessary, click or tap in the Search box, then type windows**

   As you type, Windows narrows down the search results and displays them in the Apps screen, as shown in **FIGURE B-4**. In the Apps screen search results, you can click or tap an app to open it (the first result is selected by default). For each search category, the Search panel also displays the number of matches found in each area, so you can look in different areas if you can't find what you want.

QUICK TIP

To open the Settings Search panel, press ⊞+[W]. To open the Files Search panel, press ⊞+[F].

4. **Click or tap Settings on the Search panel**

   The Settings screen appears, displaying the search results for the specified search criteria "windows".

5. **Click or tap Apps on the Search panel**

   The Apps screen reappears, displaying the search results for the specified search criteria "windows".

6. **Click or tap the Close button ✕ in the Search box**

   The Apps screen reappears. Closing the Apps screen clears the search criteria, which cancels the search and removes the search results.

7. **Point to the lower-left corner (on a computer) or swipe right from the left edge of the screen (on a mobile device), then click or tap the Start screen thumbnail**

   The Start screen reappears.

FIGURE B-3: Search panel

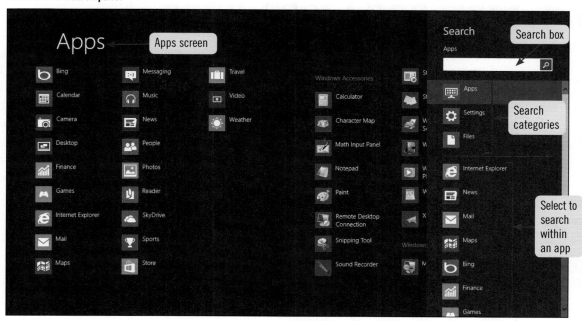

FIGURE B-4: Search panel with results in the Apps screen

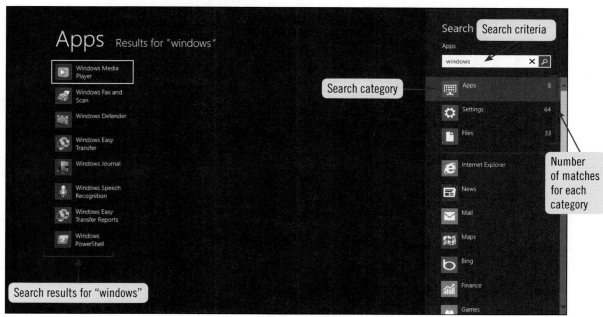

Searching with apps

When you select the Search button on the Charm bar from the Start screen, the Search panel appears, displaying a Search box, search categories, and a list of apps. You can start a search from within Windows for a specific app. For example, you can start a search on the Web using Internet Explorer or look for an e-mail message using Mail. Simply enter the search criteria in the Search box, then click or tap the app name at the bottom of the Search panel. The app opens, performs the search, and displays the results. You can customize the list of apps that appear in the Search panel by changing individual options in PC settings. Open the Charm bar, click or tap Settings, click or tap Change PC Settings, click or tap Search, then drag the slider for each app to turn it on or off. You can also set options that enable Windows to save your searches as future suggestions and show the apps you search most often at the top of the list.

Start and Close Apps

Learning
Outcomes
• Start an app
• Close an app

Starting an app is pretty straightforward in Windows 8. You can start an app from the Start screen, Apps search, or Apps search results with a simple click of a mouse or tap of your finger. When you click or tap an app tile, the app opens in full screen view, where you can start using it. As you work with an app in full screen view, you'll notice it doesn't display a visual way to close it. However, it's as simple as starting an app. You can close an app with a drag from the top edge of the screen to the bottom edge of the screen. Windows 8 is designed to work with multiple apps at the same time, so closing an app is not as typical as with previous versions of Windows unless your device is low on memory. Each time you start an app, it uses device memory, known as **RAM (random access memory)**. When you reach the memory limit for your device, you can't open any more apps unless you close one or more to free up memory space. **CASE** ▸ *To get used to working with full screen apps, you start and close them.*

STEPS

1. **With the Start screen still in view, click or tap the Maps tile, as shown in FIGURE B-5**

   The Maps app opens in full screen view. The Maps app allows you to search for a location or get directions on a map.

2. **Click or tap the lower-left corner**

   The Start screen reappears.

3. **Click or tap the Finance tile on the Start screen**

   The Finance app opens in full screen view. The Finance app provides stock information and financial news from around the world.

4. **Click or tap the lower-left corner**

   The Start screen reappears.

5. **Point to the upper-left corner, then move the mouse down (on a computer) or swipe right from the left edge of the screen, then drag back quickly (on a mobile device)**

   The Start bar appears with thumbnails for each open app.

6. **Right-click the Finance thumbnail, then click Close (on a computer) or press and drag the Finance thumbnail to the bottom edge of the screen (on a mobile device), as shown in FIGURE B-6**

   The Finance app closes and the Start screen appears.

7. **Click or tap the upper-left corner**

   The Maps app screen reappears.

8. **Point to the top edge of the screen (cursor changes to a hand), then drag down to the bottom edge of the screen**

   The Maps app closes and the Start screen appears.

FIGURE B-5: Starting an app

Finance app tile

Maps app tile

Click or tap a tile
to start an app

Windows 8

FIGURE B-6: Closing an app

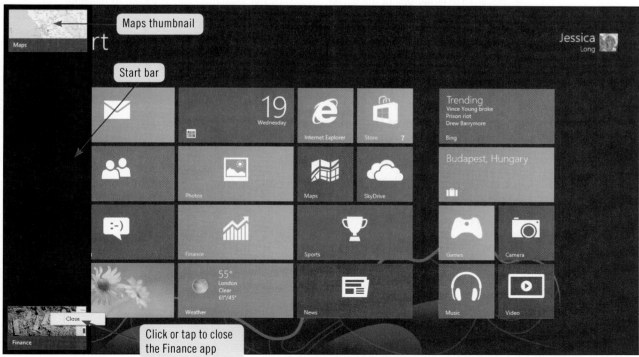

Maps thumbnail

Start bar

Click or tap to close
the Finance app

Working with Windows Apps

Work with Multiple Apps

Learning Outcomes
• Open multiple apps
• Display multiple apps on a split screen

Windows 8 was designed to work with multiple full screen apps at the same time. You can quickly switch between open apps with a click or swipe. However, sometimes you want to display more than one full screen app on the screen at the same time. For example, you might want to open the Bing Internet search engine on one part of the screen while you work with files in the desktop on another part of the screen. The **snap** feature enables you to display two apps side by side by splitting the screen with a divider, known as a **Separation bar**, as you drag one app next to another. When you snap an app to the Separation bar, one app uses one-third of the screen while the other one uses the other two-thirds of the screen. You can adjust the position of the Separation bar to show more or less of an app as you need it. The screen with multiple apps acts like a single app, not separate ones. For example, when you switch apps, only the single screen appears. **CASE** *You want to work with more than one app at the same time, so you open two apps and arrange them in a split screen.*

STEPS

1. **With the Start screen still in view, click or tap the Bing tile**
   The Bing app opens.

2. **Click or tap the lower-left corner**
   The Start screen reappears.

3. **Click or tap the Desktop tile on the Start screen**
   The desktop opens, displaying the taskbar at the bottom of the screen.

4. **Point to the upper-left corner, then drag the Bing thumbnail to the right side of the screen (on a computer) or swipe right slowly from the left edge of the screen (on a mobile device)**
   The apps snap to either side of the screen, divided by the Separation bar, as shown in FIGURE B-7.

5. **Point to the Separation bar (cursor changes to ↔), then drag it slightly to the left**
   The Separation bar moves to the left and then snaps into place, as shown in FIGURE B-8.

6. **Point to the Separation bar, then drag it to the right edge of the screen**
   The Separation bar and the app on the right (in this case, the Bing app) are removed from the split screen and the Desktop screen snaps to fill in the entire screen.

7. **Point to the top edge of the screen (cursor changes to a hand), then drag down to the bottom edge of the screen**
   The Desktop app closes and the Start screen appears.

8. **Click or tap the upper-left corner (on the computer) or swipe right from the left (on a mobile device)**
   The Bing app appears.

9. **Point to the top edge of the screen (cursor changes to a hand), then drag down to the bottom edge of the screen**
   The Bing app closes and the Start screen appears.

FIGURE B-7: Apps displayed in a split screen

Bing app

Desktop

Separation bar

Aerial shot of Whitehaven Beach, Whitsunday Island off Queensland, Australia (© imagebroker.net/Superstock)

FIGURE B-8: Split screen with Separation bar adjusted

Separation bar snapped left of the original location

Resized Desktop

Dragging the Separation bar

Aerial shot of Whitehaven Beach, Whitsunday Island off Queensland, Australia (© imagebroker.net/Superstock)

Install Apps from the Windows Store

Learning Outcomes
• Install an app from the Windows Store
• Display installation information

Windows 8 comes with a default set of apps, such as Internet Explorer, Mail, Messaging, Photos, Video, and Music, developed by Microsoft. However, many more apps, developed by third parties, are available for almost any need. You can purchase and install apps quickly and easily from the Windows Store, which you can access from the Start screen. The Windows Store organizes apps by main categories, such as Spotlight, Games, Social, Entertainment, Photo, Productivity, Tools, and Security, and then further breaks them down into All stars (top rated), Top free, and New releases to make apps easy to find and discover. If you're looking for a specific app, you can use Search on the Charm bar. Developers, including Microsoft, continually update apps to provide additional features. When an update is submitted by a developer, it appears in the Windows Store under App updates, where you can easily install it on your device. The Windows Store uses your Microsoft e-mail (the one used to sign in to Windows 8) as the basis for an account to purchase apps. If you have multiple devices, such as a desktop computer and a mobile tablet or phone, with Windows 8, you can install a purchased app on up to five of them using your Microsoft account. **CASE** ▶ *After purchasing a stand-alone device to read e-books, you decide to use the Windows Store to install the e-book app on Windows 8 to share e-books on both devices.*

STEPS

1. **With the Start screen still in view, click or tap the** Store tile, **then scroll as needed to display the Kindle app tile**

   The Windows Store app opens, as shown in **FIGURE B-9**.

2. **Click or tap the** Kindle tile **(or a tile for another app not installed on your device)**

   The app install screen appears, displaying overview information about the app, as shown in **FIGURE B-10**. You can also select the Details link or Reviews link to display detailed requirements or customer reviews for the app.

3. **Click or tap** Install

   The app install screen closes and the Windows Store screen appears. Windows starts installing the app in the background. Although the app install screen is no longer visible, you can still monitor the progress of this task. In the upper-right corner of the screen, the Windows Store provides a link to get installation status. The link name varies depending on the app name or number of apps installing.

4. **In the upper-right corner of the screen, click or tap** Installing Kindle **(or an app you installed), if available, then click or tap the** Back button ⊖

   The Windows Store screen displays status information as it installs the app. The Windows Store screen reappears.

5. **In the upper-right corner of the screen, click or tap** Updates, **if available, or skip to Step 7**

   The App updates screen appears, displaying the updates available for the apps currently installed on your device. This is where you select (with a check mark) the apps you want to update or deselect (without a check mark) the apps you don't want to update.

6. **Click or tap the** Back button ⊖

   The Windows Store screen reappears.

7. **Point to the top edge of the screen (cursor changes to a hand), then drag down to the bottom edge of the screen**

   The Windows Store app closes and the Start screen appears, displaying the tile for the newly installed app.

FIGURE B-9: Windows Store screen

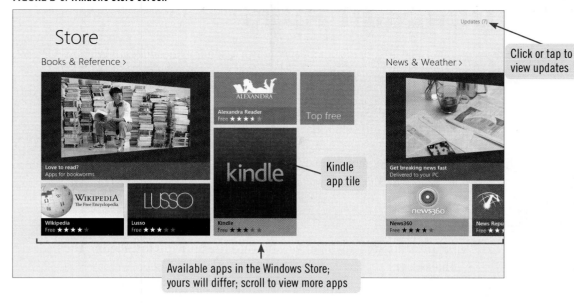

Store

Books & Reference >

News & Weather >

Updates (7)

Click or tap to
view updates

ALEXANDRA

Alexandra Reader
Free ★★★★☆

Top free

Love to read?
Apps for bookworms

kindle

Kindle
app tile

Get breaking news fast
Delivered to your PC

news360

WIKIPEDIA
The Free Encyclopedia

LUSSO

Wikipedia
Free ★★★★☆

Lusso
Free ★★★☆☆

Kindle
Free ★★★☆☆

News360
Free ★★★★☆

News Repu
Free ★★☆

Available apps in the Windows Store;
yours will differ; scroll to view more apps

FIGURE B-10: App install screen in the Windows Store

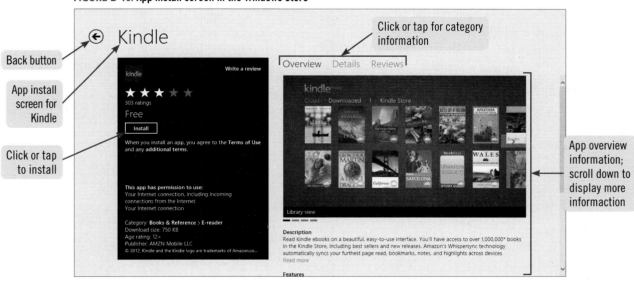

← Kindle

Click or tap for category
information

Back button

App install
screen for
Kindle

Click or tap
to install

kindle

Write a review

★★★☆☆
303 ratings

Free

Install

When you install an app, you agree to the Terms of Use
and any additional terms.

This app has permission to use:
Your Internet connection, including incoming
connections from the Internet
Your Internet connection

Category: Books & Reference > E-reader
Download size: 750 KB
Age rating: 12+
Publisher: AMZN Mobile LLC
© 2012, Kindle and the Kindle logo are trademarks of Amazon.co...

Overview   Details   Reviews

kindle
Cloud   Downloaded | Kindle Store

Library view

Description
Read Kindle ebooks on a beautiful, easy-to-use interface. You'll have access to over 1,000,000* books
in the Kindle Store, including best sellers and new releases. Amazon's Whispersync technology
automatically syncs your furthest page read, bookmarks, notes, and highlights across devices
Read more

Features

App overview
information;
scroll down to
display more
informaction

Updating apps

Developers, including Microsoft, continually update apps to provide additional features. If a new version of an app you have installed is available, Windows automatically generates an update link for you in the Windows Store on the App updates screen. To access the App updates screen, click or tap the Store tile on the Start screen, then click or tap the Updates link in the upper-right corner of the Windows Store screen. If the Updates link is not available, then all of the apps you have installed on your device are up to date with the latest version. The App updates screen automatically displays a list of apps with an available update. You can also manually check for updates; click or tap Settings on the Charm bar, click or tap Account and preferences on the Store panel, then click or tap Check for updates. From the Account and preferences screen, you can also drag a slider to enable or disable the ability to automatically download updates. The updates appear with a check mark in the upper-right corner of the tile by default to indicate you want to install the update. You can click or tap an individual tile to deselect or select the app. You can also use the buttons at the bottom of the screen to clear, select, or view the updates. When you're ready to install the selected updates, click or tap the Install button. The App updates screen closes and the Windows Store screen appears. Windows starts installing the app updates in the background.

Uninstall Apps

Learning
Outcomes
• Uninstall an app

When you install an app, including the ones that come by default with Windows 8, it takes up storage space on your computer or mobile device. If space becomes limited or you just don't use an app anymore, you can uninstall it to free up storage space. You can uninstall one or more apps at the same time from the Start or Apps screen. Simply select the one or more apps you want to uninstall, then use the Uninstall button on the App bar. After an alert message to confirm the uninstall, Windows 8 uninstalls the app. If you want to uninstall Windows Accessories and system tools, you need to turn the Windows features off under Programs within the Control Panel from the desktop, which you'll learn about in a later unit. **CASE** *After installing and using an app, you decide it doesn't meet your needs, so you uninstall it from your device.*

STEPS

1. **With the Start screen still in view, locate the app you installed in the previous lesson**
   See **FIGURE B-11**.

2. **Right-click (on your computer) or tap and hold (on a mobile device) the Kindle tile (or app tile you installed in the previous lesson)**
   The Kindle app, or the app you installed in the previous lesson, is selected on the Start screen with a check mark in the upper-right corner. The Command bar at the bottom of the Start screen displays the options for uninstalling the selected apps.

3. **Click or tap the Uninstall button ⊖ on the App bar**
   An alert message box appears, asking you to confirm the uninstall, as shown in **FIGURE B-12**.

   TROUBLE
   If prompted, follow app-specific instructions to complete the uninstall.

4. **Click or tap Uninstall in the alert message box**
   The app tile is removed from the Start screen and Windows uninstalls the app from your device.

FIGURE B-11: Start screen with installed apps

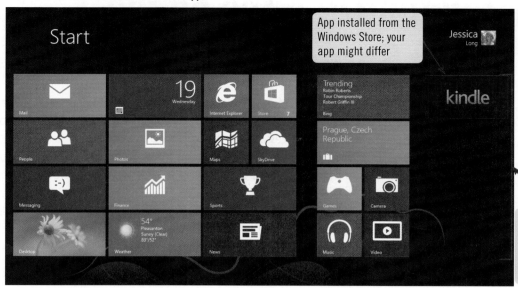

App installed from the Windows Store; your app might differ

Apps installed on the device; yours might differ

FIGURE B-12: App selected for uninstall

Check mark indicates selection

This app and its related info will be removed from this PC.

k Kindle

Uninstall

Click or tap to uninstall the selected apps

App bar for the Start screen

Viewing your apps

If you're not sure what apps you own from the Windows Store, you can display a list of them on the Your apps screen. This doesn't include any Windows 8 apps installed along with the operating system. To open the Your apps screen, click or tap the Store tile from the Start screen, click or tap Settings on the Charm bar, click or tap Account and preferences on the Store panel, then click or tap View your apps. From the list arrow on the Your apps screen, you can display all the apps you own or only the ones installed on the device. From the Your apps screen, you can install or reinstall an app or an app update. You can install a purchased app on up to five different devices using the same Microsoft account. To install an app, click or tap an individual tile to deselect or select the app, then click or tap the Install button. The Your apps screen closes and the Windows Store screen appears. Windows starts installing the apps or app updates.

Customize Apps on the Start Screen

Learning
Outcomes
• Pin apps to the
  Start screen
• Unpin apps from
  the Start screen

The Start screen is the beginning point for accessing apps and features in Windows 8. Customizing the Start screen can save you time and effort by making it easier to find the apps or accessories you use most often. You can add apps or Windows accessories to the Start screen or customize the way the Start screen looks and functions. The Start screen contains pinned items from the Apps screen. Pinned items on the Start screen are shortcuts to make it easier to open an app or accessory. The Start screen comes with a default set of pinned items when you install Windows 8. When you install an app, it's also pinned to the Start screen. The pinned items remain on the Start screen, like a pushpin holds paper on a bulletin board, until you unpin them. When you unpin an item, Windows removes the shortcut from the Start screen; however, it doesn't remove the app or accessory from your system. **CASE** *Because you work often with the Windows Media Player program, you decide to pin it to the Start screen for easy access.*

STEPS

1. **Right-click a blank area of the screen (on a computer) or swipe up from the bottom edge of the screen (on a mobile device), then click or tap the** All apps button **on the App bar**
   The Apps screen appears.

2. **Scroll as needed, then right-click (on your computer) or tap and hold (on a mobile device) the** Windows Media Player tile
   A check mark appears in the upper-right corner of the selected app tile, as shown in **FIGURE B-13**.

3. **Click or tap the** Pin to Start button ⊘ **on the App bar**
   The Apps screen remains and the app is pinned to the Start screen.

4. **Click or tap the lower-left corner**
   The Start screen appears, displaying the Windows Media Player app tile, as shown in **FIGURE B-14**.

5. **Scroll as needed, then right-click (on your computer) or tap and hold (on a mobile device) the** Windows Media Player tile
   A check mark appears in the upper-right corner of the app tile.

6. **Click or tap the** Unpin from Start button ⊗ **on the App bar**
   The Start screen appears; the tile for the Windows Media Player app tile no longer displays.

FIGURE B-13: Pin an app to the Start screen

Click or tap to pin
selected apps

App bar with options
for the selected app

Selected app to pin

FIGURE B-14: Pinned app on the Start screen

Pinned app;
your location
might differ

Changing Start screen settings

In addition to pinning and unpinning apps to the Start screen, you can also change some display options using the Start settings panel. To change Start screen settings, click or tap the Settings button on the Charm bar, click or tap Tiles on the Start panel, then specify the options you want on the Start settings panel. You can drag a slider to enable or disable the Show administrative tools. The Show administrative tools option adds Windows accessories and system tools from the Apps screen to the Start screen. Tiles on the Start screen can display information from the app for easy viewing. Sometimes this information is personal. To maintain privacy, you can click or tap the Clear button on the Start panel.

Group Apps on the Start Screen

Learning
Outcomes
• Create a group of
  app tiles
• Name a group of
  app tiles

When you view the Start screen, you notice the app tiles are arranged in groups. Grouping apps together makes it easier to locate and use them individually. You can arrange app items within an existing group or create a new group simply by repositioning them on the Start screen. When you move app tiles into groups, Windows arranges them by default within the group. Because tile sizes vary—some are smaller squares while others are larger rectangles—they don't always fit seamlessly into place. If you want the tile groups to appear more precisely, you can resize them at any time. After you organize your apps into a group, you can name each group for easy identification. You name a group by zooming out the Start screen, selecting a group, then using the Name group button on the App bar. If the name you originally chose for a group no longer fits, or you want to delete it, you can edit or remove the group name using the same method. **CASE** ▶ *Because you use your device for both work and personal tasks, you decide to group your apps on the Start screen for better organization.*

STEPS

1. **With the Start screen still in view, drag the Mail tile to the right side of the screen**

   As you drag to the right side of the Start screen, a vertical bar appears indicating a new group. The Mail tile appears in a new group, as shown in **FIGURE B-15**. The group that previously contained the Mail tile automatically arranges the tiles to fit in place.

2. **Drag the Messaging tile to the new group**

   The Messaging tile appears in the new group.

3. **Point to the lower-right corner, then click or tap the Zoom button ▬ or pinch in (on a mobile device)**

   The Start screen zooms out to display more items on the screen but in a smaller size so that it is easier to work with groups.

4. **Right-click (on your computer) or tap and hold (on a mobile device) the new group tile**

   A check mark appears in the upper-right corner of the group tile, as shown in **FIGURE B-16**.

5. **Click or tap the Name group button 🖉 on the App bar**

   The Name box appears, requesting a name for the group, as shown in FIGURE B-16. You can also use the Name box to edit or remove a group name.

6. **Type Communication in the Name box, then click or tap Name**

   The group name appears above the newly created group.

7. **Click a blank area of the Start screen (on a computer) or pinch out (on a mobile device)**

   The Start screen zooms in to display less on the screen in a larger size.

8. **Repeat Steps 3 through 7 to remove the group name, then drag the Mail tile and Messaging tile back to their original groups**

   When you remove all the tiles in a group, Windows also deletes the group name. Your Start screen appears as it did before the start of the lesson; it might vary from the one used in this book.

FIGURE B-15: Creating a new group

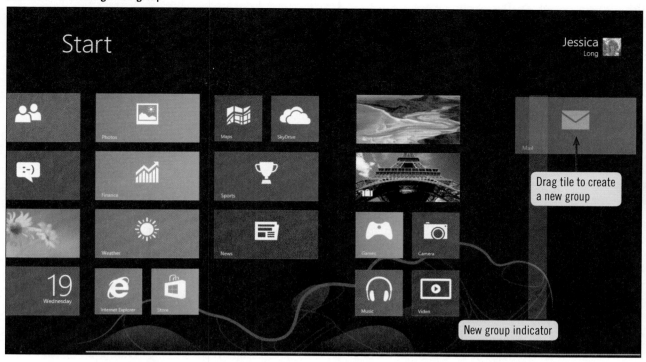

FIGURE B-16: Naming a group

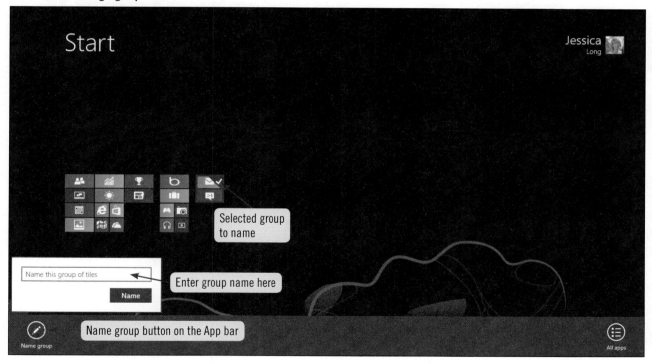

Changing app tile size

When you move app tiles into groups on the Start screen, Windows automatically arranges them in the group to fit in place. However, some tiles are smaller squares while others are larger rectangles so they don't always fit seamlessly within one another. To fix this, you can change the size of the tile. To change the size of an app tile, right-click (on your computer) or tap and hold (on a mobile device) the app tile you want to change to select it, then click or tap the Smaller button or Larger button on the App bar. You cannot select and change multiple apps at the same time.

Practice

Concepts Review

Match the statements below with the elements labeled in the screen shown in FIGURE B-17.

FIGURE B-17

1. Which element is an installed app from the Windows Store?
2. Which element installs and updates apps?
3. Which element is a pinned app from the Apps screen?
4. Which element is a new group?
5. Which element is a named group?
6. Which element zooms out to show more apps?
7. Which element searches all apps?

Match each term with the statement that describes its function.

8. Apps screen
9. Search panel
10. Start screen
11. Start screen zoomed out
12. Separation bar
13. Windows Store

a. The element you use to display Windows accessories
b. The element you use to start an app
c. The element you use to install or update apps
d. The element you use to work with group names
e. The element you use to locate apps, settings, or files
f. The element you use to work with multiple apps

Select the best answers from the following lists of choices.

14. Which screen displays all apps on a device?
   a. Start
   b. Start (zoomed out)
   c. Apps
   d. Desktop

15. Which element is *not* a category on the Apps screen?
   a. Windows Accessories
   b. Windows Ease of Access
   c. Windows Apps
   d. Windows System

16. Which element is *not* a category on the Search panel?
   a. Apps
   b. Devices
   c. Settings
   d. Files

17. Which screen does *not* allow you to start an app?
   a. Start
   b. Start (zoomed out)
   c. Apps
   d. Apps search results

18. The term RAM stands for:
   a. Relative access memory.
   b. Relative allocated memory.
   c. Random access memory.
   d. Random allocated memory.

19. Which app is installed using the Windows Store?
   a. Maps
   b. Kindle
   c. Xbox LIVE Games
   d. Messaging

20. Which task is *not* accomplished in the Windows Store?
   a. Install an app.
   b. Update an app.
   c. Uninstall an app.
   d. View your apps.

21. Which screen can you uninstall an app from?
   a. Start
   b. Desktop
   c. File Explorer window
   d. Control Panel window

22. Which method does *not* pin an app to the Start screen?
   a. Install Windows 8.
   b. Install a Windows accessory.
   c. Install an app.
   d. Use the Pin to Start button.

23. Which screen allows you to create a group?
   a. Start
   b. Start (zoomed out)
   c. Apps
   d. Desktop

24. Which screen allows you to name a group?
   a. Start
   b. Start (zoomed out)
   c. Apps
   d. Desktop

Skills Review

1. Display apps.
   a. Start Windows and sign in, if necessary.
   b. Use the App bar to show all apps.
   c. Use the Zoom feature to display Apps screen categories.
   d. Select a category.
   e. Switch to the Start screen.

2. Search for apps.
   a. Select the Search button on the Charm bar.
   b. Search **media** on the Search panel for Apps to display results.
   c. Display the search results for Settings.
   d. Use the Close button to clear the results.
   e. Switch to the Start screen.

3. Start and close apps.
   a. Open the Desktop app.
   b. Switch to the Start screen.
   c. Open the Internet Explorer app.
   d. Switch to the Start screen.
   e. Close the Internet Explorer app using the Start bar.
   f. Switch to the Desktop app.
   g. Close the Desktop app using a swipe.

4. Work with multiple apps.
   a. Open the News app.
   b. Switch to the Start screen.
   c. Open the Messaging app.
   d. Drag the News app to split the screen on the right.
   e. Drag the Separation bar to make the right screen larger.
   f. Drag the Separation bar to close the News app.
   g. Close the Messaging app.
   h. Switch to the News app, then close it.

5. Install apps from the Windows Store.
   a. Open the Windows Store app.
   b. Install an app not currently installed on your device.
   c. View status information as the app installs.
   d. Return to the Windows Store screen.
   e. Close the Windows Store app.
   f. Locate the newly installed app on the Start screen.

Skills Review (continued)

6. **Uninstall apps.**
   a. Select the app you installed in Step 5b.
   b. Uninstall the app.
   c. If prompted, follow app-specific instructions to complete the uninstall.
   d. Verify the app no longer appears on the Start screen.

7. **Customize apps on the Start screen.**
   a. Display the Apps screen.
   b. Select the Control Panel app.
   c. Pin the selected app to the Start screen.
   d. Switch to the Start screen.
   e. Unpin the Control Panel app.

8. **Group apps on the Start screen.**
   a. Drag the Games app to the right to create a new group.
   b. Drag the Music and Video apps into the new group.
   c. Zoom out the Start screen.
   d. Name the new group Entertainment.
   e. Zoom in to view the Start screen.
   f. Delete the group name Entertainment.
   g. Drag the Games, Music, and Video apps back to their original groups.

Independent Challenge 1

You are a student in a Windows 8 course and want to use a word-processing app to take notes on your computer. You want to find out what apps are installed with Windows 8 to see if there is one that fits your need. From the Start screen, use the App bar to display all of the apps installed on the device, browse through them, then search for a word-processing app.

   a. Display the Start screen.
   b. Use the Command bar to display all apps.
   c. Display the Apps screen by categories.
   d. Display the Search panel, then type **word** to display the app results.
   e. Clear the search results.
   f. Switch to the Start screen.

Independent Challenge 2

You and your classmate are working together on a project but are online at different locations. In order to perform research on the Web and simultaneously discuss project details, you want to create a split window with the Internet Explorer app on one side and the Messaging app on the other. From the Start screen, open both apps, then drag to split them on the same screen.

    a. Display the Start screen.

    b. Open the Messaging and Internet Explorer apps.

    c. Drag the Internet Explorer app to the right side of a split screen (one-third size).

    d. Drag the Messaging app to the left side of a split screen (two-thirds size).

    e. Adjust the Separation bar to expand Internet Explorer (two-thirds size).

    f. Drag the Separation bar to remove the Messaging app.

    g. Close the Internet Explorer app.

    h. Switch to the Messaging app, then close it.

Independent Challenge 3

You are a student studying for the SAT exam and want to find an educational app that will help you learn the material and provide a practice test. Use the Windows Store to find and install a free educational app for these purposes.

    a. Open the Windows Store app.

    b. Browse the Education category for a free SAT-related app.

    c. Install the SAT app.

    d. Switch to the Start Screen.

    e. Open the SAT app.

    f. Explore the SAT app.

    g. Close the SAT app.

    h. Close the Windows Store app.

    i. Switch to the Start screen.

    j. Uninstall the SAT app.

Independent Challenge 4: Explore

One of the first things people do when they start using Windows 8 is to customize the Start screen with their favorite apps or ones they will access frequently. Review your Start screen and unpin any apps that you don't think you will use. Switch to the Apps screen and pin any apps that you enjoy using, or plan to use frequently, to the Start screen. On the Start screen, arrange the related apps into groups, then name them.

    a. Display the Start screen (examine the screen so that you can restore it later).

    b. Unpin the apps you don't use.

    c. Display the Apps screen.

    d. Pin the apps you want to the Start screen.

    e. Drag to create a new group with an app.

    f. Move apps into the groups.

    g. Resize tiles (smaller or larger) as needed so they fit nicely in groups.

    h. Display settings from the Start panel, then enable the Show more tiles option.

    i. Zoom out the Start screen.

    j. Name each of the groups.

    k. Print the current Start screen.

    l. Restore the Start screen.

Visual Workshop

Re-create the screen shown in **FIGURE B-18**, which shows the Start screen.

FIGURE B-18

Getting and Sharing Information Apps

CASE ▶ Windows 8 comes with apps that help you find information and communicate with others on the Internet. You want to learn how to use apps to browse and search the Web, send and receive email and instant messages, manage calendar events, and store files online.

Unit Objectives

After completing this unit, you will be able to:

- Browse the Web with Internet Explorer
- Search the Web
- Add contacts to People
- Send messages with Mail
- Receive and respond to messages
- Chat with Messaging
- Manage events with Calendar
- Store information on SkyDrive

Files You Will Need

Holly.jpg	Steve.jpg
Jessica.jpg	Tim.jpg

©Itana/Shutterstock

Browse the Web with Internet Explorer

Learning Outcomes
• Browse Web pages
• Create browser tabs
• Use tabs to browse Web pages

The **Internet** is a global collection of millions of computers linked together to share information. The **Web** (also known as the **World Wide Web** or **WWW**) is a part of the Internet that consists of Web sites located on different computers around the world. A **Web site** contains Web pages linked together to make searching for information on the Internet easier. **Web pages** are specially formatted documents that contain highlighted words, phrases, and graphics called **hyperlinks** (or simply **links**) that open other Web pages when you click or tap them. **Web browsers** are software applications that you use to "surf the Web," or display and navigate Web pages. Internet Explorer is a Web browser from Microsoft that comes with Windows 8. As you open Web sites, you can display each site in a separate tab, so you can view multiple Web sites in a single window. A **Web address**, also called a **URL** (which stands for **Uniform Resource Locator**) is a unique place on the Internet where a Web page resides. When you enter the URL for a Web page, Internet Explorer **loads** and displays the page from the Internet. **CASE** ▶ *As an executive director at QST, you want to evaluate the Quest Specialty Travel Web site, so you open it in Internet Explorer to browse through the site.*

STEPS

1. **With the Start screen in view, click or tap the Internet Explorer tile**

   The Internet Explorer app opens in full screen view, displaying the default home page in the browser screen. The **home page**, the main Web page around which a Web site is built, appears when you start Internet Explorer. The Address bar appears at the bottom of the screen, displaying navigation and option buttons.

2. **Click or tap in the Address box on the Address bar, then type www.questspecialtytravel.com**

   Internet Explorer displays a list of tiles for frequently used or pinned Web pages. When you type a Web address in the Address box, a feature called **AutoComplete** displays a list of tiles with possible matches from addresses you've typed previously. If a suggestion in the list matches the Web address you're typing, a list appears with the items highlighted. You can click or tap a suggestion or continue to type.

   QUICK TIP
   If a Web page takes too long to load, click or tap the Stop button ✕ on the App bar.

3. **Click or tap the Go button ➡ or press Enter to load the Web page, move the pointer over Destinations, as shown in FIGURE C-1, then click or tap Destinations**

   The Destinations page loads in the browser screen. Anytime you move the pointer over a link, it changes to 🖑, and a ScreenTip with the address of the link appears, as shown in **FIGURE C-1**.

   QUICK TIP
   If a page doesn't completely load, click or tap the Refresh button ↻ on the Address bar to update it.

4. **Move the mouse, then click or tap the Back arrow on the left edge of the screen (on a computer) or swipe right from the left side of the screen (on a mobile device)**

   The Web page you previously viewed—the Quest Specialty Travel home page—reloads in the browser window. You can also click or tap the Back ⬅ or Forward button ➡ to navigate between pages.

5. **Right-click the screen (on a computer) or swipe down from the top of the screen (on a mobile device), as shown in FIGURE C-2, then click or tap the New Tab button ➕ on the App bar**

   Internet Explorer creates a new tab and displays a list of tiles for frequently used or pinned Web pages.

6. **Type www.travel.com in the Address box on the Address bar, then click or tap the Go button ➡ or press [Enter] to load the Web page**

7. **Right-click the screen (on a computer) or swipe down from the top of the screen (on a mobile device), then click or tap the Quest Specialty Travel tab on the App bar**

8. **Right-click the screen (on a computer) or swipe down from the top of the screen (on a mobile device), click or tap the Close Tab button ✕ for the Travel.com tab on the App bar to remove the tab, then click or tap a blank area or press [Esc]**

FIGURE C-1: Web page displayed in Internet Explorer browser screen

Quest Specialty Travel Web site

Link

Pointing finger cursor

ScreenTip with the address for the link

Back button

URL in Address box

Refresh button

Pin to START button

Page tools button

Forward button

Address bar

FIGURE C-2: Creating tabs in Internet Explorer

Close Tab button

New Tab button

Current tab

Tab tools button

Apps bar

Connecting to the Internet

The Internet's physical structure includes telephone lines, cables, satellites, and other telecommunications media. In many areas, **DSL (digital subscriber line)** provides a completely digital connection using telephone lines, whereas **cable modems** provide one using cable television lines. DSL and cable modems, also known as **broadband** connections, are continually connected to the Internet and use a network setup. In remote areas, or if you want a lower-cost alternative yet slower you can create a connection with a dial-up modem and telephone line, which needs to be established each time you connect to the Internet. You can avoid using physical telephone or cable lines by using a **wireless connection**, which uses radio waves or microwaves to maintain communications. Whether you use a telephone line, DSL line, cable modem, or wireless signal, Windows can help you establish a connection between your computer and the Internet. First, you need to select an **ISP (Internet service provider)**, which is a company that provides Internet access through servers connected directly to the Internet. Your ISP sets you up with an **Internet account** and connection information that provides you Internet access for a monthly rate.

Search the Web

The best way to find information on the Web is to use a search engine. A **search engine** is a program provided by a **search provider** that you access directly from Internet Explorer or through a Web site to search through a collection of Internet information to find what you want. Many search engines are available on the Web, such as Bing (default) by Microsoft, Wikipedia, Google, and Yahoo!, which you can add on to Internet Explorer. When you perform a search, you submit words or phrases, known as **keywords**, that best describe what you want to retrieve to the search engine using the Search box in the Search panel. As you type in the Search box, the search engine displays a menu list of text for the matched sites, known as **hits**. The search results of different search engines vary. If you're looking for information on a page, you can use the Find toolbar to help highlight the text you want to find. **CASE** ▶ *You decide to use Bing to search for and examine another travel-related Web site to complete a competitive review.*

STEPS

1. **Within Internet Explorer, point to the upper-right corner and move down (on a computer) or swipe left from the right edge of the screen (on a mobile device), then click or tap the Search button 🔍 on the Charm bar**

   The Search panel appears, displaying a Search box with the search engine name, Bing, by default. Internet Explorer is automatically selected as the search app. To initiate a search using Internet Explorer, you enter keywords in the Search box.

2. **Click or tap in the Search box on the Search panel, if necessary**

   The more specific your search criteria or keyword in the Search box, the better the list of matches you will receive from the search engine. Use specific words, eliminate common words, such as "a" or "the," and use quotation marks for specific phrases.

3. **Type africa**

   As you type, the Search panel displays suggestions based on your search criteria, as shown in **FIGURE C-3**.

4. **Click or tap the Search button 🔍 in the Search box, or press Enter**

   The search results for "africa" appear in order of decreasing relevance. If the search results return too many hits, you can narrow the search by adding more keywords. As you add more keywords, the search engine finds fewer, more specific Web pages that contain all of those words.

5. **Right-click the screen (on a computer) or swipe down from the top of the screen (on a mobile device)**

   The Search panel closes and the App bar appears.

6. **Click or tap the Page tools button ⊘ on the App bar, then click or tap Find on page**

   The Find bar appears at the bottom of the screen, displaying the Find box, find options, such as Previous, Next, and Close, and the number of matches.

7. **Click or tap in the Find box on the Find bar, then type africa**

   The search keyword is highlighted on the page, as shown in **FIGURE C-4**.

8. **Click or tap any link in the list of matches**

   The corresponding Web page appears in the browser window. You can click or tap links on this Web site to jump to other related ones.

9. **Point to the top edge of the screen (cursor changes to a hand), then drag down to the bottom edge of the screen**

   Internet Explorer closes and the Start screen appears.

FIGURE C-3: Search panel with search criteria displayed

FIGURE C-4: Search results with Find bar displayed

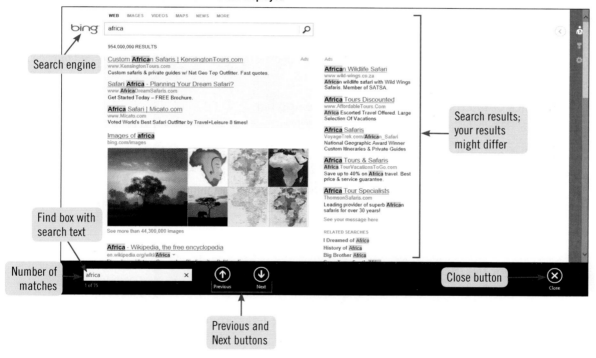

Using InPrivate browsing

If you're using a computer at a friend's house, another office, a hotel, or an Internet café and you don't want to leave any trace or evidence of your Web activity, you can use InPrivate browsing. InPrivate browsing doesn't retain or keep track of browsing history, searches, temporary Internet files, form data, cookies, or usernames and passwords. You can start InPrivate browsing from the App bar in Internet Explorer. Right-click the screen (on a computer) or swipe down from the top of the screen, click or tap the Tab tools button on the App bar, then click or tap the New InPrivate tab. When you start InPrivate browsing, Internet Explorer opens a new browser window. An InPrivate indicator icon appears in the Address bar when the feature is turned on. When you're done, simply close the browser window to end the InPrivate browsing session.

Add Contacts to People

A **contact** is a person or company with whom you communicate. Windows 8 uses the People app as a centralized place to add and manage contact information, including a person's name, address, phone, and email, which you can use in other apps, including Mail and Messaging, to communicate with others. You can create and manage contacts in People and add contacts from other online service accounts, such as Facebook, Hotmail, Twitter, Microsoft Exchange, LinkedIn, and Google. When you set up Windows 8, you also set up a specified Microsoft account, which becomes your default account and profile in People. When you open People, you can access different areas by selecting the categories at the top of the screen, either People, What's new, or Me. The People category shows you all your contacts, where you can edit them or create new ones. With the What's new category, you can display updates and notifications from your contacts. With the Me category, you can view and edit your account information. **CASE** *You want to maintain an up-to-date list of current QST employees, so you create a new contact for a recent hire.*

STEPS

TROUBLE
If prompted to sign in, enter your Microsoft account username and password.

1. **With the Start screen in view, click or tap the People tile**
   The People app opens in full screen view, displaying a list of your contacts in the main People screen. The People app allows you to create new contacts, edit existing contacts, and add accounts from online services.

QUICK TIP
To delete a contact, click or tap the contact, right-click the screen (on a computer) or swipe down from the top of the screen (on a mobile device), click or tap the Delete button on the App bar, then click or tap Delete.

2. **Right-click the screen (on a computer) or swipe down from the top of the screen (on a mobile device)**
   The App bar appears, as shown in **FIGURE C-5**, displaying options to create a new contact and provide feedback to Microsoft about the People app.

3. **Click or tap the New button ⊕ on the App bar**
   The New contact screen appears, displaying fields to specify an account type and enter contact information.

4. **Click or tap the Add Field button ⊕ next to Address, then click or tap Work on the menu**
   A set of address fields appears alongside the other default contact information fields.

5. **Enter the information as shown in FIGURE C-6**
   The contact information appears in the new contact.

6. **Click or tap the Save button 🖫 on the App bar**
   The completed contact appears, displaying the information you entered in the previous step.

QUICK TIP
To edit a contact, click or tap the contact, right-click the screen (on a computer) or swipe down from the top of the screen (on a mobile device), click or tap the Edit button on the App bar, make changes, then click or tap the Save button.

7. **Click or tap the Back button ⊖ in the upper-left corner of the screen**
   The People app main screen reappears.

8. **Point to the top edge of the screen (cursor changes to a hand), then drag down to the bottom edge of the screen**
   The People app closes and the Start screen appears.

FIGURE C-5: Displaying contacts in People

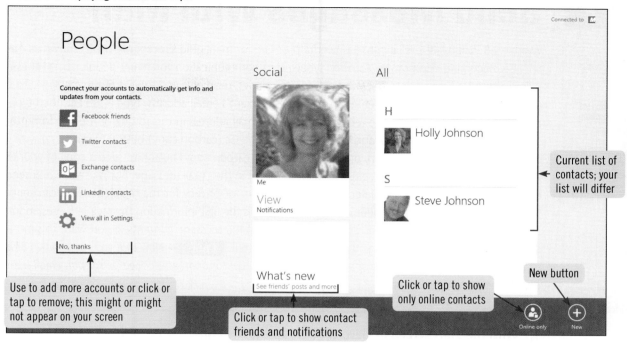

Use to add more accounts or click or tap to remove; this might or might not appear on your screen

Click or tap to show contact friends and notifications

Click or tap to show only online contacts

New button

Current list of contacts; your list will differ

FIGURE C-6: Creating a contact

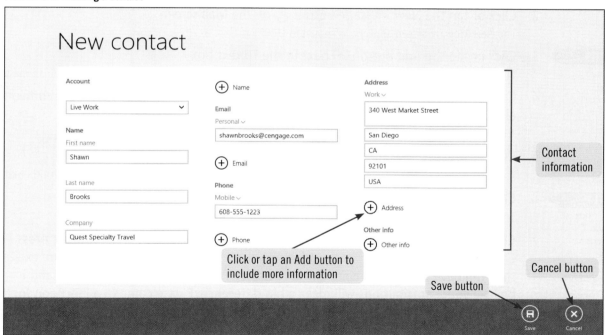

Click or tap an Add button to include more information

Contact information

Cancel button

Save button

Adding and using other accounts

In addition to using the default Microsoft account, you can add contacts from other online service accounts, such as Facebook, Hotmail, Twitter, Microsoft Exchange, LinkedIn, and Google. To add an online service account, point to the upper-right corner and move down (on a computer) or swipe left from the right edge of the screen (on a mobile device), then click or tap the Settings button on the Charm bar, click or tap Accounts on the Settings panel, click or tap Add an account, click or tap an account type, then follow the on-screen instructions to connect to the account. When your contacts update their information or send notifications, you automatically receive them in the People app.

Send Messages with Mail

Learning
Outcomes
• View email
  messages
• Create and send
  an email message
• Select email
  contacts

Windows 8 includes the Mail app, a powerful program for managing **electronic mail**, known as **email**. Email is becoming the primary form of typewritten communication for many people. Email messages follow a standard memo format, with fields for the sender, recipient, and subject of the message. To send an email message, you need to enter or select the recipient's email address, type a subject, then type the message itself. You can enter the recipient's name or email address in the To box or use the To button to select contacts from the People app. You can also use the Cc (carbon copy) button to send a copy of your email message to another person, or use the Bcc (blind carbon copy) button to send a copy of your email message to another person whose name will not appear in the email message. Bcc is useful when sending emails to a large group of unrelated people, and allows for privacy for the recipients. You can send the same message to one or more people. The subject text is the first information the recipient sees about the email, so it should provide a short, concise summary of the message contents. If you want to send a file along with your email message, you can attach the file to it. **CASE** ▶ *Now that you have Shawn Brooks's contact information in the People app, you want to send him (or another specified person) an email message about a new employee luncheon.*

STEPS

1. **With the Start screen in view, click or tap the Mail tile**

   The Mail app opens in full screen view, displaying options to send and receive email messages from different accounts.

2. **Click or tap the New Message button ⊕ on the Mail screen**

   The New Message screen appears, as shown in **FIGURE C-7**.

3. **Click or tap the Add button ⊕ next to the To text box**

   The People app opens in Mail, displaying contacts you can select from in order to address an email message.

4. **Click or tap the email address of your instructor, technical support person, or someone else you know**

   A check mark appears in the contact tile, as shown in **FIGURE C-8**.

5. **Click or tap Add**

   The recipient's name appears in the To text box. The recipient's email address is associated with the name.

6. **Click or tap in the Subject text box, then type Welcome aboard!**

   The subject text changes to "Welcome aboard!"

7. **Click or tap in the upper-left corner of the Messages pane, type Dear Shawn:, press Enter twice, type I would like to welcome you to Quest Specialty Travel. We are excited that you have joined our team. Quest Specialty Travel is a growing company, and I believe your contributions will make a big difference. Please come to a luncheon for new employees this Thursday at 12:30 in the company cafe., press Enter twice, then type Jessica Long**

   As you type, Mail automatically corrects any misspelled words that it recognizes from the default dictionary. If a red line appears under a word, Mail doesn't recognize it. You can right-click or tap and hold to display a menu with suggestions or an option to add the word to the dictionary.

8. **Click or tap the Send button ⊜ on the New Message screen**

   The New Message screen closes and the Mail screen reappears. The email message is sent automatically to the recipient.

FIGURE C-7: New Message screen

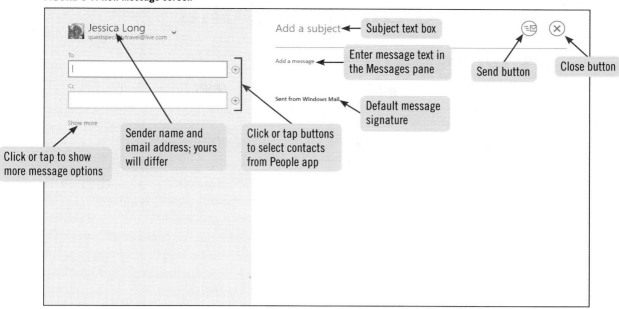

- Subject text box
- Send button
- Close button
- Enter message text in the Messages pane
- Default message signature
- Click or tap buttons to select contacts from People app
- Sender name and email address; yours will differ
- Click or tap to show more message options

FIGURE C-8: Selecting recipients for an email message

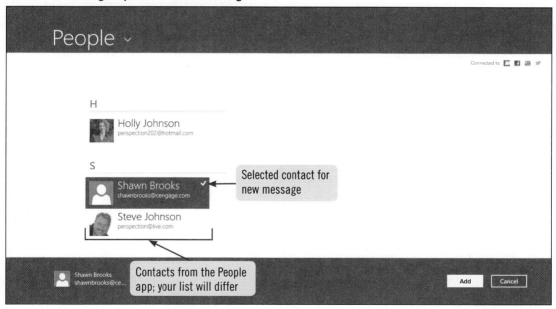

- Selected contact for new message
- Contacts from the People app; your list will differ

Formatting content in email messages

When you click or tap in the Message text area of an email message, the App bar appears with formatting options, which include Font, Font color, Highlight, Bold, Italic, Underline, Bulleted list, and More. To apply formatting, click or tap to place the insertion point or select text in the message text, click or tap a button on the App bar, then select an option, if prompted. In addition to these typical text formatting options, you can also insert graphical symbols called **emoticons**, such as a happy face, which help convey your emotions, or graphical animations, called **winks**. To insert an emoticon, click or tap to place the insertion point in the message text, click or tap the Emoticons button on the App bar, click or tap a category icon, such as People or Travel, at the top of the panel, then click or tap an icon. The More button on the App bar allows you to apply other options to an email message. You can specify a message priority (high, normal, or low), add the Bcc box, and undo or redo the most recent command.

Receive and Respond to Messages

You can receive email anytime—even when your computer is turned off. When you start the Mail app, the program automatically checks for new email messages from the selected account and continues to check periodically while the program is open. You can also retrieve your email messages manually with the Sync button. You can add more accounts, such as Microsoft Exchange or Google, and switch between them at any time by using the Accounts panel under Settings. New messages appear in boldface in the Inbox along with any messages you haven't stored elsewhere or deleted. Unsolicited mass email, known as **spam**, is automatically placed in the Junk folder, where you can review and delete later. You can respond to a message in two ways: You can reply to it, which creates a new message addressed to the sender(s) and other recipients, or you can forward it, which creates a new message you can send to someone else. In either case, the original message appears in the message response. As you create a message, Mail automatically saves it in the Drafts folder until you send it in order to protect its content. Once you send a message, it is placed temporarily in the Outbox, a folder for storing outgoing messages, until the action is completed. A copy of the outgoing message is also placed in the Sent Items folder for reference later. **CASE** *To prepare for the new employee luncheon, you want to forward a relevant email message you received to your assistant at Quest Specialty Travel.*

STEPS

1. **Have the email recipient to whom you sent the email message send a reply back to you**

2. **With the Mail app in view, right-click the screen (on a computer) or swipe down from the top of the screen (on a mobile device)**

   The App bar appears, as shown in **FIGURE C-9**, displaying options to move messages to folders, mark messages as unread, and manually check for new email.

3. **Right-click the screen (on a computer) or swipe down from the top of the screen (on a mobile device), then click or tap the Sync button ⊜ on the App bar**

   When you receive new email, the messages are placed in the Inbox folder in the Folders list. The Folders list appears, displaying folders for storing and managing email messages. The folders include Inbox, Drafts, Sent Items, Outbox, Junk, and Deleted Items.

4. **Click or tap the email message you received from Step 1**

   The Reading pane displays the email message selected in the Message list.

5. **Click or tap the Respond button ⊖ on the Mail screen, then click or tap Forward**

   The Forward Message screen opens, as shown in **FIGURE C-10**, displaying the original email subject title in the Subject text box with the prefix "Fw:" (short for Forward) and the original message in the message box. The Respond menu allows you to also Reply and Reply All email messages.

6. **Click or tap in the To text box, type the email address of your instructor, technical support person, or someone else you know, then select a contact if available**

   As you type, any matches from existing contacts appear in a drop-down list.

7. **Click or tap in the upper-left corner of the Message text box, type** Please add Shawn Brooks to Thursday's luncheon guest list**, then click or tap the Send button ⊜ on the Forward Message screen**

   The Forward Message screen closes and the Mail screen reappears. The email message is automatically sent.

8. **Point to the top edge of the screen (cursor changes to a hand), then drag down to the bottom edge of the screen**

   The Mail app closes and the Start screen appears.

FIGURE C-9: Mail screen with Inbox

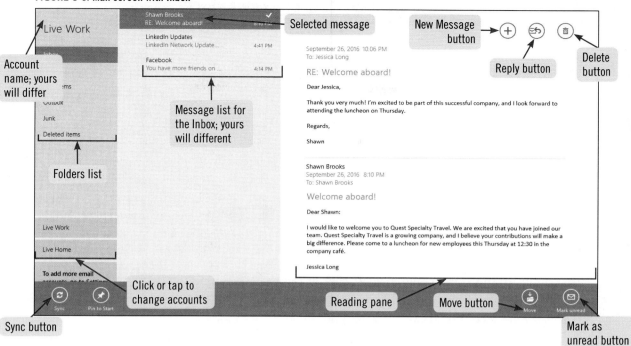

Account name; yours will differ

Selected message

New Message button

Reply button

Delete button

Message list for the Inbox; yours will different

Folders list

Click or tap to change accounts

Reading pane

Move button

Mark as unread button

Sync button

FIGURE C-10: Forward message screen

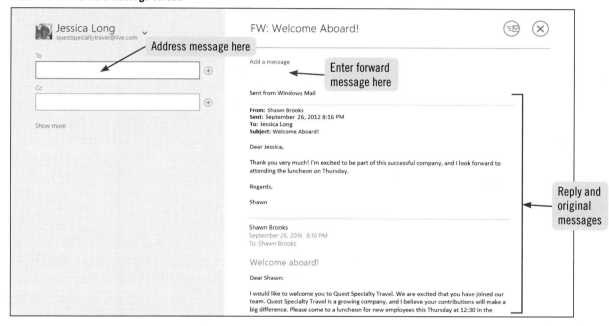

Address message here

Enter forward message here

Reply and original messages

Attaching a file to an email message

You can easily share a file, such as a photo or a document, using email by attaching it to an email message. Upon receiving the email, the recipient can open the file in the program that created it or save it. For example, suppose that you are working on a report with a colleague in another part of the country. After you finish the report, you can attach the report file to an email message and send the message to your colleague, who can then open, edit, and print the report. To attach a file to an email

message, create the message (using New, Reply, Reply all, or Forward options), right-click the screen (on a computer) or swipe down from the top of the screen (on a mobile device), click or tap the Attachments on the App bar, browse and select a file, then click or tap Attach. When you reply to a message that has an attachment, the attachment isn't returned to the original sender. However, when you forward an attachment, it is included along with the message.

Chat with Messaging

Learning Outcomes
• View instant message threads
• Create an instant message
• Send and respond to instant messages

Messaging is an instant messaging app that allows you to send and receive instant messages. An **instant message (IM)** is an online typewritten conversation in real time between two or more contacts. Whereas email messages collect in an email app and can be viewed at a later time, instant messages can only be exchanged if both parties are online. An instant message conversation consists of text exchanges, called a **thread**. As part of the text exchange, you can insert emoticons just like in an email. The Messaging app screen includes a Threads pane for tracking your conversations, a Messages pane that contains each conversation you have in the currently selected thread, and a text box for adding comments to that thread. Messaging tracks the online status of each participant in a thread and supports multiple services, which includes Windows Messenger and Facebook. Messaging also supports notifications, which appear as floating "toasts" near the upper right of the screen. **CASE** *You want to talk to an associate about the company's next stockholders meeting, so you decide to use instant messaging to communicate.*

STEPS

QUICK TIP
To change your online status, click or tap the Status button on the App bar, then click or tap Available or Invisible.

1. **With the Start screen in view, click or tap the Messaging tile**

   The Messaging app opens in full screen view, displaying options to send and receive instant messages.

2. **Click or tap the New message button ⊕ on the App bar**

   The People app opens in Messaging, displaying contacts you can select to address an instant message. The People app only shows you those contacts who are connected to a compatible service and are currently online.

3. **Click or tap the Holly Johnson name or the email address of your instructor, technical support person, or someone else you know**

   A check mark appears in the contact tile, as shown in **FIGURE C-11**.

TROUBLE
If no contacts are available, have your contact change his/her IM status to available, then wait or click Invite on the App bar, click Add a new friend, then follow the online instructions.

4. **Click or tap Choose**

   The recipient's name appears selected in the Threads pane. The online status, including online or offline, for you and your recipient appears as a text indicator under the pictures and as a color bar next to the pictures in the Messages pane. A vertical green bar indicates an available online status, while no bar indicates an offline or not available status.

5. **Click or tap in the Message text box, if necessary, then type the message shown in the top part of the Messages pane in FIGURE C-12**

   The text automatically wraps in the Message text box, so you don't need to use the enter key

6. **Press Enter**

   The instant message is sent to your online contact.

7. **Have your contact (Holly) type the message shown in the Messages pane in FIGURE C-12, and send it to you, then continue back and forth to complete the conversation; click or tap the Emoticons button ☺, then click or tap the ☺ icon to insert it in the conversation**

   The Messages pane displays the instant message conversation.

QUICK TIP
To delete a thread, select the thread, right-click the screen (on a computer) or swipe down from the top of the screen (on a mobile device), click or tap the Delete button on the App bar, then click or tap Delete.

8. **Point to the top edge of the screen (cursor changes to a hand), then drag down to the bottom edge of the screen**

   The Messaging app closes and the Start screen appears.

FIGURE C-11: Selecting recipients for an instant message

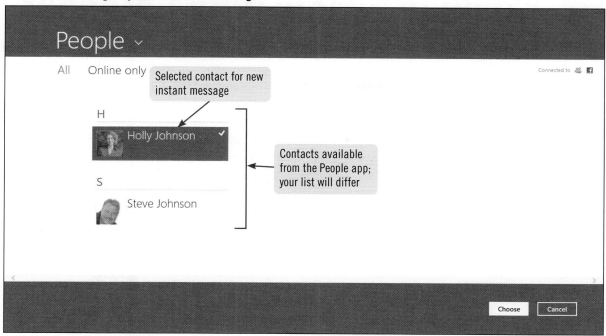

FIGURE C-12: Instant message conversation

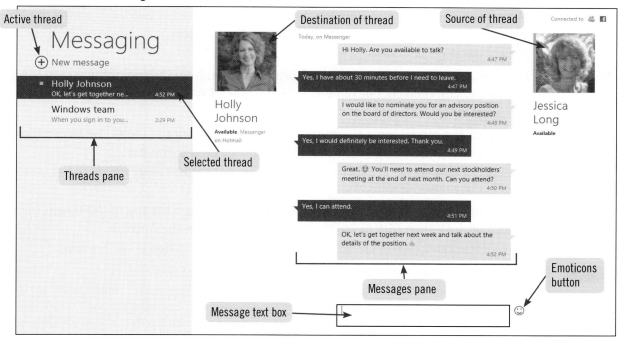

Adding instant message accounts

Windows Messenger is the default account that Messaging uses to have instant messaging conversations. However, you can also use other online services, including Facebook, to have an instant messaging conversation. To add another account, click or tap the Connected to icon at the top-right of the screen, click or tap Add an account in the Accounts panel, click or tap an account type, then follow the on-screen instructions to connect to the service.

Manage Events with Calendar

Learning Outcomes
• View a calendar of events
• Create a calendar event

The Calendar app allows you to update the appearance and organization of events on your calendar in order to make things less cluttered and easier to read. You can use Calendar to schedule time for completing specific tasks, appointments, meetings, vacations, holidays, or any other activity. You can adjust the Calendar screen to show events using the Day, Week, or Month format. When you display the Calendar screen using the Day format, for example, you can view events for the current day, as well as what is going on tomorrow. Creating events is simple: Just click or tap on the date that you want and add your new event details. You can specify to which calendar to add the event, where and when the event takes place, how long the event will last, how often the event occurs, whether you want a reminder notice, your status (Free, Busy, Tentative, Out of office, or Working elsewhere), and whether to make the event private. When you specify a reminder notice, Calendar displays a notification anywhere in Windows 8, which you can select to display the event. If the event is a meeting, you can invite contacts to attend. Calendar comes with multiple calendars for different purposes, which include Main (with the username), Birthday, Personal, Holidays, and Work. Each calendar uses a different color for easy identification and use. You can show or hide calendars to focus on the events most important to you. The Birthday calendar even includes notices coming from social networks. **CASE** *You want to attend the new employee luncheon, so you schedule the event in your calendar.*

STEPS

1. **With the Start screen in view, click or tap the Calendar tile**
   The Calendar app opens in full screen view, displaying your calendar in the Month format for the current month, as shown in **FIGURE C-13**.

2. **Move your mouse (on a computer), then click the Right arrow button ▷ on the upper-right corner of the screen or swipe left (on a mobile device)**
   The next month on the calendar appears.

3. **Right-click the screen (on a computer) or swipe down from the top of the screen (on a mobile device), then click or tap the Today button 🔘 on the App bar**
   The current day appears in dark gray in the Month format.

4. **Right-click the screen (on a computer) or swipe down from the top of the screen (on a mobile device), then click or tap the Day button 🔘 on the App bar**
   A detailed schedule appears in an hourly format for today and tomorrow, where you can click or tap to add or edit the information.

5. **Right-click the screen (on a computer) or swipe down from the top of the screen (on a mobile device), then click or tap the Month button 🔘 on the App bar**
   The current month appears in the Month format with today's date highlighted in a dark gray.

6. **Double-click or double-tap the next Thursday on your calendar**
   The New Calendar Event screen appears. This is where you can specify to which calendar to add the event, where and when the event takes place, how long the event will last, how often the event occurs, whether you want a reminder notice, your status, and whether to make the event private.

7. **Enter the information and specify the settings shown in FIGURE C-14 (use next Thursday's date)**
   The New Calendar Event screen shows the completed event information.

8. **Click or tap the Save this event button 🔘 on the New Calendar Event screen**
   The day specified in the event appears in the Month format.

9. **Point to the top edge of the screen (cursor changes to a hand), then drag down to the bottom edge of the screen**
   The Calendar app closes and the Start screen appears.

FIGURE C-13: Calendar screen in Month format

FIGURE C-14: Creating a calendar event

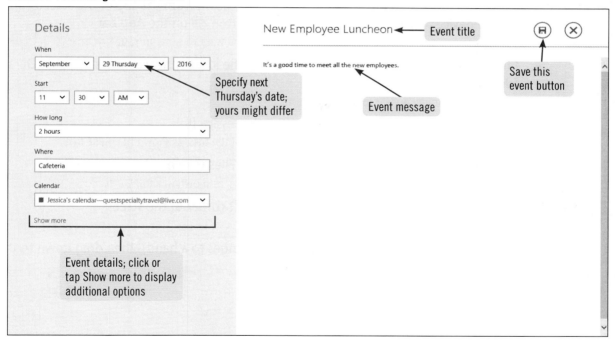

Working with existing events

After you create an event, you can edit or delete it. You can edit or delete a single occurrence of an event or all occurrences. In any of the format views, click or tap the event, click or tap Change one or Change all, if necessary. To edit the event, make changes to event details, then click or tap the Save this event button. To delete the event, click or tap the event, click or tap the Delete button on the top-right of the screen then click or tap Delete to confirm.

Store Information on SkyDrive

Learning Outcomes
- View files on a SkyDrive
- Add files to a SkyDrive

SkyDrive is an online file hosting service that allows you to upload and sync files to and then access them from the SkyDrive app in Windows 8, a Web browser at SkyDrive.com, or a mobile device, including a Windows phone, Apple iPhone or iPad, or Android. SkyDrive allows you to organize your files so that you can share them with contacts, make them public, or keep them private. The online service offers 7 GB of free storage for new users; however, additional storage is available for purchase. SkyDrive comes with a default set of folders—Documents, Favorites, Pictures, and Public (Shared)—you can use to store your files. Depending on your SkyDrive setup, your folders might differ. When you store files on SkyDrive, it automatically makes them available on your other devices without having to sync them. The files you store in your Public (Shared) folder are available for anyone to view and edit. You can view a file on the SkyDrive by clicking or tapping it. When you view some files, such as Microsoft Office documents, your Web browser opens, where you can view and edit them using a WebApp. **CASE** *You have some recent employee photos that you want to store and share with other QST departments so you add them on your SkyDrive.*

STEPS

1. **With the Start screen in view, click or tap the SkyDrive tile, then sign in to your Microsoft account, if prompted**
   The SkyDrive app opens in full screen view, displaying folder tiles to access the files on the SkyDrive.

2. **Click or tap the Pictures tile on the SkyDrive screen**
   The Pictures screen opens, displaying the files in the Pictures folder.

3. **Right-click the screen (on a computer) or swipe down from the top of the screen (on a mobile device), then click or tap the Upload button ⬆ on the App bar**
   The Files screen appears, where you can select the files you want to store on your SkyDrive.

4. **Click or tap the Files down arrow, navigate to the location where you store your Data Files, then select the Photos folder**
   The files in the folder appear in the Files screen.

5. **Click or tap the Holly file, then click or tap the Jessica file**
   A check mark appears in the upper-right corner of each of the tiles, as shown in **FIGURE C-15**.

6. **Click or tap the Add to SkyDrive button on the Files screen**
   The files are added to the Pictures folder on your SkyDrive, as shown in **FIGURE C-16**.

7. **Click or tap the Back button ⬅ in the upper-left corner of the screen**
   The main screen for the SkyDrive app appears.

8. **Point to the top edge of the screen (cursor changes to a hand), then drag down to the bottom edge of the screen**
   The SkyDrive app closes and the Start screen appears.

FIGURE C-15: Selecting files for the SkyDrive

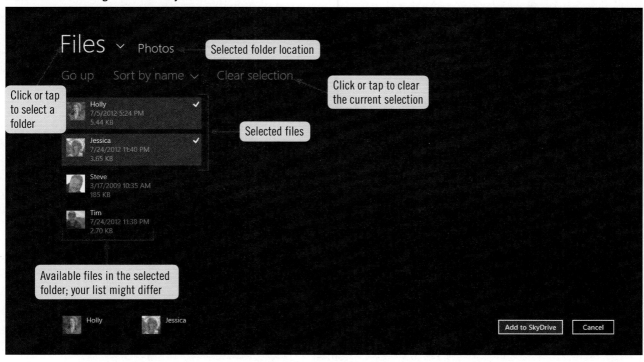

FIGURE C-16: Viewing files on the SkyDrive

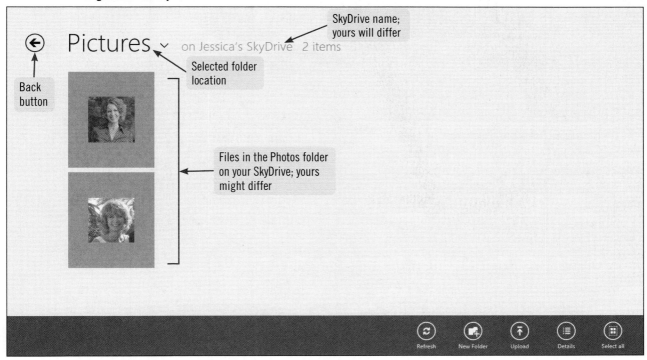

Practice

Concepts Review

Match the statements below with the elements labeled in the screen shown in FIGURE C-17.

FIGURE C-17

1. Which element lets you send email messages?
2. Which element lets you send instant messages?
3. Which element lets you manage events?
4. Which element lets you add contacts?
5. Which element lets you browse the Web?
6. Which element lets you store files online?

Match each term with the statement that best describes it.

7. Web
8. Internet
9. Instant message
10. Email
11. Web address
12. Web browser

a. A way to surf the Web
b. A typewritten conversion
c. A URL
d. An electronic message
e. Global collection of linked Web pages
f. Global collection of linked computers

Select the best answers from the following lists of choices.

13. **Which is a global collection of linked computers?**
    a. Internet
    b. Web
    c. URL
    d. ISP

14. **The term URL stands for:**
    a. Uniform Resource Locator.
    b. Universal Resource Locator.
    c. Uniform Result Locator.
    d. Universal Result Locator.

15. **The term ISP stands for:**
    a. Internet service provider.
    b. Internet search provider.
    c. International service provider.
    d. International search provider.

16. **The search results from a search engine are called:**
    a. Keywords.
    b. Matches.
    c. Hits.
    d. Phrases.

17. **Which of the following means private carbon copy?**
    a. Cc
    b. Bcc
    c. To
    d. None of the above

18. **Which of the following is *not* a way to respond to an email?**
    a. Reply
    b. Reply All
    c. Inbox
    d. Forward

19. **When you receive an email message, Mail stores it in which folder?**
    a. Outbox
    b. Junk
    c. Inbox
    d. Drafts

20. **When you receive a spam email message, Mail stores it in which folder?**
    a. Outbox
    b. Junk
    c. Inbox
    d. Drafts

21. **When you save an email message, Mail stores it in which folder?**
    a. Outbox
    b. Sent Items
    c. Inbox
    d. Drafts

22. **When you send an email message, you first send it to the:**
    a. Outbox.
    b. Sent Items folder.
    c. Inbox.
    d. Drafts folder.

23. **An instant message conversation consists of a(n):**
    a. thread.
    b. notification.
    c. emoticon.
    d. wink.

24. **Which option is *not* a Calendar app format?**
    a. Day
    b. Two Day
    c. Week
    d. Month

25. **Which calendar is *not* a Calendar app format?**
    a. Home
    b. Work
    c. Holidays
    d. Birthday

26. **Which folder is *not* a default folder on a SkyDrive?**
    a. Documents
    b. Pictures
    c. Favorites
    d. Videos

Skills Review

1. **Browse the Web with Internet Explorer.**
   a. Open the Internet Explorer app.
   b. Type **www.cengage.com** in the Address box, then press [Enter].
   c. Explore the Web site by using the scroll box, toolbar, and hyperlinks.
   d. Type **www.cbssports.com** in the Address bar, then press [Enter].
   e. Follow the links to investigate the content.
   f. Use the Back button to return to any page on Cengage.com.
   g. Use the Forward button to return to the Sportsline.com home page.
   h. Add a new tab.
   i. Type **www.loc.gov** in the Address box, then press [Enter].
   j. Delete the tab.

2. **Search the Web.**
   a. Open the Search panel for Internet Explorer.
   b. Click in the Search box.
   c. Type **job computer training**.
   d. Press [Enter].
   e. Use the Find on Page command to highlight the search text for computer training.
   f. Click a link to a Web site from the list of search results.
   g. Close the Internet Explorer app.

3. **Add contacts to People.**
   a. Open the People app.
   b. Create a new contact.
   c. Type **Grace** in the First name text box, press [Tab], then type **Wong** in the Last name text box.
   d. Type **gwong@questspecialtytravel.com** in the Email box.
   e. Type **Quest Specialty Travel** in the Company text box.
   f. Save the contact.
   g. Close the People app.

4. **Send messages with Mail.**
   a. Open the Mail app.
   b. Create a new email message.
   c. Use the To button to address the email message.
   d. Select the email address of your instructor, technical support person, or someone else you know.
   e. Add the contact to the email message.
   f. Type **Financial Update Request** in the Subject text box.
   g. In the Messages pane, type **Grace: Please send year-end financial report ASAP. Thanks.**
   h. Send the email message.

5. **Receive and respond to messages.**
   a. Have the email recipient to whom you sent the email message send a reply back to you.
   b. Use the Sync button to receive messages.
   c. Display the Folders pane.
   d. In the Folders pane, click Inbox, then click the message you just received.
   e. Forward the email message.
   f. Type your email address in the To box, then compose a response in the Messages pane.
   g. Send the email message.
   h. Close the Mail app.

Skills Review (continued)

6. Chat with Messaging.

    a. Open the Messaging app.

    b. Create a new instant message.

    c. Select the name of your instructor, technical support person, or someone else you know.

    d. Select the contact.

    e. Type **Status Report** in the Subject text box.

    f. In the Message text box, type and send a message, then wait for a response.

    g. Continue to converse in this manner.

    h. When you're done, delete the thread.

    i. Close the Messaging app.

7. Manage events with Calendar.

    a. Open the Calendar app.

    b. Display the next month on your calendar.

    c. Display today's calendar.

    d. Display the Day format.

    e. Display the Month format.

    f. Create a new event for next Monday with information of your choice.

    g. Save the event.

    h. Open the event, then delete it.

    i. Close the Calendar app.

8. Store information on SkyDrive.

    a. Open the SkyDrive app.

    b. Open the Pictures folder on your SkyDrive.

    c. Add files to your SkyDrive.

    d. Navigate to the drive and folder where you store your Data Files, then select the Photos folder.

    e. Select the **Tim** file, then select the **Steve** file.

    f. Add the files to your Documents folder on your SkyDrive.

    g. Go back to the SkyDrive screen.

    h. Close the SkyDrive app.

Independent Challenge 1

You will soon graduate from college with a degree in business management. Before entering the workforce, you want to make sure that you are up to date on all advances in the field. You decide that checking the Web would provide the most current information. In addition, you can search for companies with employment opportunities.

    a. Open Internet Explorer from the Start screen and use the app to investigate the business-related sites listed in **TABLE C-1**, or search for other business sites if these are not available.

    b. Open three sites in separate tabs.

    c. Click the appropriate links on the page to locate information about employment opportunities that sound interesting to you.

    d. When you find a relevant page, use the Print button on the App bar to print the page.

    e. Close the Internet Explorer app.

TABLE C-1: Business-related sites

Career Builder	www.careerbuilder.com
Monster	www.monster.com
Jobs	www.jobs.com

Independent Challenge 2

As president of Auto Metals, you just negotiated a deal to export metal auto parts to an assembly plant in China. Your lawyer, Jack Blea, drew up a preliminary contract. You want to send Jack an email indicating the terms of the deal so he can finish the contract.

    a. Open the Mail app from the Start screen.

    b. Create a new message.

    c. Type **jblea@blealaw.com** in the To text box, then type **China Deal Contract** in the Subject text box.

    d. Enter the following message:

        Dear Jack,

        I have completed the negotiations with the assembly plant. Please modify the following terms in the contract:

        1. All parts shall be inspected before shipping.

        2. Ship 100,000 units a month for 4 years with an option for 2 more years.

        Sincerely yours,

        [your name]

    e. Within the email message, insert an emoticon or wink.

    f. Send the email to Jack Blea.

    g. Delete any email responses to the Jack Blea email.

    h. Display the Sent Items folder.

    i. Delete the email to Jack Blea in the folder.

    j. Close the Mail app.

Independent Challenge 3

You are working in a regional office as a financial service advisor for Point Financial Services. You've recently invested in a new money market fund. As the financial markets move up and down during the day, you want to send instant message updates to clients and other advisors at the main office.

    a. Open the People app.

    b. Select a partner who has access to the Messaging app in Windows 8, then add your partner as a contact.

    c. Close the People app.

    d. Choose a time for instant messaging, then open the Messaging app.

    e. Create a new instant message with your contact.

    f. Wait for a response, then continue to converse in this manner within the thread.

    g. During the conversation, insert an emoticon or a wink.

    h. When you are done, delete the conversation.

    i. Close the Messaging app.

    j. Open the People app.

    k. Delete any contacts that you added.

    l. Close the People app.

Independent Challenge 4: Explore

Whether you are a student or a businessperson, managing your schedule is an important part of daily life. The Calendar app in Windows 8 helps you keep track of your events and tasks and provides reminder notifications before they occur. Use the Calendar app to manage your events for a week.

a. Open the Calendar app.

b. Enter at least three events for your schedule for the current week. Include an event 20 minutes from now with a 15-minute reminder.

c. View your calendar of events by the day, week, and month.

d. Close the Calendar app.

e. Wait for your next event to occur.

f. When the notification appears, view it in your calendar.

g. Close the Calendar app again.

Visual Workshop

Re-create the screen shown in **FIGURE C-18**.

FIGURE C-18

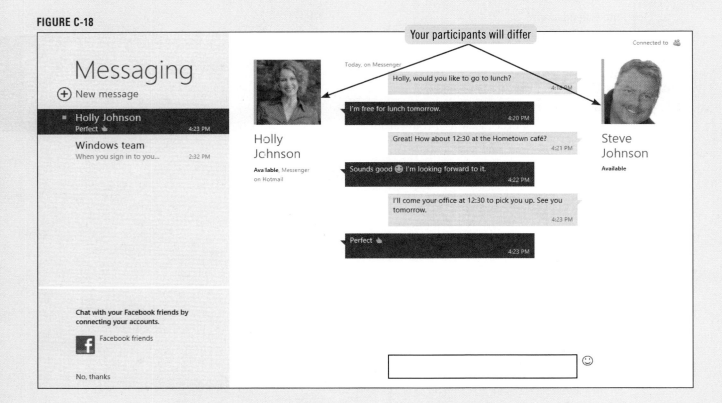

Getting and Sharing Information Apps

Working with Media Apps

CASE Windows 8 comes with apps that help you find information and use media on the Internet. You want to learn how to use apps to get news, financial, sports, maps, travel, and weather information; get and play music, videos, and games from the Xbox LIVE online store; and read documents.

Important: Before you start this lesson, place the Photos folder in the Pictures folder under Libraries, then place the Media folder in the Videos folder under Libraries. At the end of the unit, delete these folders.

Unit Objectives

After completing this unit, you will be able to

- Get information with media apps
- Take photos and video with the camera
- View photos and videos
- Get and play music or videos
- View and play games
- Use Windows Media Player
- Work with media from the desktop
- View and read documents

Files You Will Need

Holly.jpg	WIN D-1.wmv
Jessica.jpg	WIN D-2.wma
Steve.jpg	WIN D-3.xps
Tim.jpg	WIN D-4.pdf

©Itana/Shutterstock

Get Information with Media Apps

Windows 8 comes with a host of media-related apps that allow you to get specialized information, capture photos and video, watch movies and TV shows, listen to music, and play games. If you need information on a specific topic, Windows has specialized apps, such as Bing, Finance, Maps, News, Sports, Travel, and Weather, that provide targeted content supplied by Microsoft Bing. For example, if you want to find out the latest travel news, all you need to do is start the Travel app. **TABLE D-1** provides information on each of the specialized media information apps. Many of these media apps also allow you to customize the display, so you can focus on the information you want, rather than just the information available. This reduces the amount of searching you need to perform to find what you need. If you need to search the Web for information, instead of using Internet Explorer, you can use the Bing app, which provides a full screen approach to displaying search suggestions and results to make the process easier. You can access the media apps from the Start or All apps screen. **CASE** *As a travel consultant at QST, part of your job is to be aware of the latest trends in travel. To browse through travel-related materials, you decide to open the Travel app and the Bing app to search for travel information.*

STEPS

1. **With the Start screen in view, as shown in FIGURE D-1, click or tap the** Travel tile
   The Travel app opens in full screen view, displaying featured destinations, panoramas, and magazine articles. A panorama provides a 360-degree view of a destination.

2. **Move the mouse (on a computer) to display the scroll bar, then drag the white scroll box to the right or swipe your finger (on a mobile device) left from the right side of the screen**
   The screen scrolls to the right to display the additional app features.

3. **Click or tap an image or article, then scroll to view it**
   The image or article appears.

4. **Click or tap the** Back button ⊝
   The Home screen for the Travel app appears.

5. **Point to the top edge of the screen (cursor changes to a hand), then drag down to the bottom edge of the screen**
   The Travel app closes and the Start screen appears.

6. **Click or tap the** Bing tile
   The Bing app opens in full screen view, displaying a featured image along with suggested links at the bottom of the screen.

7. **Click or tap in the** Search box, **type** travel, **then click or tap the** Search button ⌕ **or press** [Enter]
   As you type, a list of tiles with suggested sites or topics appears. When you select a tile or enter search criteria, a list of links appears, in this case travel links.

8. **Click or tap a link, then scroll to view it**
   The image or article appears, where you can scroll to view the image or information.

9. **Point to the top edge of the screen (cursor changes to a hand), then drag down to the bottom edge of the screen**
   The Bing app closes and the Start screen appears.

FIGURE D-1: Viewing the Start screen with media information apps

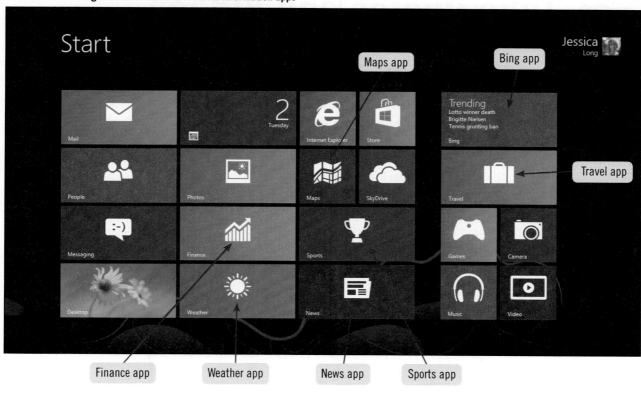

TABLE D-1: Media information apps

app	used to
Bing	Search the Web for information
Finance	Display financial information, including stock exchanges, interest rates, and business news
Maps	Display maps and get directions
News	Display top stories in local, national, and global news
Sports	Display the most recent sports news and scores
Travel	Display the latest trends and news in travel; get hotel and flight information
Weather	Display the latest weather for local, national, and global locations

Working with tiles

The live tiles on the Start screen provide quick status information that relates to each app. For example, the tile for the Finance app displays current stock information from the different exchanges. The information on the live tiles continually changes. If you don't want to display live tile information, you can clear the tile information for all tiles by using the Tiles command on the Settings panel; simply click or tap the Settings button on the Charm bar. If you only want to clear live tile information for specific tiles, you can turn live tiles on and off on an individual basis. Simply right-click or tap-hold a tile on the Start screen to select it with a check mark, then click the Turn live tile on or Turn live tile off button on the App bar.

Take Photos and Video with the Camera

Learning Outcomes
• Capture and play a video
• Take a photo
• Delete a video and delete a photo

With the Camera app that comes with Windows 8, you can use a digital camera to capture a still photo or video. To use the Camera app to take photos and video, you need to have a digital camera, such as a webcam, installed on your device. When you open the Camera app for the first time, you're asked to allow or block the use of your webcam and microphone. Once you capture a photo, you can preview and crop it as desired in the Camera app using the Crop button on the App bar. When you capture a video, you can preview and trim it if necessary in the Camera app using the Trim button on the App bar, and then play it back in the Camera app. After you capture a photo or video, it's automatically saved in the Camera Roll folder within the Pictures library folder. You can also view a photo or play a video and manage individual files in the Photos app or in File Explorer. If you don't like the way a photo or video came out or no longer want it, you can delete it at any time. **CASE** ▶ *As a travel consultant at QST, you use many travel videos and photos for company purposes. You try out the Camera app to see how effectively it can take a video and a photo.*

STEPS

1. **With the Start screen in view, click or tap the Camera tile, then if necessary click or tap Allow, if prompted to enable the use of your webcam and microphone**

   The Camera app opens in full screen view. The Home screen displays the video image from the current view of your computer's digital camera. The App bar, which appears at the bottom of the window, provides buttons that allow you to change camera options, switch to video mode, or use a timer before taking a photo or video.

2. **Click or tap the Video mode button ⊙ on the App bar to select it, if necessary**

   When the Video mode button is selected ⊙, the Camera app captures video. See **FIGURE D-2**. When it is not selected ⊙, the Camera app captures a photo.

3. **Click or tap the screen to start the video, then in 10 seconds or so click or tap the screen again to pause it**

   The Camera app captures a video from the digital camera. Note that when the video starts, a timer appears in the lower-right corner to indicate the length of the video.

4. **Click or tap the Video mode button ⊙ on the App bar to deselect it, click or tap the screen to take a photo, then click or tap the screen again**

   The Camera app takes a photo from the digital camera, and then the Home screen appears.

5. **Move the mouse (on a computer), then click the Back arrow ◄ twice or swipe right from the left side of the screen twice (on a mobile device)**

   The photo image appears, followed by the still image for the video.

6. **Click or tap the screen to play the video, click or tap to display the progress bar, then click or tap again to pause it**

   The video you recorded in Step 3 plays, as shown in **FIGURE D-3**, and then pauses. The App bar appears, displaying a progress bar, adjustable playhead, and buttons to delete and trim the start or end of the video.

7. **Click or tap the Delete button 🗑 on the App bar, click or tap the screen again, then click or tap the Delete button again**

   The video is deleted, and then the photo is deleted. The Home screen appears.

8. **Point to the top edge of the screen (cursor changes to a hand), then drag down to the bottom edge of the screen**

   The Camera app closes and the Start screen appears.

FIGURE D-2: Capturing a video

Back Arrow button

Camera options button

Timer button

Selected Video mode button

FIGURE D-3: Playing a video

Forward Arrow button

00:06

00:15

Trim

Delete

Video timeline

Progress bar

Playhead

Trim button

Delete button

Working with Media Apps

View Photos and Videos

Learning Outcomes
• View photos or videos
• Display a photo slide show

The Photos app that comes with Windows 8 provides a centralized place to store and view your photos, pictures, and videos from the Pictures library, SkyDrive, Facebook, Flickr, or any attached devices, such as a camera. The Pictures library is stored locally on your device. You can manage photos and pictures in the Pictures library from File Explorer in the desktop. Photos and videos you capture using the Camera app are automatically saved in the Pictures library folder in the Camera Roll folder. SkyDrive is a cloud-based storage device where you can share photos and other documents; you can access and manage files on SkyDrive from the SkyDrive app. Facebook and Flickr are online social networking services that allow you to store photos and videos along with other information. Within the Photos app, you can navigate or view photos and videos with a simple click or tap of a folder or image. Within a folder, you can scroll left or right or zoom in or out to view your photo or video differently. When you display a photo or video, you can use the Back or Forward arrow or a swipe left or right to quickly display other media elements in the folder. **CASE** *After taking some current employee photos and storing them in the Pictures library, you want to view them using the Photos app.*

STEPS

QUICK TIP
To import media, connect the camera, click or tap the Import button on the App bar, select the device, select the images, then click or tap Import.

1. **With the Start screen in view, click or tap the Photos tile**

   The Photos app opens in full screen view, displaying the Home screen with folders for Pictures library, SkyDrive, Devices, Facebook photos, and Flickr photos, as shown in **FIGURE D-4**. The image content in the folder, as well as subfolders, appears in the tile for easy identification.

2. **Click or tap the Pictures library tile**

   The Pictures library folder appears, displaying the contents of the folder, either folders or files.

3. **Click or tap the Camera Roll tile, click any available video to start it, then click the video**

   The video plays using the Camera app. When you click the video while it is running, a progress bar appears at the bottom of the screen.

4. **Click or tap the Back button ⬅ twice, then click or tap the Photos tile**

   The Photos folder appears, displaying the contents of the folder, as shown in **FIGURE D-5**. You can click or tap an image to display it. To navigate through the images in the folder, you move your mouse (on a computer), then click or tap the Back or Forward arrows, or swipe left or right (on a mobile device).

QUICK TIP
To zoom in or out, move the mouse, then click or tap the Zoom in button ➕ or Zoom Out button ➖ or pinch in or out.

5. **Click or tap an image**

   The image zooms in.

6. **Right-click the screen (on a computer) or swipe down from the top of the screen (on a mobile device), then click or tap the Slide show button ⊙ on the App bar**

   A slide show appears displaying all the images in the folder in alphabetical order every two seconds or so.

7. **Click or tap the screen**

   The slide show stops at the currently displayed image.

QUICK TIP
To set an image as the lock screen, app tile, or app background, click or tap the Set as button on the App bar, then click or tap a command.

8. **Click or tap the screen, then click or tap the Back button ⬅ until the Home screen appears**

   The Home screen for the Photos app appears.

9. **Point to the top edge of the screen (cursor changes to a hand), then drag down to the bottom edge of the screen**

   The Photos app closes and the Start screen appears.

FIGURE D-4: Viewing the Home screen for the Photos app

Images from folder appear on the tile; yours might differ

Hide

Add a device to see photos

Hide

f
See yours here

See yours here

Pictures library   SkyDrive   Devices   Facebook photos   Flickr pho

Folder tiles on the Home screen

FIGURE D-5: Viewing photos in a folder

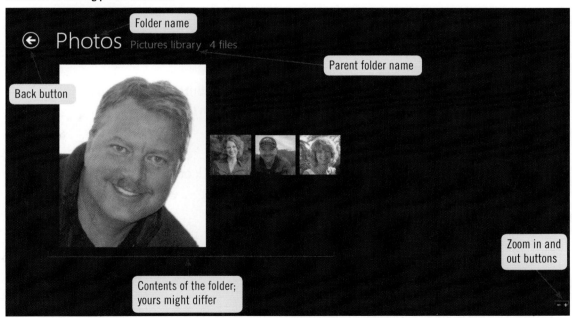

Folder name

← Photos Pictures library 4 files

Parent folder name

Back button

Zoom in and out buttons

Contents of the folder; yours might differ

Working with options and accounts in the Photos app

With the Options panel in the Photos app, you can set options to shuffle photos on the app tile and show or hide photos or videos from the different locations on your system. Click or tap the Settings button on the Charm bar, click or tap Options, then select from the available options. You can also quickly hide a storage location, such as Pictures library, SkyDrive, Facebook, Flickr, or Devices, by clicking or tapping the Hide button on the tile located on the Home screen of the Photos app. With the Photos app, you can view photos and videos stored on both Facebook and Flickr online services. After you connect the online service to your Microsoft account (which you only need to do once within Windows 8), you can set options to enable or disable the settings you want. For example, you can select or clear the View your Facebook photos and videos check box to show or hide them. You can access the online service options by using the Options panel in the Photos app, which opens your Web browser, displaying the available settings.

Get and Play Music or Videos

Learning Outcomes
• View music from Xbox LIVE
• Play music from Xbox LIVE

With the Music and Video apps that come with Windows 8, you can listen to music or watch videos located in the Music or Videos library folders or on the Xbox LIVE online service. With Xbox LIVE, you can buy and play music from the Xbox Music Store from the Music app, or rent or buy and watch videos from the movies store or television store from the Video app. To use Xbox LIVE and make purchases, you need to log in with an existing Xbox account or your Microsoft account. The Music app is organized by the following categories: my music, now playing, xbox music store, and most popular; the Video app is organized by my videos, spotlight, movies store, and television store. Each store is further organized into more detailed categories, including featured, new releases, top selling, genres, and studios or networks. If you can't find a song or video, you can use the Search button on the Charm bar to locate it. If you have your Xbox 360 console connected to your device, you can get media for (requires the free Xbox SmartGlass app from the Windows Store) and play media on the console. **CASE** *You like to play music in the background while you work, so you decide to use the Music app to find an appropriate selection.*

STEPS

1. **With the Start screen in view, click or tap the Music tile**
   The Music app opens in full screen view, displaying the Home screen with the following categories: my music, now playing, xbox music store, and most popular, as shown in **FIGURE D-6**.

2. **Click or tap xbox music store**
   The Xbox Music Store appears, displaying a list of categories on the left and albums on the right.

3. **Click or tap a category, then click or tap an album**
   A window appears, displaying the album cover, name, list of songs, and options to preview, buy, or find out more about the artist.

   QUICK TIP
   To buy music, click or tap the Buy album or Buy song button for a selected item, then follow the purchase instructions.

4. **Click or tap a song, then click or tap the Preview button ⊙ next to it**
   The Apps bar appears displaying the selected song, and then it starts to play.

5. **Click or tap the Pause button ⏸ on the App bar**
   The song is paused. See **FIGURE D-7**.

   QUICK TIP
   To repeat the song or to shuffle songs, click or tap the Repeat or Shuffle button on the App bar to toggle on or off.

6. **Click or tap off the App bar to dismiss it, then click or tap off the Album screen**
   The Album screen closes and the Xbox Music Store appears.

7. **Click or tap the Back button ⊙**
   The Home screen for the Music app appears.

8. **Point to the top edge of the screen (cursor changes to a hand), then drag down to the bottom edge of the screen**
   The Music app closes and the Start screen appears.

FIGURE D-6: Viewing the Music app with xbox music

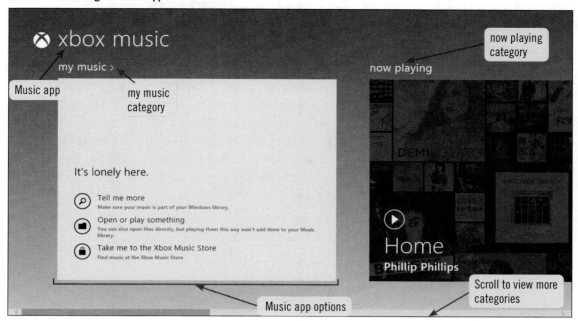

FIGURE D-7: Playing a song

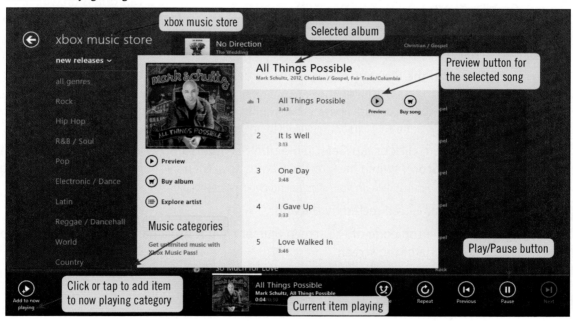

Playing media in the Video app

You can play movies and television shows in the Video app using a similar method as you would use to play music in the Music app. Click or tap the Video app tile on the Start screen, click or tap a movie or show from one of the categories or click or tap a category name to view additional content. In the movie store or television store, click or tap a category, then click or tap a movie or show. For movies, click or tap the Buy button to make a purchase, the Explore button to find out more information, or the Play trailer button to preview. For television shows, click or tap the View seasons to display and buy episodes or the Explore seasons to find out more information. After you select an episode you want, click or tap the Buy episode button, then follow the instructions to purchase it from Xbox LIVE. You will find that some movies or shows are free of charge. Click or tap the Back button to return to previous screens.

View and Play Games

**Learning
Outcomes**
• View games in
the Windows
games store
• Play a game from
the Windows
games store
• Install and unin-
stall a game from
the Windows
game store

With the Games app that comes with Windows 8, you can play local or online games from either the Windows games store or Xbox 360 games store. For Windows games, you can buy and install them from the Windows Store. For Xbox 360 games, you can buy a game for and play a game on Xbox 360. To use Xbox LIVE and make purchases, you need to log in with an existing Xbox account or your Microsoft account. To play Xbox 360 games, you need to connect the console to your device and install the free Xbox SmartGlass app from the Windows Store. If you can't find a game, you can use the Search button on the Charm bar to locate it. As a game player, you can create an **avatar**—a character that represents you—and profile for use during games, as well as view your gaming achievements. **CASE** ➤ *In your off-hours from work you like to play games, so you decide to check out what's available using the Games app.*

STEPS

1. **With the Start screen in view, click or tap the** Games tile

    The Games app opens in full screen view, displaying the Home screen with the following categories: spotlight, game activity, windows games store, and xbox 360 games store.

2. **Click or tap** windows games store

    The windows games store appears, displaying a list of available games for Windows.

3. **Click or tap the** Wordament **game, or another free game if this one is unavailable**

    A game preview screen appears, displaying information about the game as well as buttons to play the game and explore more information about the game. A button to play a trailer about the game may also appear. See **FIGURE D-8**.

4. **Click or tap the** Play button ▷ **on the screen**

    The game app opens or a message appears indicating the game is not currently installed. If it's not installed and you are working on a lab device, obtain permission from your instructor or technical support person to install it, then complete Steps 5 through 9. Otherwise, skip to Step 6.

5. **If prompted, click or tap** Get *"game title"* from the Store, **click or tap** Install, **close the Windows Store, switch back to the Games app, then click or tap the** Play button **again**

    The game app is installed on your system and appears on the Start screen.

QUICK TIP
To preview a game,
click or tap the Play
trailer button, if
available, on the
game preview
screen.

6. **Play the game as directed by the app**

7. **Point to the top edge of the screen (cursor changes to a hand), then drag down to the bottom edge of the screen**

    The installed game app closes and the Start screen appears.

8. **Click the upper-left corner (on a computer) or swipe right from the left side of the screen (on a mobile device) to switch to the Games app, point to the top edge of the screen (cursor changes to a hand), then drag down to the bottom edge of the screen**

    The Games app closes and the Start screen appears.

9. **If you installed a game, right-click or tap-hold the game tile, click or tap the** Uninstall **button** ⊖ **on the App bar, then click or tap** Uninstall

    The installed game app is removed from your system and the Start screen appears.

FIGURE D-8: Viewing a game from the windows games store

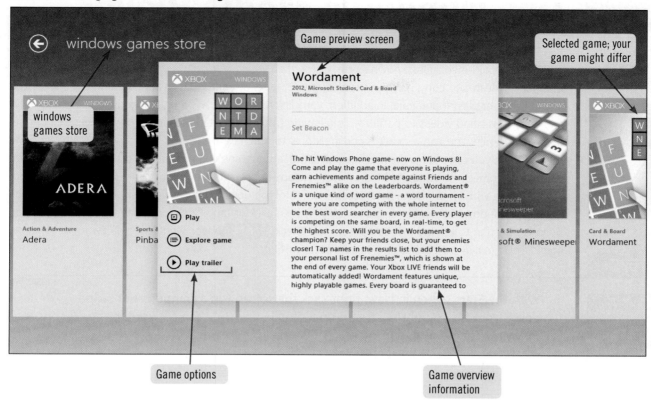

Game preview screen

Selected game; your game might differ

windows games store

windows games store

ADERA

Action & Adventure
Adera

Sports &

Pinba

◎ XBOX WINDOWS

W O R
N T D
E M A

Wordament
2012, Microsoft Studios, Card & Board
Windows

Set Beacon

The hit Windows Phone game- now on Windows 8!
Come and play the game that everyone is playing,
earn achievements and compete against Friends and
Frenemies™ alike on the Leaderboards. Wordament®
is a unique kind of word game - a word tournament -
where you are competing with the whole internet to
be the best word searcher in every game. Every player
is competing on the same board, in real-time, to get
the highest score. Will you be the Wordament®
champion? Keep your friends close, but your enemies
closer! Tap names in the results list to add them to
your personal list of Frenemies™, which is shown at
the end of every game. Your Xbox LIVE friends will be
automatically added! Wordament features unique,
highly playable games. Every board is guaranteed to

▣ Play

≡ Explore game

▶ Play trailer

crosoft
inesweeper

& Simulation
soft® Minesweepe

W
N
E

N F
E U
W N

Card & Board
Wordament

Windows 8

Game options

Game overview information

Accessing your Xbox account

After you accept the terms of use for Xbox LIVE when you access it for the first time in the Games, Music, or Video apps, you can use Account Preferences to view your Xbox account information. Click or tap the Settings button on the Charm bar, click or tap Account on the Settings panel, then click or tap a link to an account area, such as Xbox LIVE Membership, Xbox Music Pass, Redeem Code, and Manage Payment Options.

Viewing and changing player information

In the Games app, you can create or customize an avatar—a character that represents you in the game—edit or share a player profile, and view player achievements. After you open the Games app, scroll all the way to the left to display the current player information. To create or customize an avatar, click or tap Create Avatar or Customized Avatar, select the style and features you want, then click the Save button. To edit a profile, click or tap the Edit Profile button, specify a name, motto, location, and bio, then click or tap Save. To share your profile with others, click or tap the Share Profile button, click or tap the app you want to use on the Share panel, then use the app to send it.

Use Windows Media Player

Learning
Outcomes
• View media in
Windows Media
Player
• Play a video using
Windows Media
Player

Windows 8 comes with a built-in accessory called Windows Media Player, which you can use to play video, audio, and mixed-media files, known as **clips**, stored on your system, a CD, a DVD, a local network, or the Internet. You can also copy, or **rip**, individual music tracks or entire CDs to your system and create your own jukebox or playlist of media. In addition, you can create, or **burn**, your own audio CDs or data DVDs and copy music and videos to portable digital audio players and PCs, such as an MP3 player, cell phone, or mobile device. You can also access online stores to purchase music and other media. With Windows Media Player, you can modify the media, control the settings, and change the player's appearance, or skin. Windows 8 comes with Windows Media Player version 12; however, new versions are periodically released. To make sure you are using the most recent version of Windows Media Player, right-click or tap-hold the taskbar in Windows Media Player, point to Help, then click or tap Check for updates. You must have an open connection to the Internet to perform this check. **CASE** *You want to learn how to use Windows Media Player to play travel video and audio clips for customers.*

STEPS

1. **With the Start screen in view, right-click the screen (on a computer) or swipe down from the top of the screen (on a mobile device), then click or tap the All apps button ⊞ on the App bar**
   The All apps screen appears, displaying all the apps on your system.

2. **Under Windows Accessories, click or tap the Windows Media Player tile**
   The Windows Media Player window opens in the desktop. A taskbar with tabs is at the top of the window and player controls that look and function similar to those on a CD or DVD player are along the bottom. The Library window opens by default, as shown in **FIGURE D-9**, displaying media you currently have stored on your system.

3. **In the Windows Media Player window, select the Videos library, then double-click or double-tap the WIN D-1 file**
   A video clip of wildlife opens and plays once in the Now Playing window, a smaller more compact window, as shown in **FIGURE D-10**.

4. **Click the Turn repeat on button 🔁 at the bottom of the Media Player**
   The media clip plays continuously, or **loops** in the Now Playing window.

5. **After the video clip repeats several times, click the Stop button ⏹, then click or tap the Turn repeat off button 🔁**
   The looping feature turns off and the video clip ceases. You can control the playback of media in the Windows Media Player window or from the taskbar.

6. **Click or tap the Switch to Library button ⊞ in the upper-right corner of the Now Playing window**
   The Library window opens in Windows Media Player.

7. **Click or tap the Close button ✕ in the Windows Media Player window**
   The Windows Media Player app closes and the desktop appears.

8. **Point to the top edge of the screen (cursor changes to a hand), then drag down to the bottom edge of the screen**
   The Desktop app closes and the Start screen appears.

FIGURE D-9: Library window in Windows Media Player

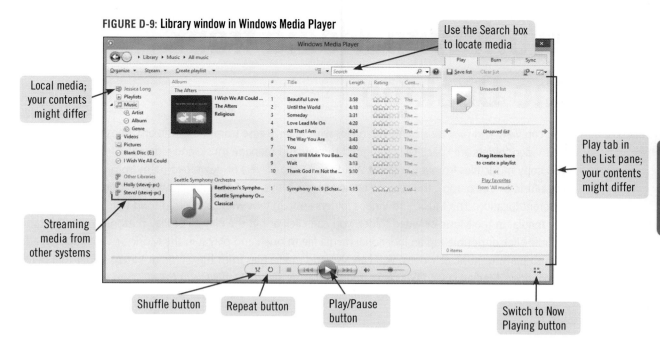

Use the Search box to locate media

Local media; your contents might differ

Play tab in the List pane; your contents might differ

Streaming media from other systems

Shuffle button   Repeat button   Play/Pause button   Switch to Now Playing button

FIGURE D-10: Playing a video clip in the Now Playing window

Video title

Switch to Library button

View full screen button

Drag to rewind or forward media   Repeat button   Stop button   Mute button   Volume button

Playing media from other systems or the Internet

You can use Windows Media Player to play media available on the Internet or a network, such as videos, live broadcasts, and music tracks. You can stream the media directly from another system on your network over the Internet, or from a Web site, or you can download the media file to your system. Delivering high-quality, continuous video, live broadcasts, sound, and music playback is known as **streaming media**. When you stream media, the video or music starts playing while the file is being transmitted to you from a network or over the Internet. The streaming media is not stored on your system. If you have media on another system over a network, HomeGroup (a home-sharing network), or the Internet, you can use commands on the Stream menu to allow access and control of the media on your system. You can access the

streaming media from the Navigation pane just your like local media. To stream media from the Internet, locate the Web site that contains the media you want to play, click or tap the link to the media, then wait for Windows Media Player to start (if necessary) and the first data bits to be transmitted to a temporary memory storage area called a **buffer** and for the media to start playing automatically. The buffer continues to download the media as Window Media Player plays the media in the buffer. When you download a media file, you have to wait for the entire file to be transferred to your system before you can play or work with it. To download a media file, use a Web browser to locate it from the Internet, then click or tap the download link to download and save it locally.

Work with Media from the Desktop

Learning Outcomes
• Play a media file from the desktop
• Add a media file to a playlist

You can view and play music and video files with relative ease from the Music or Videos folder. The Music and Video folders are specifically designed to play and manage music and video files, respectively. When you copy music files from a CD (from Windows Media Player) or download them from the Internet (from the Music or Video app), the files are copied to the Music or Videos folder by default unless you specify a different location. The Music and Videos folders contain tabs with specialized tools that can help you play the media. In the Music or Video folder, you can click or tap the Play all or Play button on the Play tab or double-click or double-tap an individual media file to open and play it in the Music or Video app. In addition to playing music or videos, you can also add media files from the Music or Videos folder to a playlist in Windows Media Player. **CASE** *You mostly use your desktop while in the office, so you decide to try to play some music from the File Explorer window.*

STEPS

1. **With the Start screen still in view, click or tap the Desktop tile, then click or tap the File Explorer button 📁 on the taskbar**

   The File Explorer window opens in front of the desktop.

2. **In the File Explorer window, navigate to the Videos folder where you store your Data Files, then double-click or double tap the Media folder**

   The contents of the Videos folder appears in the File Explorer window.

3. **Click or tap the WIN D-2 file, then click or tap the Play tab under Music Tools**

   When you select a music or video file, the Play tab appears under Music Tools or Video Tools with buttons to play the selected file in the Music or Video app, as shown in **FIGURE D-11**.

TROUBLE
If a dialog box opens asking you how to open the WMA file, click or tap Music.

4. **Click or tap the Play button ▷ on the Play tab**

   The Music app opens and starts to play the song. When the song is over, the Home screen for the Music app appears, displaying the song in the now playing area.

5. **Point to the top edge of the screen (cursor changes to a hand), drag down to the bottom edge of the screen, then click the upper-left corner (on a computer) or swipe right from the left side of the screen (on a mobile device)**

   The Music app closes and the Start screen appears, then the Desktop app appears, displaying the File Explorer window. The WIN D-3 file remains selected.

6. **Click or tap the Add to playlist button ▷ on the Play tab, then click or tap the Windows Media Player button on the taskbar**

   The Windows Media Player app opens in a minimized window. The Windows Media Player app button appears on the taskbar.

7. **Click or tap the Switch to Library button ⊞ in the upper-right corner of the Now Playing window**

   The Windows Media Player app closes and the desktop appears.

8. **Click or tap the Close button ✕ in the Windows Media Player window and in the File Explorer window**

   The Windows Media Player and File Explorer app close and the desktop appears.

9. **Point to the top edge of the screen (cursor changes to a hand), then drag down to the bottom edge of the screen**

   The Desktop app closes and the Start screen appears.

FIGURE D-11: Viewing media files in File Explorer

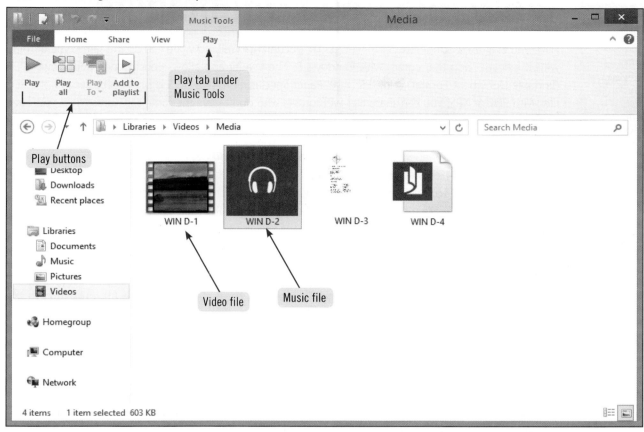

Creating a sound file

Using Sound Recorder and a microphone, you can record your own sound files. Sound Recorder creates Windows Media Audio files with the .wma file extension. Sound Recorder doesn't play sounds; you can play your recording in a digital media player, such as the Music app or Windows Media Player. Before you can use Sound Recorder, you need to have a sound card, speakers, and a microphone installed on your PC computer. In the Start screen, click or tap the All apps button on the App bar, then click or tap Sound Recorder. In the Sound Recorder app, click or tap the Start Recording button, then record the sounds you want. When you're finished recording, click or tap the Stop Recording button, select a folder, type a name for the file, then click or tap Save. When you're done, click or tap the Close button.

Associating a sound with an event

Besides customizing the desktop appearance of Windows, you can also add sound effects to common Windows commands and functions, such as starting and exiting Windows, printing complete, opening and closing folders, or emptying the Recycle Bin. You can select a **sound scheme** (a collection of sounds associated with events), or you can mix and match sound files to create your own collection for your PC computer. You need to use Wave files with the .wav file extension. If you put WAV files in the Media folder, located in the Windows folder, the sound files appear in the Sounds list. In the desktop, click the Settings button on the Charm bar, click or tap Control Panel, then click or tap the Sound icon in Small icons or Large icons view. In the dialog box, click or tap the Sounds tab, click or tap an event to which you want to associate a sound, click or tap the Sounds list arrow, then select a sound, or click or tap Browse and locate the sound file you want to use. Click or tap Save As, type a name for the sound scheme, then click or tap OK. To select a sound scheme, click or tap the Sound Scheme list arrow, then select a scheme. When you're done, click or tap OK.

View and Read Documents

Learning Outcomes
• Open a document using the Reader app
• View a document using the Reader app

Have you ever used Adobe Reader to view a PDF document? Well, now you can do the same type of thing with the Reader app that comes with Windows 8. The Reader app allows you to open and browse PDF (Portable Document Format) and XPS (XML Paper Specification) files. XPS is Microsoft's version of a PDF file. With PDF or XPS, you can share files with others who don't have the same software. When you open a PDF or XPS document, it looks the same on the destination as it would on the source. In addition to the Reader app, you can also open XPS documents with the XPS Viewer, a Desktop app that comes with Windows 8. In XPS Viewer, you can also set permissions and add digital signatures to protect the document from unauthorized viewing and printing. You create an XPS document, either an XPS Document (.xps) or OpenXPS Document (.oxps), by printing it with the Microsoft XPS Document Writer printer from within an app, such as Microsoft Word or WordPad. **CASE** ➤ *You want to view the Company Information Sheet XPS document, so you decide to open it using the Reader app.*

STEPS

1. **With the Start screen still in view, right-click the screen (on a computer) or swipe down from the top of the screen (on a mobile device), then click or tap the** All apps button ⊞ **on the App bar**

   The All apps screen appears, displaying all the apps on your system.

2. **Click or tap the** Reader tile

   The Reader app opens in full screen view, displaying the Home screen with a Browse tile for opening documents and tiles for opening any recent files.

3. **Click or tap the** Browse tile

   The Files screen appears, where you can select the files you want to open.

4. **Click or tap the** Files down arrow, **navigate to the Videos folder where you store your Data Files, then click or tap the** Media folder

   The files in the folder appear in the Files screen.

5. **Click or tap the** Win D-3 file

   A check mark appears in the upper-right corner of the file tile, as shown in **FIGURE D-12**.

6. **Click or tap the** Open button **on the Files screen**

   The file is opened in the Reader screen.

7. **Right-click the screen (on a computer) or swipe down from the top of the screen (on a mobile device), then click or tap the** One page button ⊕ **or the** Continuous button ⊕ **on the App bar**

   The view changes to display one page at a time (horizontally or vertically) on the screen, as shown in **FIGURE D-13**. The App bar provides options to find text, change the display view, and open and save documents. In addition, the More button provides options to close a file, get document information, and rotate a document.

8. **Click or tap the** More button ⬤ **on the App bar, then click or tap** Close file

   The document closes and the Home screen for the Reader app appears.

9. **Point to the top edge of the screen (cursor changes to a hand), then drag down to the bottom edge of the screen**

   The Reader app closes and the Start screen appears.

FIGURE D-12: Selecting files to open in the Reader app

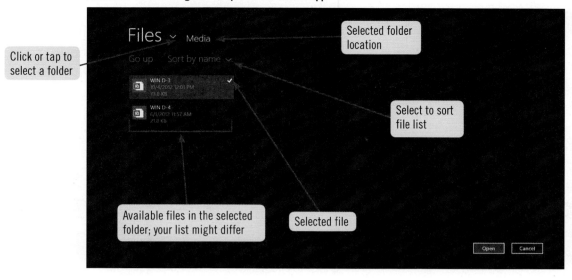

Click or tap to select a folder

Selected folder location

Select to sort file list

Available files in the selected folder; your list might differ

Selected file

FIGURE D-13: Viewing a document in the Reader app

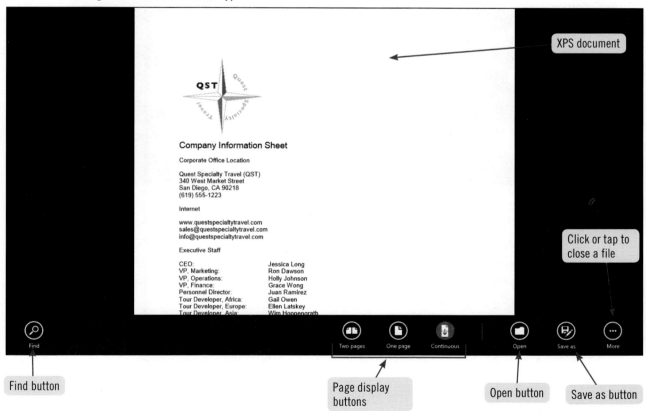

XPS document

Click or tap to close a file

Find button

Page display buttons

Open button

Save as button

Creating an XPS document

You create an XPS document by printing it with the Microsoft XPS Document Writer printer from within an app, such as Microsoft Word or WordPad. To create an XPS document, open the app and document you want to create as an XPS document, click or tap the File tab or menu, click or tap Print, select Microsoft XPS Document Writer as your printer, click or tap Print, specify a location, name the XPS document, select a format, either XPS Document (.xps) or OpenXPS Document (.oxps), then click or tap Save. The OpenXPS Document format is a new file format supported only by Windows 8; you can't view an OpenXPS Document on earlier versions of Windows.

Practice

Concepts Review

Match the statements below with the elements labeled in the screen shown in FIGURE D-14.

FIGURE D-14

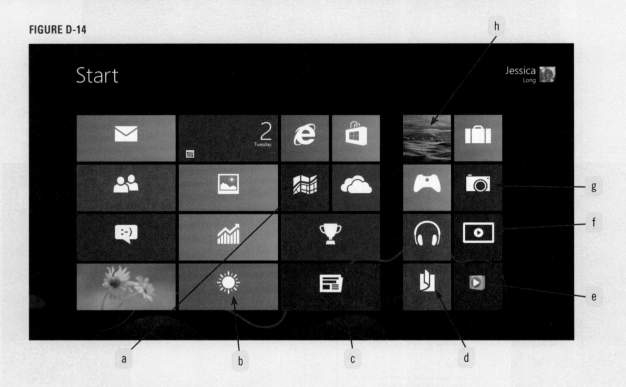

1. **Which element lets you find directions?**
2. **Which element lets you search the Web?**
3. **Which element lets you create a video?**
4. **Which element lets you play music?**
5. **Which element lets you play movies?**
6. **Which element lets you get the weather?**
7. **Which element lets you read the news?**
8. **Which element lets you view documents?**

Match each term with the statement that best describes it.

  9. **Rip**   **a.** A cloud-based storage area
10. **SkyDrive**   **b.** A temporary memory storage area
11. **Buffer**   **c.** A way to continuously play media
12. **Stream**   **d.** A way to copy media
13. **Loop**   **e.** A way to continuously play media repeatedly

Select the best answers from the following lists of choices.

14. **Which app allows you to display travel information?**
    a. Bing
    b. Weather
    c. Maps
    d. News

15. **Which folder does the Camera app use to store photos and videos?**
    a. Camera
    b. Camera Roll
    c. Videos
    d. Pictures

16. **Which of the following is *not* a folder in the Photos app?**
    a. SkyDrive
    b. Facebook
    c. Pictures library
    d. Documents

17. **Which of the following is *not* a Music app category?**
    a. my music
    b. featured
    c. now playing
    d. most popular

18. **Which of the following is *not* a Video app category?**
    a. my videos
    b. spotlight
    c. video store
    d. movies store

19. **Which of the following categories allows you to buy games for use on Windows 8?**
    a. Windows games store
    b. Xbox 360 games store
    c. Games store
    d. Xbox games store

20. **When you create a CD or DVD, the process is known as:**
    a. ripping.
    b. burning.
    c. copying.
    d. synchronizing.

21. **Which of the following apps allows you to play music and videos?**
    a. Music
    b. Video
    c. Windows Media Player
    d. Camera

22. **The term PDF stands for:**
    a. Portable Document File.
    b. Portable Document Format.
    c. Page Document File.
    d. Page Document Format.

23. **The term XPS stands for:**
    a. XML Paper Specification.
    b. XML Page Specification.
    c. XML Paper Specialization.
    d. XML Page Specialization.

24. **Which of the following commands allows you to create an XPS document?**
    a. Save
    b. Print
    c. Export
    d. Publish

Skills Review

1. **Get information with media apps.**
   a. Open the News app.
   b. Scroll through the content.
   c. Click or tap an image or article, then scroll to view it.
   d. Go back to the Home screen.
   e. Close the News app.
   f. Open the Bing app.
   g. Search for **news**.
   h. Click or tap a link, then scroll to view it.
   i. Close the Bing app.

Skills Review (continued)

2. Take photos and video with the camera.

  a. Open the Camera app.

  b. Select Video mode, if necessary.

  c. Click or tap to start the video, then end it.

  d. Deselect Video mode.

  e. Click or tap to take a photo.

  f. View the video, then play it.

  g. Delete the video.

  h. View the photo, then delete it.

  i. Close the Camera app.

3. View photos and videos.

  a. Open the Photos app.

  b. Open the Pictures library folder.

  c. Open the Photos folder.

  d. Click or tap an image.

  e. Start a slide show.

  f. View the slide show, then stop it.

  g. Go back to the Home screen.

  h. Close the Photos app.

4. Get and play music or videos.

  a. Open the Music app.

  b. Display the Xbox Music Store.

  c. Select a category, then select an album.

  d. Select a song, then preview it.

  e. Pause the song.

  f. Go back to the Home screen.

  g. Close the Music app.

5. View and play games.

  a. Open the Games app.

  b. Display the Windows games store.

  c. Click or tap a free game.

  d. Play the game.

  e. If prompted, install it, switch back to the Games app, then play the game as directed by the app.

  f. Close the game app, the Games app, and Windows Store app.

  g. If you installed an app, uninstall it.

6. Use Windows Media Player.

  a. Open the Windows Media Player app from the All apps screen.

  b. Select the Videos library.

  c. Open and start the WIN D-1 video.

  d. Turn repeat on.

  e. Stop the video, then turn repeat off.

  f. Switch to the library.

  g. Close Windows Media Player.

  h. Close the Desktop app.

7. Work with media from the desktop.

  a. Open the Desktop app.

  b. Start File Explorer.

  c. Navigate to the Videos folder from the location where you store your Data Files, then open the Media folder.

  d. Select the WIN D-3 music file.

  e. Play the music file (Music app opens).

  f. Close the Music app, then switch back to the desktop.

  g. Add the selected file to the playlist.

  h. Switch to the library.

  i. Close the Windows Media Player app.

  j. Close the Desktop app.

8. View and read documents.

  a. Open the Reader app from the All apps screen.

  b. Browse to the Videos folder from the location where you store your Data Files, then open the Media folder.

  c. Select the WIN D-4 file, then open it.

  d. Change the view between One page and Continuous.

  e. Use the More button to close the file.

  f. Close the Reader app.

Independent Challenge 1

You are working in a regional office as a financial service advisor for Point Financial Services. You want to monitor the financial markets as they move up and down during the day, so you can advise your clients appropriately. You decide to use the Finance app to quickly check the market data and the Bing app to research companies on the upswing.

a. Open the Finance app.
b. Scroll through the finance informaton.
c. Identify and track the following financial data for a week:
  • Dow and Nasdaq
  • Top five gainers for the day
  • Mortgage rates for the day
d. Read and print a financial article.
e. Close the Finance app.
f. Open the Bing app.
g. Search for one of the companies you tracked.
h. View and print information about the company.
i. Close the Bing app.

Independent Challenge 2

You are in the process of looking for a job. You want to capture a photo to insert into your written résumé as well as put together a video résumé. Before you get started on the video portion, take a moment to write out a basic script about your qualifications and how you want to present yourself. You decide to use the Camera app to capture the video and take a photo to complete the project.

a. Open the Camera app.
b. Select Video mode, if necessary.
c. Click or tap to start the video, read the script, then end it.
d. Deselect Video mode.
e. Click or tap to take a photo.
f. View the video, then play it.
g. View the photo.
h. Close the Camera app.
i. Open the Photos app.
j. Open the Pictures library folder.
k. Open the Camera Roll folder.
l. Play the video and view the photo.
m. Select the video and photo, then delete them.
n. Close the Photos app.

Independent Challenge 3

You are a college student majoring in music. As part of your studies, you need to listen to different types of music and identify the unique styles of each one. You want to use the Xbox Music Store to locate music from different genres, and then preview the songs to complete your assignment.

a. Open the Music app.
b. Display the Xbox Music Store.
c. Preview at least two songs in the following genres:
  • Rock
  • Hip Hop
  • Country
  • Classical
  • Jazz or Blues
d. Identify the artist and song in a document.
e. Close the Music app.

Independent Challenge 4: Explore

Whether you are a student or a businessperson, taking a vacation is important to get away from the daily grind and enjoy some time away from everyday life. The Travel app in Windows 8 enables you to look for travel destinations, make flight and hotel reservations, and use planning tools to create the vacation you always wanted to take. Use the Travel app to plan a weeklong trip anywhere in the world.

a. Open the Travel app.
b. View any destinations provided or use Destinations on the Apps bar.
c. Use Flights and Hotels on the App bar to plan reservations.
d. Use Best of Web on the App bar to use tools.
e. Document and print your travel plans.
f. Close the Tavel app.

Visual Workshop

Re-create the screen shown in **FIGURE D-15**, which shows an avatar and a profile in the Games app.

FIGURE D-15

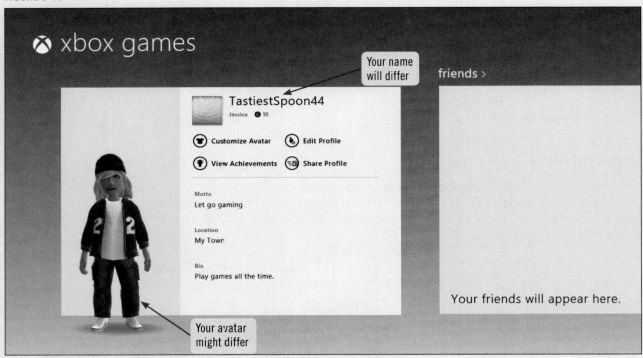

Managing Files and Folders in the Desktop

CASE Windows 8 comes with File Explorer, which helps you organize and keep track of files and folders. You want to learn how to use File Explorer to access and work with files, folders, drives, and disks on your local, homegroup, and network computers.

Unit Objectives

After completing this unit, you will be able to

- Open File Explorer
- View files and folders
- Navigate a folders list
- Create and rename files and folders
- Search for files and folders

- Organize files and folders
- Copy and move files and folders
- Delete and restore files and folders
- Work with libraries

Files You Will Need

Quest Travel (folder)
  Advertising (folder)
    QST Ad Copy.rtf
  Company (folder)
    QST Company Info.rtf
    QST Fact Sheet.rtf
    QST People.rtf
    QST Press Release.rtf
  Letters (folder)
    Business Letters (folder)
      C&N Printing.rtf
      IRS Letter.rtf

Personal Letters (folder)
  Eric Shubel.rtf
  Tracy Teyler.rtf
Marketing (folder)
  QST Focus.rtf
  QST Logo.bmp
  QST New Logo.bmp
Tours (folder)
  QST Tours.rtf
To Do List.rtf

©Itana/Shutterstock

Open File Explorer

File management is organizing and keeping track of files and folders. Working with poorly managed files is like looking for a needle in a haystack—it is frustrating and time consuming to search through irrelevant, misnamed, and out-of-date files to find the one you want. Windows allows you to organize folders and files in a file hierarchy, imitating the way you store paper documents in real folders. Just as a filing cabinet contains several folders, each containing a set of related documents, and several dividers grouping related folders together, a file hierarchy allows you to place files in folders, then place folders in other folders, so that your files are organized and easier to find. Windows 8 provides you with a main file management window called File Explorer. File Explorer contains a toolbar, a Navigation pane, a Details pane, a menu bar (which might not be visible), a status bar (which might not be activated) providing information about the contents of the window, and a list of contents. The Navigation pane displays links to common folder and drive locations, including Favorites, Libraries, Homegroup (a shared home network), Computer, and Network. **Libraries** are special folders that catalog files and folders in a central location, regardless of where you actually store them on your hard drive, to make finding files easier. **CASE** *You are a newly hired marketing specialist at Quest Specialty Travel (QST). Ron Dawson, your Marketing Manager, sends you a list of upcoming projects. You want to review the files on your computer and organize them as your first task.*

STEPS

1. **With the Start screen in view, click or tap the** Desktop tile
   The Desktop screen appears, displaying the desktop and taskbar.

2. **Click or tap the** File Explorer button 📁 **on the taskbar**
   The File Explorer window opens, displaying the contents of the Libraries folder. File Explorer comes with four default libraries: Documents, Music, Pictures, and Videos.

3. **Click or tap** Computer **in the Navigation pane**
   The Computer window opens, as shown in **FIGURE E-1**, displaying the contents of your computer, including all disk drives, removable storage devices, and network locations, which are denoted inside a set of parentheses with a letter (assigned by the device in alphabetical order) and a colon. **TABLE E-1** lists the typical drives on a computer and how to use them.

4. **Double-click or double-tap the** drive **or click or tap a location in the Navigation pane where you store your Data Files**
   The folders contained on the disk drive open in the window. When you open a disk drive or folder, the Address bar adds the new location to the list. In this example, the Documents folder is now listed in the Address bar after Computer.

5. **Double-click or double-tap the** folder **where you store your Data Files**
   The folder contains the Quest Travel folder, which contains the Data Files for this unit.

6. **Double-click or double-tap the** Quest Travel folder
   The folders and files in the Quest Travel folder display in the window: Advertising, Company, Letters, Marketing, Tours, and To Do List. The file is represented by an icon that indicates the application it was created with. For example, the To Do List.rtf file was created in WordPad.

7. **Double-click or double-tap the** Company folder
   The Company folder opens, displaying four files, which were created in WordPad.

FIGURE E-1: Computer window

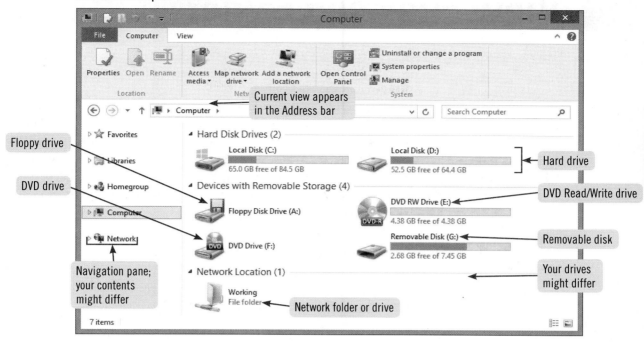

TABLE E-1: Typical disk drives

icon	type	description
	Local	A hard magnetic disk on which you can store large amounts of data. The disk is typically not removable from the computer.
	Removable	A removable disk on which you can store computer data, such as a Flash memory card or Flash or USB drive.
	Compact Disc-Read-Only Memory (CD-ROM)	An optical disc on which you can stamp, or burn, up to 1 GB (typical size is 650 MB) of data in only one session. The read-only disc cannot be erased or burned again with additional new data.
	Compact Disc-Recordable (CD-R)	A type of read-only CD on which you can burn up to 1 GB of data in multiple sessions. The disc can be burned again with additional new data, but cannot be erased.
	Compact Disc-Rewritable (CD-RW)	A type of CD on which you can read, write, and erase data, just like a removable or hard disk.
	Digital Video Disc (DVD)	A type of read-only optical disc that holds a minimum of 4.7 GB, enough for a full-length movie.
	Digital Video Disc-Recordable (DVD-R)	A type of read-only DVD on which you can burn up to 4.7 GB of data in multiple sessions. The disc can be burned again with new data, but cannot be erased.
	Digital Video Disc-Rewritable (DVD-RW)	A type of DVD on which you can read, write, and erase data, just like a hard disk.
	Network drive	A location on a network drive.

© 2014 Cengage Learning

Opening a document with a different program

Most documents on your desktop are associated with a specific program. For example, if you double-click a document whose filename ends with the three-letter extension .txt, Windows automatically opens the document with Notepad, a text-only editor. There are situations, though, when you need to open a document with a program other than the one Windows chooses, or when you want to choose a different default program. For example, you might want to open a text document in WordPad rather than Notepad so that you can add formatting and graphics. To do this, right-click or tap-hold the document icon you want to open, point to Open with on the shortcut menu, then click or tap the application you want to use to open the document, or click or tap Choose default program to access more program options.

View Files and Folders

If you have more than one folder opened in a window, you can move quickly between them using the Address bar and navigation buttons. When you open a folder, Windows keeps track of your previously viewed locations. To go back or forward to a folder you already viewed, click the Back or Forward button, or click the Recent locations list arrow next to the Forward button to display a menu of places you viewed two or more locations ago. The Address bar displays the path you have taken, separated by arrows, to get from a disk drive to your current folder location. To quickly go back to a folder within the path, click the folder name in the Address bar or click an arrow to view the contents of each folder. You can also change the way you view file and folder icons using the Layout view buttons on the View tab. The Large, Medium, and Small Icons view displays icons in different sizes, sorted alphabetically in rows, with the name of the file or folder below each icon. When you view files using one of the Icon views, some file types, such as a bitmap, display **Live icons** (or thumbnails), which display the first page of documents, the image of a photo, or the album art for songs, making it easier to find exactly what you are looking for. The other views—Details, Tiles, and Content—display additional information, such as file type, date modified, and size, about the file or folder. **CASE** *As you continue to browse QST files and folders, you want to move between them and, depending upon the information you need, change the way you view them.*

STEPS

1. **Click or tap the Back button ⊖ to the left of the Address bar**

   The contents of the Quest Travel folder open in the Quest Travel window in Tiles view, as shown in **FIGURE E-2**. Each time you click ⊖, you are brought back to the previous folder or drive you viewed.

2. **Click or tap the drive or click or tap the location where you store your Data Files in the Address bar**

   In this example, the Libraries folder is listed in the Address bar. The contents of the drive open in the window. Instead of reopening folders, the ⊖ will return you to the previous folder you viewed.

3. **Click or tap ⊖ to the left of the Address bar, then double-click or double-tap the Advertising folder in the window**

   The contents of the Advertising folder open in the window. Instead of using the Back button, you can use the Recent locations list arrow to display a list of the drives and folders you recently viewed.

4. **Click or tap the Recent locations list arrow to the left of the Address bar, then click or tap Quest Travel in the menu**

   The contents of the Quest Travel folder reopen in the window.

5. **Click or tap the View tab, then click or tap the Layout More button on the View tab**

   The View options expand to show all the layout views: Extra Large, Large, Medium, and Small icons and List, Details, Tiles, and Content.

6. **Point to the Details button ▤, then click or tap the Details button ▤ on the View tab**

   The Quest Travel window changes to Details view, which shows the name and the date that each file or folder was last modified and the type and size of the file, as shown in **FIGURE E-3**. Pointing to a view button previews the view changes while clicking or tapping a view button accepts the view changes.

7. **Click or tap the Tiles button ▤ on the View tab**

   The display changes to Tiles view. You can also use the Address bar to navigate between folders and drives instead of the Back and Forward buttons.

8. **Click or tap Computer in the Address bar or click or tap the leftmost arrow or double arrow ⪻ in the Address bar, then click or tap Computer on the menu**

   The Computer window opens, displaying the drives on your computer. The ⪻ icon in the Address bar indicates the path is too big to fit in the Address bar.

FIGURE E-2: Viewing files and folders in Tiles view

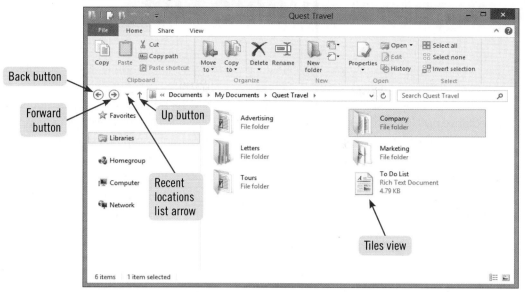

FIGURE E-3: Viewing files and folders in Details view

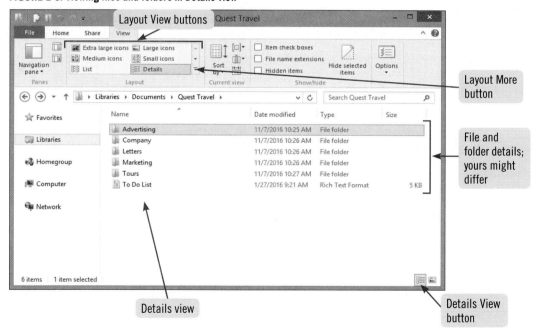

Customizing Details view

When you view files and folders in Details view, a default list of file and folder information appears, which consists of Name, Size, Type, and Date Modified. If the default list of file and folder details doesn't display what you need, you can add and remove any file and folder information. If you need to change the way Windows sorts your files and folders, you can use the column indicator buttons in the right pane. Clicking or tapping one of the column indicator buttons, such as Name, Size, Type, or Date Modified, sorts the files and folders by the type of information listed in the column. To change the details shown, right-click or tap-hold a column heading in Details view, then click or tap the detail you want to show or hide. To see more details or to change the list order, right-click or tap-hold a column title, then click or tap More. You can also drag a column heading to move it quickly to a new position.

Navigate a Folders List

Learning Outcomes
- Display a folders list
- Navigate a folders list

If you are working in File Explorer, you can use the Navigation pane to display and manage files and folders. File Explorer splits the window into two panes, or frames, as shown in **FIGURE E-4**, which allows you to view information from two different locations simultaneously. The Navigation pane on the left displays all of the drives and folders on your computer or network, while the right pane displays the contents of the selected drive or folder. This arrangement enables you to view the file hierarchy of your computer or network and the contents of a folder at the same time. The Navigation pane is organized into five categories: Favorites, Libraries, Homegroup, Computer, and Network. The Navigation pane displays the file hierarchy of the drives and folders for each category in a **folders list**. Using the Expand indicator ▷ and Collapse indicator ◢ to the left of an icon in the Navigation pane allows you to display different levels of the drives and folders on your computer without opening and displaying the individual contents. With its split window, the folders list in the Navigation pane makes it easy to copy, move, delete, and rename files and folders. **CASE** *You want to use the folders list in the Navigation pane to quickly move to QST folders within folders without opening and displaying the contents of each folder in the file hierarchy.*

STEPS

1. **Click or tap the** Back button ⊝ **to the left of the Address bar**

   The Quest Travel folder opens, displaying folders and files in Tiles view.

2. **In the Navigation pane, point to** Libraries **or** Computer **in the folders list where you store your Data Files, then click or tap the** Expand indicator ▷ **that appears next it**

   The folder expands to display its folder structure in the Navigation pane, including a file hierarchy of the currently selected folder or disk. You can access all folders and drives from the folders list in the Navigation pane. Note that the contents of your folders list will vary, depending on the programs and files installed on your computer as well as the location where Windows is installed on your hard drive or network.

3. **Click or tap the** Expand indicator ▷ **next to the folder where you store your Data Files, then continue to click or tap the** Expand indicator **to display the Letters folder**

   The Letters folder expands to display its folder structure, as shown in **FIGURE E-4**. Because you did not click the folder icon, the right pane still displays the contents of the Quest Travel folder. The Expand indicator ▷ changes to the Collapse indicator ◢, indicating the subfolders on the drive or in the folder. When neither ▷ nor ◢ appears next to an icon, the item has no folders in it. However, it might contain files, whose names you can display in the right pane by clicking the folder name.

4. **Click or tap** Business Letters **in the folders list**

   The two files in the Business Letters folder display in the right pane, as shown in **FIGURE E-5**. When you click a folder or drive in the folders list, its contents open in the right pane.

5. **Click or tap** ▷ **next to the Letters folder in the folders list**

   The folders in the Letters folder collapse and no longer appear in the folders list. Because you did not click the Letters folder icon, the right pane still displays the contents of the Business Letters folder.

6. **Click or tap** Letters **in the folders list**

   The contents of the Letters folder open in the right pane.

7. **Double-click or double-tap the** Business Letters **folder in the right pane**

   The right pane redisplays the contents of the Business Letters folder. When you double-click a drive or folder in the right pane, the right pane of the window shows the contents of that item. When you double-click a file, the program associated with the file starts and opens the file in the program window.

FIGURE E-4: Folders list in the Navigation pane

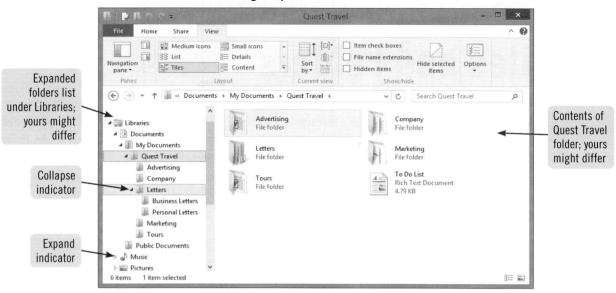

Expanded folders list under Libraries; yours might differ

Collapse indicator

Expand indicator

Contents of Quest Travel folder; yours might differ

FIGURE E-5: Business Letters folder

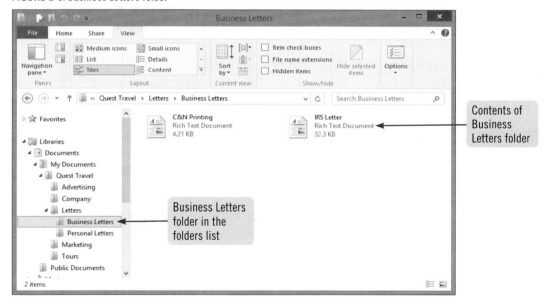

Contents of Business Letters folder

Business Letters folder in the folders list

Customizing the Favorites list

The Favorites list in the Navigation pane provides links to commonly used folders and saved searches to reduce the number of clicks or taps it takes to locate a file or folder. Windows provides a default list of Favorites, including Desktop, Downloads, and Recent Places. You can customize the Favorites list in the Navigation pane to include the folders or saved searches you use most often. You can also move current links, add or rename folders, save searches, or remove items. To move a link, drag an item in the Navigation pane to a higher or lower position. To add a link to the Favorites list, drag an item from its original location in a folders list or in the Folder window to a new position in the Favorites list. To rename or remove a link, right-click or tap-hold the link, then click or tap Rename or Remove on the shortcut menu. If the Navigation pane gets cluttered, you can restore it back to its original default items. Simply right-click or tap-hold Favorites in the Navigation pane, then click or tap Restore favorite links on the shortcut menu.

Create and Rename Files and Folders

Learning
Outcomes
• Create a new
 folder
• Rename a file

A file hierarchy allows you to place files in folders, then place folders in other folders, so that your files are organized and easier to find. To create a hierarchy, you create new folders within disks or folders and then store files within them. To create a folder, you select the location where you want the new folder to go, create the folder, then name the folder. You should name each folder meaningfully, so that just by reading the folder's name you know its contents. Once you have named a folder or file, you can rename it at any time. **CASE** *You want to create a set of new folders to hold the files for the Quest Travel Spring Specials and to rename at least one file with a more appropriate name.*

STEPS

1. **In the Navigation pane, click Quest Travel in the folders list**

   The contents of the Quest Travel folder open. To create a new folder, you use the New folder button on the toolbar.

TROUBLE
If the folder name is not highlighted, click or tap the folder, then click or tap New folder so that a rectangle surrounds it and the folder name is highlighted.

2. **Click or tap the Home tab, if necessary, then click or tap the New folder button on the Home tab**

   A new folder, temporarily named New folder, appears highlighted with a rectangle around the title in the right pane of the window, as shown in **FIGURE E-6**. To enter a new folder name, you simply type the new name; the text you type replaces the selected text.

3. **Type Spring Specials, then press [Enter]**

   The Spring Specials folder appears in both panes. When you create a new folder, the icon for the new folder is placed in the list of files and folders in the right pane. You can rearrange, or sort, the icons in the folder to make them easier to find.

QUICK TIP
To create a new file, right-click or tap-hold a blank area in File Explorer, point to New, then click or tap the type of file you want.

4. **In the right pane, double-click or double-tap the Spring Specials folder**

   There aren't any contents to display in the right pane because the folder is empty; no new files or folders have been created or moved.

5. **Right-click or tap-hold anywhere in the right pane, point to New on the shortcut menu, click or tap Folder, type Spring Ad Pages as the new folder name, then press [Enter]**

   The new folder named Spring Ad Pages appears in the right pane. When you right-click or tap-hold, the commands on the shortcut menu differ, depending on the item or the Windows features installed on your computer. If you point to the Spring Specials folder in the folders list, the Expand indicator appears, indicating that this folder contains other folders or files.

6. **Click or tap Quest Travel in the Address bar**

   The contents of the Quest Travel folder open. If a current filename is not useful, you can use the Rename command to change it.

QUICK TIP
To quickly change a file or folder name, select the icon, click or tap the name, then type a new name.

7. **Click or tap the To Do List file in the right pane, then click or tap the Rename button 🔲 on the Home tab**

   The filename appears highlighted, as shown in **FIGURE E-7**. If a filename includes an extension, it's not highlighted.

8. **Type Important, then press [Enter]**

   The file originally called To Do List is renamed Important and retains its format as a Rich Text Document.

FIGURE E-6: Creating a new folder

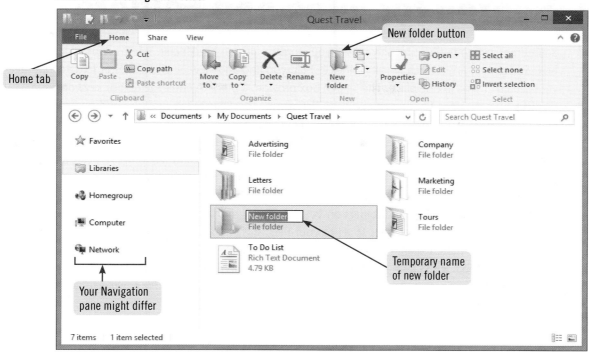

FIGURE E-7: Renaming a file

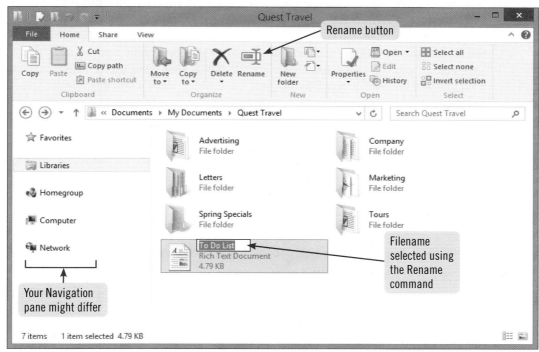

Changing the layout of File Explorer windows

Windows gives you the option to customize the layout for each File Explorer window depending on the information the window contains. The layout for each File Explorer window can include a menu bar, Details pane, Preview pane, and Navigation pane. The Navigation pane appears by default. The View tab contains buttons to show or hide the layout elements. To show or hide the Preview pane or Details pane, click the Preview pane button or Details pane button. To show or hide the Navigation pane, click the Navigation pane button arrow, then click or tap Navigation pane.

Search for Files and Folders

Learning Outcomes
• Search for files or folders
• Change search criteria
• Cancel a search

Sometimes remembering precisely where you stored a file can be difficult. Windows provides a Search box, Search tab, and Search Results folder to help you find and view all of the files or folders that meet your search criteria in one place. The Search box provides a place to enter the text or keywords that you want to find within a file or in a file or folder name. The Search tab provides additional options to change the search location or refine the search along with the criteria in the Search box. You can change the search location to the current folder, all subfolders, libraries, the entire computer, or the Internet. The refine search options give you ways to narrow down a search to find files or folders by other criteria, such as name, title, author, location, date (taken, modified, or created), size, or **tags**, which are user-defined file properties. The Search Results folder is accessible from any folder window with the Search box to help you locate files and folders on your computer, homegroups, and the Internet. The Search Results folder provides easy access to all of your files, such as documents, pictures, music, and email, and folders that match search criteria you set in a single view. Items that match the search criteria appear highlighted. **CASE** *You need to access a file that was created several months ago with preliminary notes for the Spring Specials. Ron Dawson does not know the exact title of the file or where it was stored. You want to do a search for this file and move it to the Spring Specials folder.*

STEPS

1. **Click or tap in the Search box to the right of the Address bar**

   The Search tab under Search Tools appears and a Search box menu opens, if available, displaying recently performed searches and advanced search options, known as **filters**. A filter narrows the search to display only items that meet the criteria. After a moment, the menu closes. By default, a search occurs in the folder that is currently open, as well as any subfolders in it, but you can specify any location on your computer to search. Just type the name of the folder or file you want to find or the part you know for certain in the Search box. If you don't know the name of the file, but do know some text contained in the file, you can enter that text. You want to search in the Quest Travel folder, which is the current folder.

2. **Type qst in the Search box**

   As you type, files that contain the text you typed as part of their filename display highlighted in the Search Results pane, as shown in **FIGURE E-8**. Notice that this automatically occurred without you pressing [Enter]. If any folders in the Quest Travel folder or its subfolders had names that contained QST, their names would appear as well. Notice that the Address bar displays "Search Results in Quest Travel" to indicate the location of the search. If you don't find the file you want, you can perform an advanced search.

3. **Click or tap the Size button 🖥 Size ▾ on the Search tab**

   The Size menu lists size options, which include Empty (0 KB), Tiny (0–10 KB), Small (10–100 KB), Medium (100 KB–1 MB), Large (1–16 MB), Huge (16–128 MB), and Gigantic (> 128 MB).

4. **Click or tap Medium (100 KB–1 MB) on the menu**

   The Search program finds and lists all the corresponding files and folders that meet the criteria and displays them in the Search Results pane. See **FIGURE E-9**. The search criteria you selected specified that you only wanted to find document files that were larger than 100 KB, yet smaller than 1 MB in size. Notice that the criteria in the Search box changes to "qst size:medium" to reflect the search options.

5. **Click or tap the Close button ☒ in the Search box**

   The search criteria is removed from the Search box.

6. **Click or tap the Recent searches button 🕘 on the Search tab**

   A Search box menu opens, displaying recent searches and search filter options at the bottom. The current menu displays "qst" and "qst size:medium."

7. **Click or tap the Close search button ✖ on the Search tab**

   The Search tab closes and the files and folders in the Quest Travel folder display in the right pane.

FIGURE E-8: Performing a search

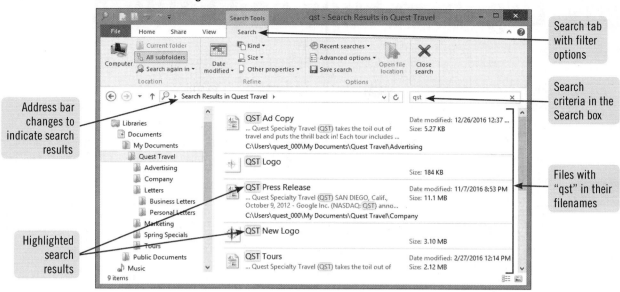

Address bar changes to indicate search results

Highlighted search results

Search tab with filter options

Search criteria in the Search box

Files with "qst" in their filenames

FIGURE E-9: Results from a filtered search

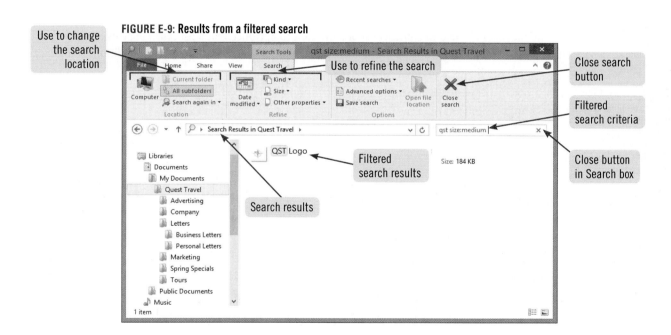

Use to change the search location

Use to refine the search

Search results

Close search button

Filtered search criteria

Close button in Search box

Filtered search results

Saving a search

If you frequently perform the same search, you can save your search results just like you would a file and perform or modify the search again later. Once your search is completed, click or tap the Save search button on the Search tab to open the Save As dialog box. The default file type in the Save as type box is Saved Search (*.search-ms). Type a name for the search, then click or tap Save. The search is saved by default in the Searches folder, which you can open by clicking or tapping Favorites or Searches in the Navigation pane. To run a saved search, double-click or double-tap it in the Searches window, or click or tap it in the Navigation pane. Like any file or folder icon, you can move a saved search from the Searches folder to the Favorite section in the Navigation pane to make it more accessible. When you no longer need a saved search, you can select it, press [Delete], then click or tap Yes to confirm.

Organize Files and Folders

Learning Outcomes
• Sort files and folders
• Filter files and folders

In File Explorer windows, files appear in lists with headings at the top. You can use the headings to change how files are displayed in the window. There are several ways to organize your files by using file list headings, including sorting, filtering, and grouping. **Sorting** displays files and folders in alphabetical order, either A to Z or Z to A. **Filtering** displays only files and folders with the properties you select by heading type. When you apply a filter to a heading, a check mark appears in the column heading, indicating a filter is enabled. If a filter doesn't display the files you want in the selected folder, you can use the Subfolders option to include them in an expanded search. **CASE** *You want to use sorting and filtering to help you find specific Quest Specialty Travel files.*

STEPS

1. **Click or tap the Details button ⊞ in the lower-right corner of the window, if necessary**

   The contents of the Quest Travel folder appear in Details view.

QUICK TIP

To sort items by a column, click or tap the Sort by button on the View tab, then click or tap an option.

2. **Click or tap the Name column heading**

   The file list is sorted in alphabetical order from Z to A. When you click a column heading, the file list is sorted in order by that column. Clicking the column toggles between sorting the list in ascending to descending order and descending to ascending order.

3. **Click or tap the Name column heading again**

   The file list is resorted in alphabetical order from A to Z. Notice that a list arrow appears at the end of the Name column heading. The Name column heading list arrow allows you to access additional filtering and grouping commands.

QUICK TIP

To add a column in Details view, click or tap the Add columns button on the View tab, then click or tap an option.

4. **Point to the Name column heading, then click or tap the Name column heading list arrow**

   A menu opens, as shown in **FIGURE E-10**. This menu displays commands to filter files and folders to help you find what you're looking for. If you only want to view files in a certain group, you can select one of the filtering options.

5. **On the menu, click or tap the I - P check box to select it, then click or tap off the menu to close it**

   The window displays only the files that meet the I - P filter, as shown in **FIGURE E-11**. A check mark appears in the Name column heading to indicate a filter is applied to the view.

QUICK TIP

To group items, click or tap the Group by button on the View tab, then click or tap an option.

6. **Click or tap the Name column heading check mark, click or tap the I - P check box to clear it, then click off the menu to close it**

   All of the search results for the Quest Travel folder open in Details view. The Address bar displays "Search Results in Quest Travel" to indicate the results of the search. The file list in the Quest Travel folder is restored back to its original state.

7. **Click or tap the View tab, click the Layout More button, if necessary, then click or tap the Tiles button ⊞**

   The contents of the Quest Travel folder appear in Tiles view.

FIGURE E-10: Menu to filter files and folders

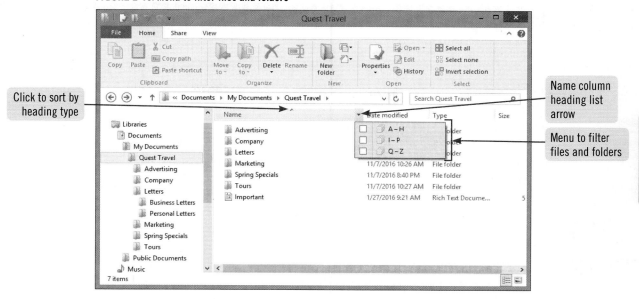

Click to sort by heading type

Name column heading list arrow

Menu to filter files and folders

FIGURE E-11: Filtering files and folders

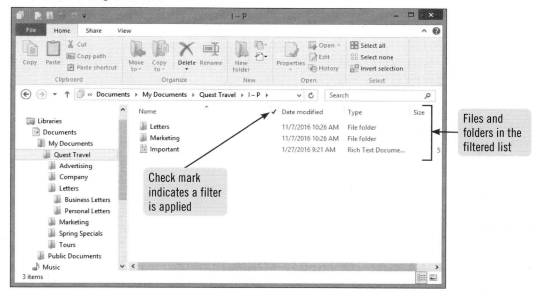

Files and folders in the filtered list

Check mark indicates a filter is applied

Adding property tags to files

When you create a file, Windows automatically adds **properties** to the files, such as the filename, creation date, modified date, and size. These properties are important to Windows; however, they might not be useful to you when you are searching for a file. You can create your own custom properties called tags to make it faster and easier to locate files in the future. A **tag** can be anything you choose, such as "QST" or "Important." You can add or modify tag properties for most files. However, there are some

exceptions, such as plain text (.txt) or Rich Text Format (.rtf) files. You can add or modify properties using the Tags box in the Details pane in a File Explorer window, the Details tab in the Properties dialog box, or in the Save As dialog box. If you want to remove some or all of the property information in a file, you can quickly remove it using the Properties dialog box. To open the Properties dialog box for a file, select the file, then click or tap the Properties button on the Home tab.

Copy and Move Files and Folders

Learning Outcomes
• Copy files or folders
• Move files or folders

Eventually you will need to move or copy a file from one folder to another. This can be accomplished using a variety of methods. If the file or folder and the location where you want to move it are visible in a window or on the desktop, you can simply drag the item from one location to the other. Moving a file or folder on the same disk relocates it, whereas dragging it from one disk to another copies it so that it appears in both locations. One way to make sure that you move or copy an item properly is to right-click the file or folder, drag the item to the destination location while still holding down the right mouse button, then choose the appropriate command from the shortcut menu. When the destination folder or drive is not visible in a File Explorer window, you can use the Cut, Copy, and Paste commands on the Home tab or a shortcut menu. **CASE** *As you continue to organize QST files, you want to move a file, make a copy of another file, and then place the copy of the file in a folder.*

STEPS

QUICK TIP

To select files or folders that are not consecutive, press and hold [Ctrl], then click or tap each item in the right pane.

1. **In the Navigation pane, click or tap Company in the folders list**

   The contents of the Company folder open in the window. When moving or copying files or folders, make sure the files or folders you want to move or copy appear in the right pane. To move a file, you drag it from the right pane to the destination folder in the folders list.

2. **Drag the QST Press Release.rtf file in the right pane across the vertical line separating the two panes to the Marketing folder in the folders list, as shown in FIGURE E-12, then release the mouse button or your finger**

   Once you release the mouse button, the QST Press Release.rtf file is relocated to the Marketing folder. If you decide that you don't want the file moved, you could move it back easily using the Undo command on the Organize button menu.

3. **Click or tap Marketing in the folders list**

   The QST Press Release file is now more appropriately located in the Marketing folder.

4. **Point to the QST New Logo.bmp file, press and hold the right mouse button (on a computer) or tap and hold (on a mobile device), drag the file across the vertical line separating the two panes to the Advertising folder, then release the mouse button or your finger**

   As shown in FIGURE E-13, a shortcut menu appears, offering a choice of options.

QUICK TIP

To copy a file quickly from one folder to another on the same disk, select the file, press and hold [Ctrl], then drag the file to the folder.

5. **Click or tap Copy here on the shortcut menu**

   The original QST New Logo file remains in the Marketing folder, and a copy of the file is placed in the Advertising folder. Another way to copy or move the file to a new location is by right-clicking a file in the right pane, then clicking the appropriate option on the shortcut menu.

6. **Click or tap Advertising in the folders list**

   A copy of the QST New Logo file is now located in the Advertising folder.

FIGURE E-12: Moving a file from one folder to another

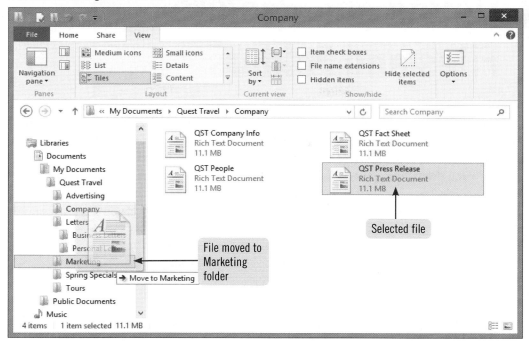

FIGURE E-13: Copying a file from one location to another

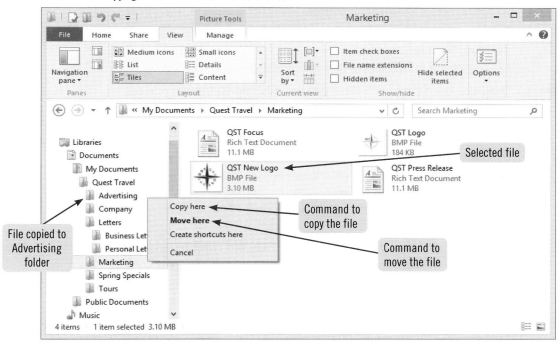

Sending files and folders

When you right-click or tap-hold most objects on the desktop or in the File Explorer window, the Send To command is often one of the choices on the shortcut menu. This command enables you to move a file or folder to a new location on your computer. For example, you can send a file or folder to a USB drive to make a quick backup copy of the file or folder, to a mail recipient as an email message, or to the desktop to create a shortcut. You can also use the Send To command to move a file or folder to the Documents folder. To send a file or folder, right-click or tap-hold the file or folder you want to send, point to Send To on the shortcut menu, then click or tap the destination you want.

Delete and Restore Files and Folders

Learning
Outcomes
• Delete files or
  folders
• Restore files or
  folders

When you organize the contents of a folder, disk, or the desktop, you will inevitably find ones that you no longer need. It is easy to **delete**, or remove, items from any of these locations. The **Recycle Bin**, located on your desktop, is a temporary storage area for deleted files. If you delete a file or folder from the desktop or from the hard drive, it automatically gets placed into the Recycle Bin. The Recycle Bin stores all the items you delete from your hard disk, so that if you accidentally delete an item, you can remove it from the Recycle Bin to restore it. If the deletion is a recent operation, you can also use the Undo command on the Organize button menu to restore a deleted file or folder. However, if you delete a file from a removable disk, such as a USB drive, it is permanently deleted, not stored in the Recycle Bin. **TABLE E-2** summarizes deleting and restoring options. **CASE** *You find a file in the Quest Travel folder that is no longer relevant. You want to delete this file, as well as a practice restoring a file using the Recycle Bin in case you make a mistake and delete a file by mistake in the future.*

STEPS

TROUBLE
If the folder is not
visible, click or tap
the Expand indicator
▷ next to the
Letters folder.

1. **If necessary, move and resize the window so that you can see the Recycle Bin icon on the desktop, then click or tap Personal Letters in the folders list**

    Because you cannot restore files deleted from a removable disk, you must move a file from the drive where your Data Files are located to the desktop.

2. **Point to the Eric Schubel.rtf file in the right pane, press and hold [Ctrl], drag it to the desktop, then release [Ctrl]**

    The Eric Schubel file is copied to the desktop, as shown in FIGURE E-14.

TROUBLE
If a message box
appears, click or tap
Yes to confirm the
deletion.

3. **Drag the Eric Schubel.rtf file from the desktop to the Recycle Bin**

    The Recycle Bin icon should look like it contains paper.

4. **Click or tap the Minimize button** ▬ **in the Personal Letters folder window**

5. **Double-click or double-tap the Recycle Bin icon on the desktop**

    The Recycle Bin window opens, containing the Eric Schubel.rtf file and any other deleted files. Like most other windows, the Recycle Bin window has an Address bar, a Search box, a toolbar, and the Details pane. Your deleted files remain in the Recycle Bin until you empty it, permanently removing the contents of the Recycle Bin from your hard drive.

6. **Select the Eric Schubel.rtf file in the Recycle Bin window, as shown in FIGURE E-15, then click or tap the Restore the selected items button** ▧ **on the toolbar**

    The file is restored back to its previous location on the desktop. It is intact and identical to the form it was in before you deleted it.

7. **Click or tap the Close button** ❌ **in the Recycle Bin window, then click or tap the File Explorer button on the taskbar**

    The Recycle Bin window closes, and the File Explorer opens displaying the contents of the Personal Letters window with the Eric Schubel.rtf file restored.

8. **Select the Eric Schubel.rtf file on the desktop, press [Delete], then click or tap Yes to confirm the deletion, if necessary**

    The Eric Schubel.rtf file is again moved to the Recycle Bin.

9. **Right-click or tap-hold the Recycle Bin, click or tap Empty Recycle Bin, then click or tap Yes to confirm the deletion**

    The Eric Schubel.rtf file is permanently deleted from the Recycle Bin and your computer.

FIGURE E-14: Selecting a file to drag to the Recycle Bin

FIGURE E-15: Deleted file from the desktop in the Recycle Bin

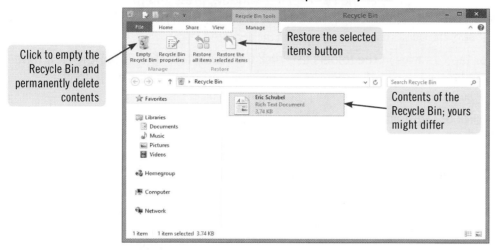

TABLE E-2: Deleting and restoring files

ways to delete a file or folder	ways to restore a file or folder from the Recycle Bin
Select the file or folder, click or tap the Delete button on the Home tab	Select the file or folder, click the Restore the selected items or Restore all items button
Select the file or folder, then press [Delete]	Click or tap the Undo button on the Quick Access toolbar
Right-click or tap-hold the file or folder, then click Delete	Right-click or tap-hold the file or folder, then click Restore
Drag the file or folder to the Recycle Bin	Drag the file or folder from the Recycle Bin to any location

© 2014 Cengage Learning

Recycle Bin properties

You can adjust several Recycle Bin settings by using the Properties option on the Recycle Bin shortcut menu or the Recycle Bin Properties button on the Manage tab under Recycle Bin Tools. For example, if you want to delete files placed in the Recycle Bin immediately, right-click or tap-hold the Recycle Bin, click or tap Properties, then click or tap the "Don't move files to the Recycle Bin. Remove files immediately when deleted." check box to select it. Also, if you find that the Recycle Bin is full and cannot accept any more files, you can increase the amount of disk space allotted to the Recycle Bin by changing the value in the Maximum size text box.

Work with Libraries

Libraries are special folders that catalog files and folders in a central location, regardless of where you actually store them on your hard drive. A library can contain links to files, other folders, and other subfolders anywhere on your system. You can also share entire libraries as easily as you can share individual directories or files. Windows comes with four libraries already in place: Documents, Music, Pictures, and Videos. You can create additional ones at any time. After you have a library in place, you can use your mouse or the Properties dialog box to include or remove folders and set options to optimize, share, and display the library. After you add one or more folders to a library, Windows tracks your selected folders and updates them automatically in libraries whenever you change their contents. When you open a library, a detailed grouping view of the library indicates the files and subfolders within the monitored folders, letting you easily browse for the file or folder you want to open. **CASE** *You access the same QST company files on a regular basis. Rather than locating a specific folder using the traditional method, you want to create a library and place a folder in it for easy access and use.*

STEPS

1. **In the Navigation pane of the File Explorer window, press and hold [Ctrl], drag the Quest Travel folder to an empty area of the desktop, then release [Ctrl]**
   A duplicate of the Quest Travel folder appears on the desktop.

2. **Click or tap Libraries in the folders list, click the Home tab, click or tap the New item button, click or tap Library from the menu, type Business, then press [Enter]**
   The new Business library appears in both panes, as shown in **FIGURE E-16**.

3. **Right-click or tap-hold the Quest Travel folder on the desktop, point to Include in library on the shortcut menu, then click or tap Business**
   The Business library window opens, displaying the contents of the library in a detailed grouping view, as shown in **FIGURE E-17**. If you're not sure where a file is located, you can use the Arrange by option to display the library contents by folder, date modified, tag, type, or name. **Grouping** displays a sequential list of all of the files by heading type.

4. **Double-click or double-tap the Important.rtf file in the Business library, add a bulleted item Gather year-end financial data to the bottom of the current list, then click or tap the Save button 🖫 on the Quick Access toolbar and Close button ✕ in WordPad**
   The updated file and the WordPad program close.

5. **Double-click or double-tap the Quest Travel folder on the desktop, double-click or double-tap the Important.rtf file to review the change, change Gather to Review, then click or tap the Save button on the Quick Access toolbar and Close button in WordPad**
   The updated file and the WordPad program close. The changes you made to the Important file from the original folder are saved and will appear when you access the file from the original or library location.

6. **Click or tap the Expand arrow next to the Business Library in the Navigation pane, if necessary, right-click or tap-hold the Quest Travel folder in the Business library, click Remove location from library, then click or tap the Close button ✕ in the Business window**
   The folder location included in the Business library is removed from the library.

7. **Click or tap the Business library in the Navigation pane, press [Delete], then click or tap Yes to confirm the deletion, if necessary**
   The Business library is permanently deleted from your computer.

8. **Click or tap the Quest Travel folder on the desktop, press [Delete], click or tap Yes to confirm the deletion, if necessary, then click or tap the Close button in the window**
   The Quest Travel folder on the desktop is permanently deleted and the Libraries window closes.

FIGURE E-16: Creating a library

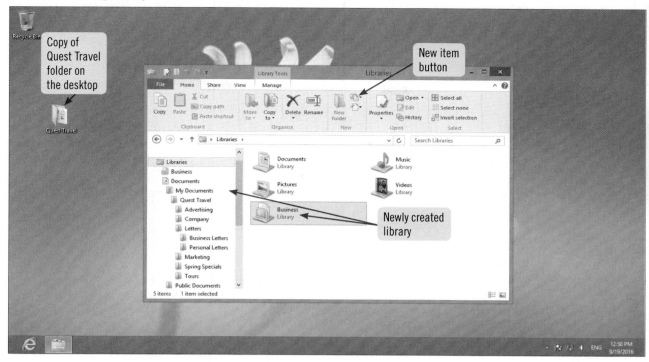

FIGURE E-17: Adding a folder to a library

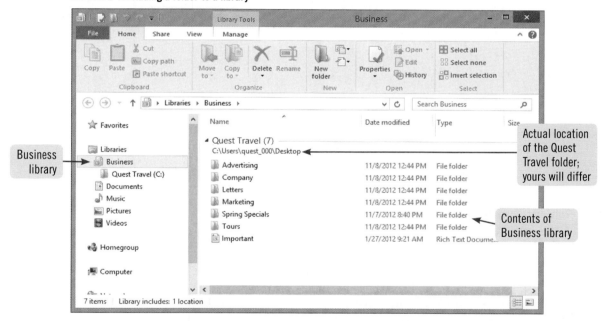

Creating and working with shortcuts on the desktop

It can be challenging to access a file or folder buried several levels down in a file hierarchy. You can create shortcuts to the items you use most frequently. A **shortcut** is a link that you create to access a particular file, folder, or program on your hard disk or on a network. Once you create a shortcut, you can place the icon representing it anywhere that is convenient for you to access it; the actual file, folder, or program remains stored in its original location. To create a shortcut on the desktop, right-click or tap-hold an icon, then click or tap Create shortcuts. All shortcuts are named the same as the files to which they link, but with the word Shortcut at the end of the original name; the file icon includes an arrow. You can also place shortcuts to frequently used files, folders, and programs on the taskbar by simply dragging the shortcut file, folder, or program to the taskbar. When you release the mouse or finger, the item appears on the taskbar.

Practice

Concepts Review

Match the statements below with the elements labeled in the screen shown in FIGURE E-18.

FIGURE E-18

1. Which element contains items to be deleted or restored?
2. Which element is copied or moved to the desktop?
3. Which element do you click or tap to collapse a folder?
4. Which element do you click or tap to expand a folder?
5. Which element do you click or tap to change the view?
6. Which element is stored in its original location?
7. Which element is stored in a library?

Match each term with the statement that best describes it.

8. Recycle Bin   a. A display of drives and disks
9. Filtering   b. A display of files and folders
10. Grouping   c. A storage area for deleted files
11. Computer window   d. A display of library files
12. File Explorer window e. A display of files by properties

Select the best answers from the following lists of choices.

13. **The File Explorer window is used to:**
    - **a.** Delete files.
    - **b.** Add folders.
    - **c.** Manage drives and disks.
    - **d.** All of the above

14. **Which of the following is *not* an option in the Navigation pane of the File Explorer window?**
    - **a.** Libraries
    - **b.** Workgroup
    - **c.** Favorites
    - **d.** Network

15. **Which of the following is *not* writable?**
    - **a.** Hard drive
    - **b.** Removable drive
    - **c.** CD-RW
    - **d.** DVD

16. **Which of the following is *not* an available view in File Explorer?**
    - **a.** Content
    - **b.** Tiles
    - **c.** Icon
    - **d.** List

17. **Which of the following is *not* a column heading in Details view?**
    - **a.** Content
    - **b.** Size
    - **c.** Type
    - **d.** Date Modified

18. **Which of the following is *not* a default favorite?**
    - **a.** Documents
    - **b.** Desktop
    - **c.** Downloads
    - **d.** Recycle Bin

19. **Which of the following is *not* a layout pane?**
    - **a.** Details
    - **b.** Search
    - **c.** Preview
    - **d.** Navigation

20. **Which of the following displays only files and folders with properties you select by heading type?**
    - **a.** Sort
    - **b.** Group
    - **c.** Filter
    - **d.** Stack

21. **Which of the following displays files and folders in alphabetical order?**
    - **a.** Sort
    - **b.** Group
    - **c.** Filter
    - **d.** Stack

22. **Which of the following is a method for copying a file or folder?**
    - **a.** Press and hold [Ctrl], then drag the folder or file.
    - **b.** Drag the folder or file on the same disk drive.
    - **c.** Double-click the folder or file.
    - **d.** Click the folder or file, then click Copy.

23. **Which of the following locations is *not* a valid place from which to delete a file and send it to the Recycle Bin?**
    - **a.** Removable disk
    - **b.** File Explorer window
    - **c.** Hard drive
    - **d.** Computer window

24. **Which of the following is *not* a default library?**
    - **a.** Documents
    - **b.** Music
    - **c.** Movies
    - **d.** Pictures

25. **What graphical element appears on a shortcut icon?**
    - **a.** Pencil
    - **b.** Chain link
    - **c.** Pointer
    - **d.** Arrow

Skills Review

1. **Open File Explorer.**
   a. Start the Desktop app.
   b. Open File Explorer using the taskbar.
   c. Display the Computer window.
   d. Navigate to the Quest Travel folder from the location where you store your Data Files.
   e. Double-click the Letters folder, then double-click the Personal Letters folder.

2. **View files and folders.**
   a. Change to List view.
   b. Click or tap the Back button to the left of the Address bar, then open the Business Letters folder.
   c. Click or tap the Quest Travel list arrow in the Address bar, then click or tap Tours.
   d. Click or tap the Recent locations list arrow, then click or tap Quest Travel.
   e. Change to Details view, then change to Content view.
   f. Change to Tiles view.

3. **Navigate a folders list.**
   a. Expand the folders list for the folder from the location where you store your Data Files.
   b. Expand the folders list for the Quest Travel folder.
   c. Expand the folders list for the Letters folder.
   d. Collapse the folders list for the Letters folder.
   e. Click or tap the Quest Travel folder in the folders list.
   f. Double-click or double-tap the Marketing folder in the right pane.

4. **Create and rename files and folders.**
   a. In the Marketing folder, create a new folder.
   b. Name the new folder **Logos & Images**.
   c. Rename the Logos & Images folder to **Logos**.
   d. Rename the file QST Focus to **About QST**.

5. **Search for files and folders.**
   a. Search in the Quest Travel folder for files or folders that are named or contain the word **logo** as part of the filename.
   b. Narrow down the search to only files with a size greater than 1 MB (Large).
   c. Click or tap the Close button in the Search box to clear the search criteria.

6. **Organize files and folders.**
   a. Display the Marketing folder in Details view.
   b. Filter the Name column by Q–Z.
   c. Sort the contents of the window alphabetically.
   d. Remove the filter Q–Z.
   e. Display the Marketing folder in Tiles view.

7. **Copy and move files and folders.**
   a. Select the QST Press Release file in the right pane, then click or tap the Copy button on the Home tab.
   b. Display the Company folder.
   c. Click or tap the Paste button on the Home tab.
   d. Switch back to the Marketing folder.
   e. Move the QST New Logo file into the Logos folder.
   f. Move the QST Logo file into the Logos folder.
   g. Move the Tours folder into the Marketing folder.

Skills Review (continued)

8. Delete and restore files and folders.

  a. Open the Quest Travel folder, then resize it, if necessary, to display part of the desktop.

  b. Copy the Marketing folder to the desktop.

  c. Drag the Marketing folder from the desktop to the Recycle Bin, then click or tap Yes to confirm the deletion, if necessary.

  d. Double-click or double-tap the Recycle Bin.

  e. Select the Marketing folder, then click or tap the Restore the selected items button on the Manage tab.

  f. Close the Recycle Bin window.

  g. Drag the Marketing folder from the desktop back to the Recycle Bin.

  h. Right-click or tap-hold the Recycle Bin, click or tap Empty Recycle Bin, then click or tap Yes to confirm the deletion.

9. Work with libraries.

  a. Open the Quest Travel folder, if necessary.

  b. Copy the Company folder to an empty area of the desktop.

  c. Display the Libraries folder.

  d. Create a library named **Business**.

  e. Include the Company folder on the desktop in the Business library.

  f. Open the QST Fact Sheet file, add the zip code **92101** to the Head Office Location, save the file, then close the program.

  g. Remove the Company folder from the library.

  h. Delete the Business library.

  i. Delete the Company folder on the desktop.

  j. Close all File Explorer windows, then close the Desktop app.

Independent Challenge 1

You are vice president of a packaging manufacturing company, Xpress Packaging, and you need to organize your Windows files and folders. In addition to folders for typical business-related functions, such as correspondence, contracts, inventory, and payroll, you have folders related to company functions, such as manufacturing and material suppliers.

  a. In File Explorer from the Desktop app, create a new folder named **Xpress Packaging** on the desktop within which the files and folders for this independent challenge will reside.

  b. Open File Explorer, display Libraries, then create a library named **Xpress**.

  c. Include the Xpress Packaging folder in the Xpress library.

  d. Create folders in the Xpress Packaging folder named **Manufacturing, Material Suppliers, East Coast**, and **West Coast**.

  e. Move the East Coast and West Coast folders into the Material Suppliers folder.

  f. Create a blank file using WordPad, add your name, then save it as **Suppliers Bid.rtf** in the Manufacturing folder.

  g. Move the Suppliers Bid.rtf file into the Material Suppliers folder.

  h. Copy the Suppliers Bid.rtf file into the Manufacturing folder and rename the copied file **Manufacturing Bids.rtf**, then display the Manufacturing folder.

  i. Copy the Xpress Packaging folder to the location where you store your Data Files.

  j. Remove the Xpress Packaging folder from the Xpress library.

  k. Delete the Xpress library.

  l. Delete the Xpress Packaging folder on the desktop.

  m. Close all windows, then close the Desktop app.

Independent Challenge 2

You are the president of MO PC, a mobile computer accessories company, and you use Windows to organize your business files. You want to create folders to keep your computer organized. As you create files, you save them in the appropriate folders.

    a. In File Explorer from the Desktop app, create a new folder named **MO PC** on the desktop within which the files and folders for this independent challenge will reside.

    b. Open File Explorer, display Libraries, then create a library named **Company**.

    c. Include the MO PC folder in the Company library.

    d. Create folders in the MO PC folder named **Advertising** and **Customers.**

    e. Use WordPad to create a letter welcoming new customers. Add your name, print, then save it as **Customer Letter.rtf** in the Customers folder.

    f. Use WordPad to create a list of five business management tasks to do. Save it as **Business Plan.rtf** in the MO PC folder.

    g. Use Paint to create a simple logo, add your name, print, then save it as **MO Logo.bmp** in the MO PC folder.

    h. Move the MO Logo file into the Advertising folder.

    i. Create a shortcut to the MO Logo file in the MO PC folder.

    j. Delete the Business Plan file, then restore it.

    k. Copy the MO PC folder to the location where you store your Data Files.

    l. Remove the MO PC folder from the Company library.

    m. Delete the Company library.

    n. Delete the MO PC folder on the desktop.

    o. Close all windows, then close the Desktop app.

Independent Challenge 3

As a human resources manager at Just in Time Books, one of your responsibilities is to create and organize company files and folders. You need to organize the folders and files on the company's computer for new employees at store locations around the world.

    a. In File Explorer from the Desktop app, open the Computer window, then open the drive and folder from the location where you store your Data Files.

    b. Create a new folder named **Just in Time Books** on the desktop within which the rest of the organization of files and folders for this independent challenge will appear.

    c. Open File Explorer, display Libraries, then create a library named **JITB**.

    d. Include the Just in Time Books folder in the JITB library.

    e. Create a file using WordPad listing at least six international store locations (city and country). Save it as **New Store Locations.rtf** in the Just in Time Books folder.

    f. Create a file using WordPad listing at least four employee names with your name being the last one. Print and save it as **Employee App.rtf** in the Just in Time Books folder.

    g. In the Just in Time Books folder, create folders named **Store Locations** and **Employees**.

    h. In the Employees folder, create four new folders representing each employee, one of which is yourself.

    i. Copy the Employee App.rtf file into each of the employee folders, then rename each file as **Employee *Name*.rtf**, replacing "Name" with each employee's name.

    j. In the folder named Store Locations, create a new folder named **New Stores**.

    k. Move the New Store Locations file to the New Stores folder.

    l. Display the contents of the Just in Time Books folder in the File Explorer window, then search for "Employee" using the Search box.

Independent Challenge 3 (continued)

m. Create an advanced search using the Date modified option as it relates to the date when you created the files.

n. Copy the Just in Time Books folder to the location where you store your Data Files.

o. Remove the Just In Time Books folder from the JITB library.

p. Delete the JITB library.

q. Delete the Just in Time Books folder on the desktop.

r. Close all windows, then close the Desktop app.

Independent Challenge 4: Explore

Many people have collections of something—recipes, books, music, DVDs, and so on. Take something you have collected and organize the different items into categories to help keep files and folders organized in the future.

a. In File Explorer from the Desktop app, create a new folder named **My Collection** within which the files and folders for this independent challenge will reside. Replace the word *Collection* in the folder name with the items you collect; for example, if you collect recipes, name the folder My Recipes.

b. Open File Explorer, display Libraries, then create a library named **Collections**.

c. Include the My Collection folder in the Collections library.

d. Create four files using WordPad and save them with names relating to your collection in the My Collection folder; for example, a collection of recipes might include files named French Bread.rtf, Torte.rtf, Sweet Bread.rtf, and 7-Layer Chocolate.rtf.

e. In the My Collection folder, create at least two folders related to your collection; for example, if you collect DVDs, you might create folders named Comedies and Thrillers.

f. Move the files into the appropriate folders.

g. Open one of the folders, then create at least two subfolders.

h. Move files into the subfolders if appropriate.

i. Copy the My Collection folder to the location where you store your Data Files.

j. Remove the My Collection folder from the Collections library.

k. Delete the Collections library.

l. Create a shortcut on the desktop to one of the files in the My Collection folder.

m. Drag the My Collection folder on the desktop to the Recycle Bin.

n. Open the Recycle Bin, then restore the folder.

o. Delete the My Collection folder and the shortcut file.

p. Close the Computer window, then close the Desktop app.

Windows 8

Visual Workshop

Re-create the screen shown in **FIGURE E-19**, which displays the Search Results window with files from the drive and folder where you store your Data Files.

FIGURE E-19

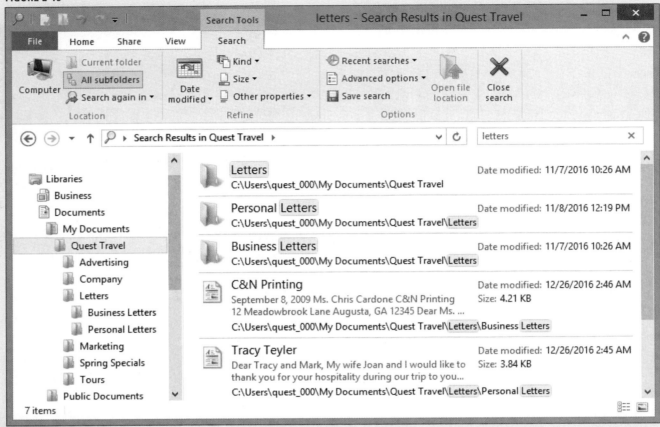

Customizing Windows

CASE ▶ Windows 8 allows you to customize the way you work to suit your objectives and preferences. You want to view and customize your settings in order to use them to personalize Windows 8. Important: If you are concerned about changing aspects of Windows 8 and do not want to customize, simply read through this unit without completing the steps.

Unit Objectives

After completing this unit, you will be able to:

- View Windows settings
- Personalize the Start and Lock screen
- Change user account settings
- Change notification settings
- Change search settings

- Change general settings
- Change share and privacy settings
- Use the Control Panel
- Personalize the desktop

Files You Will Need

QST New Logo.bmp

©Itana/Shutterstock

View Windows Settings

Windows 8 allows you to customize your work environment to suit your objectives and preferences. You can customize Windows 8 by accessing PC settings from the Charm bar or by using the Control Panel from the desktop. PC settings provide the options you need for using Windows in full screen view with metro apps, while the Control Panel provides the options you need for customizing the desktop and other advanced Windows settings. Some options overlap between PC settings. The PC settings screen displays a list of categories, including Personalize, Users, Notifications, Search, Share, General, Privacy, Devices, Ease of Access, Sync your settings, HomeGroup, and Windows Update, where you can specify the options you want. For example, you can personalize the Lock screen, Start screen, and account picture, and specify general options to set the time, app switching, spelling, and language. You can also set options to refresh, remove, or reinstall Windows 8. When you set an option in PC settings, it takes effect immediately unless otherwise indicated. When you're finished adjusting your settings, you can close the PC settings screen like any other app. **CASE** *You are an IT specialist at Quest Specialty Travel. Part of your job is to set up computers and mobile devices for employees. You want to review the available options for customizing Windows 8.*

STEPS

1. **With the Start screen in view, point to the upper-right corner and move down (on a computer) or swipe left from the right edge of the screen (on a mobile device)**
   The Charm bar opens, displaying Windows options.

QUICK TIP
To display the
Settings panel, press
⊞+[I].

2. **Click or tap the Settings button on the Charm bar**
   The Settings panel opens, as shown in **FIGURE F-1**, displaying settings for the Start screen at the top and Windows PC settings at the bottom. The settings at the top adjust based on the current screen you are working in, such as the Start screen or an app screen. The Windows PC settings at the bottom don't change based on the current screen. Within the Settings panel, you can access network options, adjust the volume, change monitor brightness, set notifications, shut down the power, or select a keyboard language.

3. **Click or tap Change PC settings on the Settings panel**
   The PC settings screen opens, as shown in **FIGURE F-2**. The Personalize category at the top is selected in the left pane and options for that category are displayed along the top of the right pane. The Personalize category includes three options: Lock screen, Start screen, and Account picture.

4. **Point to any of the categories in the left pane of the PC settings screen, then scroll down**
   The scroll bar allows you to view all of the categories.

5. **Point to any of the options in the right pane of the PC settings screen, then scroll down**
   The scroll bar allows you to view all options in the category.

6. **Click or tap Account picture in the right pane**
   Account picture options for your PC appear in the right pane.

7. **Click or tap Ease of Access in the left pane**
   Ease of Access options for your PC appear in the right pane.

FIGURE F-1: Settings panel

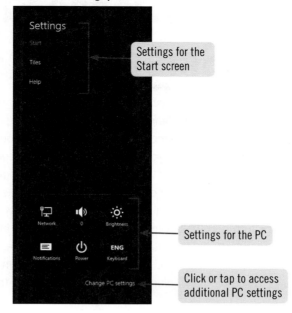

Settings for the
Start screen

Settings for the PC

Click or tap to access
additional PC settings

FIGURE F-2: PC settings screen

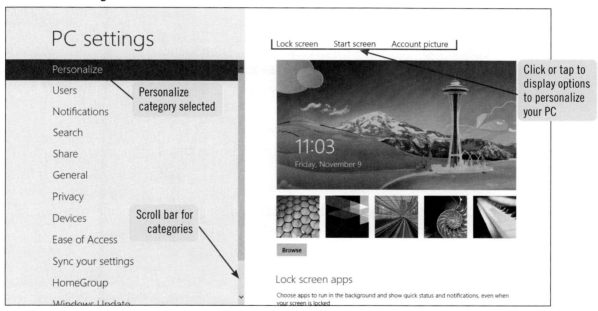

Personalize
category selected

Scroll bar for
categories

Click or tap to
display options
to personalize
your PC

Setting Ease of Access options

If you have difficulty using a mouse or keyboard, have slightly impaired vision, or are deaf or hard of hearing, you can adjust the appearance and behavior of Windows 8 to make your system easier for you to use. The Ease of Access Center allows you to configure Windows for specific vision, hearing, and mobility needs. You can also answer a few questions about your daily PC use that can help Windows recommend appropriate accessibility settings and programs. Within the Ease of Access Center, you can set options for the High Contrast color scheme to make everything on the screen appear bigger or you can change the thickness of the cursor to make it easier to see. You can also specify an Ease of Access feature (Narrator, Magnify, or On-Screen Keyboard) to access with a keyboard shortcut. To set Ease of Access settings, click or tap the Settings button on the Charm bar, click or tap Change PC settings on the Settings panel, click or tap Sync your settings, then select the options you want. To open the Ease of Access Center, press ⊞+[U], or click or tap All apps on the App bar, click or tap Control Panel, click or tap Ease of Access, then click Ease of Access Center.

Personalize the Start and Lock Screen

Learning Outcomes
• Customize the Start screen
• Customize the Lock screen

The Start screen provides a central place to access apps, utilities, and device settings. When you start Windows 8 and sign in, the Start screen appears, displaying app tiles in groups with information and notifications. You can customize the Start screen with a background design and color; in Windows, color selections can be applied to background design, text, and selection color. The Lock screen is a security feature that helps prevent others from accessing your device. It appears when you start Windows 8, switch users, or put Windows to sleep. You can customize the Lock screen by changing its picture and displaying app status information and notifications so that you can bypass the start-up screen. You can also select up to seven apps to run in the background of the Lock screen. In addition, you can select one app to display more detailed status information. For example, you can select the Weather app so that the temperature and forecast for your selected city displays on the Lock screen. **CASE** ▷ *As you continue to review Windows 8 settings as part of your IT job at QST, you want to examine the Start and Lock screen options.*

STEPS

1. **With the PC settings screen in view, click or tap Personalize in the left pane**

   The Personalize category appears, displaying the subcategories Lock screen, Start screen, and Account picture in the right pane.

2. **Click or tap Start screen, if necessary, in the right pane**

   The Start screen appears, as shown in **FIGURE F-3**.

3. **Note the current background design (first row, first box by default), then click or tap a background design of your choice**

   The background design changes in the preview and on the Start screen.

4. **Note the current background color (ninth box by default), then click or tap a background color of your choice**

   The background color changes in the preview and on the Start screen.

5. **Click or tap the original background design, then click the original background color**

   The background design and color change back to the original settings.

6. **Click or tap Lock screen**

   The Lock screen appears, as shown in **FIGURE F-4**.

7. **Note the current background image, then click a background image of your choice**

   The background image changes in the preview and on the Lock screen.

8. **Click or tap the original background image**

   The background image changes back to the original setting.

FIGURE F-3: Customizing the Start screen

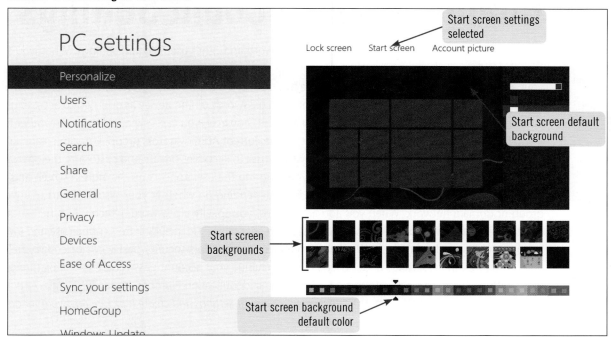

FIGURE F-4: Customizing the Lock screen

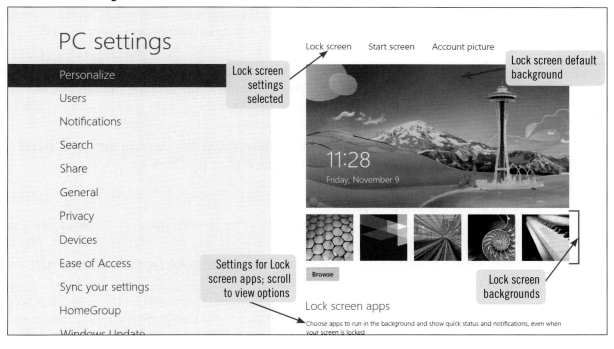

Adding Lock screen apps

In addition to the current time and date, the Lock screen also includes status information and notifications for selected apps, such as new email messages, instant messages, or calendar appointments. This allows you to get status information and notifications without having to unlock your system. To add Lock screen apps, click the Settings button on the Charm bar, click Change PC settings, click or tap Personalize in the PC settings screen, click Lock screen, scroll the right panel to the bottom, as necessary, click or tap an Add button (+), then select an available app. To remove an app, click or tap the app icon, then click or tap another app, or click or tap Don't show quick status here link or Don't show detailed status on the lock screen link.

Change User Account Settings

Learning Outcomes
• View user account settings
• Create a picture password

With PC settings, you can change your sign-in password and other user account settings. When you sign in with a Microsoft account, your account settings are maintained online. You can continue to manage your account online or change it to a local one for use only on the current device. The advantage of maintaining a local account is that it keeps usernames and passwords on the device as opposed to accessing the information online. If you choose to use a local account, however, you can't sync settings to any other PCs. If you have an administrator account or belong to the current Administrators group, you can create a new user account with a separate identity. This allows the user to keep files private and customize the operating system with personal preferences. The name you assign to the user appears on the Sign-in screen and the Start screen. The steps to add user accounts differ, depending on whether your system is part of a workgroup or domain network. When you add an account, you specify a password, which you can change at any time. Good passwords are typically at least seven characters and include letters (uppercase and lowercase), numbers, and symbols. In Windows 8, you can use multiple security passwords or codes, such as text or pictures. In PC settings under Users, you can change your account password, create a picture password with gestures, or create a four-digit PIN (Personal Identification Number) code. **CASE** As part of your IT responsibilities at QST, you want to view user account settings and create a picture password for added security.

STEPS

1. **With the PC settings screen in view, click or tap Users in the left pane**

   The Users category appears, as shown in **FIGURE F-5**, displaying user account options, including settings to switch to a local or online account, change your password, create a picture password, create a PIN (Personal Identification Number), change access to wake the PC, and add user accounts.

2. **If necessary, scroll down the options list in the Users category in the right pane, click or tap Create a picture password, type your password at the prompt, then click or tap OK**

   The Welcome to picture password screen appears. The picture password provides another way to access your system. You can have multiple passwords for an account.

3. **Click or tap Choose picture, select the document QST New Logo in the Quest Travel folder where you store your Data Files, then click or tap Open**

   The QST New Logo displays in right pane.

4. **Click or tap Use this picture**

   The QST New Logo is selected as the background image for the picture password. The Set up your gestures screen appears.

5. **Draw three gestures on your picture, as shown in FIGURE F-6, repeat your three gestures again to confirm, then click or tap Finish**

   As you finish drawing a gesture, an arrow appears to show you the direction. The PC settings screen appears. Note that the Create a picture password button changes to the Change picture password button and the Remove button appears next to the Change picture password button.

6. **Press ⊞+[L]**

   The Lock screen appears.

7. **Click or tap the Lock screen, then draw the three gestures from Step 5 on your background image**

   The PC settings screen appears, displaying the Users category in the left pane.

8. **Click or tap Remove in the right pane**

   The picture password is removed. The Change picture password button changes back to Create a picture password button.

FIGURE F-5: Viewing user account settings

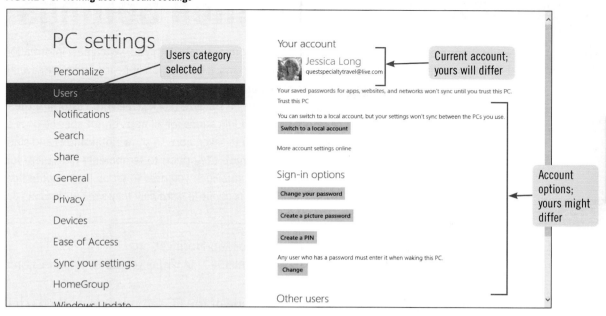

FIGURE F-6: Creating a picture password

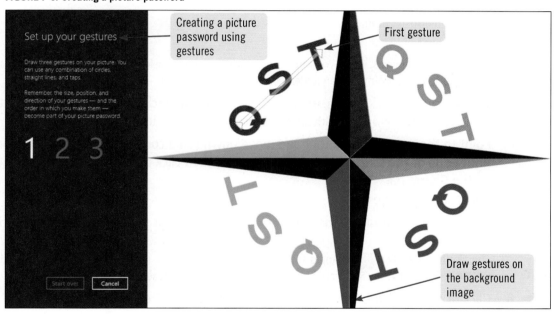

Deleting an account

If you have an administrator account or are a member of the Administrators group, you can delete an existing account. When you delete an account, you have the choice to delete or keep its contents. If you keep the contents, Windows automatically saves the content of the User's desktop and Documents, Favorites, Music, Pictures, and Video folders to a new folder (named the same as the user) on your desktop. The steps to delete user accounts differ, depending on whether your system is part of a domain network or a shared/workgroup system. To delete an account, click or tap All apps on the App bar on the Start screen, click or tap Control Panel, then click or tap the User Accounts icon in Small icons or Large icons view. Click or tap Manage another account, select the account you want to delete, click or tap Delete the account, click or tap Delete Files to remove all account files or Keep Files to save account folders (with username) to the desktop, click or tap Delete Account, then click or tap the Close button.

Change Notification Settings

Notifications are a way for Windows 8 and apps to communicate with you. When new information is available within an app or an action is requested by Windows, a notification appears. There are several types of notifications: a pop-up (also known as toast), a Start screen tile or badge, and a Lock screen icon. You can change notifications settings under Notifications or Personalize (Lock screen) to customize the way they work. For example, you can enable or disable app notifications for all apps or just specific ones as well as play sounds. For the Lock screen, you can specify up to seven apps to show notifications and status. If you find you are receiving too many notifications, you have the option to temporarily hide them for 1, 3, or 8 hours at a time. **CASE** ► *As part of your IT responsibilities, you need to set up the computers and mobile devices for all QST employees. You want to enable notifications to learn how they work in Windows 8.*

STEPS

1. **With the PC settings screen in view, click or tap Notifications**
   The Notifications category appears, as shown in **FIGURE F-7**, displaying general and app-specific notification options.

2. **Point to any of the options in the right pane of the PC settings screen, then scroll down**
   The scroll bar allows you to view all of the options in the Notifications category.

3. **Under Notifications in the right pane, drag the Show app notifications on the lock screen slider to On, if necessary**
   This option displays notifications on the Lock screen.

4. **Press ⊞+[L]**
   The Lock screen appears, where you can view notification icons. The icons that appear are the ones specified on the Lock screen settings screen under Personalize in PC settings.

5. **Click or tap the Lock screen, enter your password, then click or tap the Submit button**
   The PC settings screen appears with the Notifications category selected.

6. **Point to the upper-right corner and move down (on a computer) or swipe left from the right edge of the screen (on a mobile device), then click or tap the Settings button ⚙ on the Charm bar**
   The Settings panel appears.

7. **Click or tap the Notifications button ▤ on the Settings panel, then click or tap Hide for 1 hour**
   The Notifications icon 🕐 changes to include a timer to indicate notifications are hidden, as shown in **FIGURE F-8**. Note that the Show app notifications settings in the PC settings screen are now turned off.

8. **Click or tap off of the Settings panel to exit the panel, then drag the Show app notifications slider in the PC settings screen to On**
   Notifications are turned on in the PC settings screen.

FIGURE F-7: Viewing notifications settings

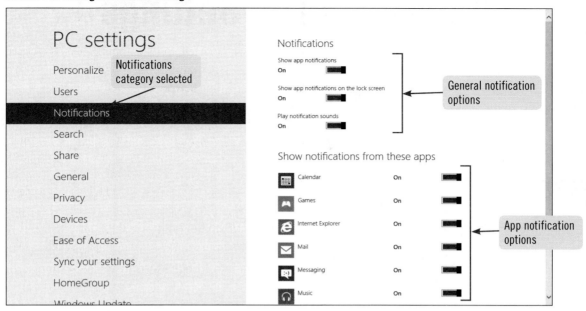

FIGURE F-8: Hiding Notifications using the Settings panel

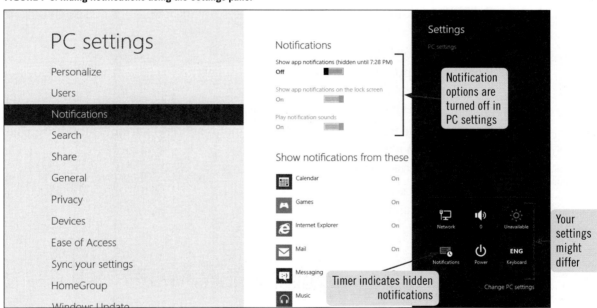

Syncing Windows settings on other devices

When you sign in to Windows 8 with a Microsoft account, you can enable the system to automatically synchronize your system and some app settings with other devices that utilize the same Microsoft sign-in information. You can also enable or disable sync settings for the entire device or enable or disable individual settings. Finally, you can sync the settings on your current device for personalized settings (Start screen, Lock screen, and Account picture), desktop personalization, passwords (only when trusted),

Ease of Access, language preferences, app settings, browser settings, and other Windows settings (File Explorer, mouse, and more). If your device is connected over a metered connection (based on minutes), you can specify whether or not to sync settings. To set sync settings, click or tap the Settings button on the Charm bar, click or tap Change PC settings on the Settings panel, click or tap Sync your settings, then select the options you want.

Change Search Settings

**Learning
Outcomes**
• View search
settings
• Change app
search settings

When you use the Search button on the Charm bar to locate information on the Web or within an app, you can also set options under PC settings to customize the way it works. For example, you can set options to show the apps you search for most often at the top of the Search panel, let Windows save your searches as future search suggestions, or clear the search history in Windows. You can also enable or disable the use of specific apps on the Search panel when searching for information. This can be useful to shorten up the list of apps on the Search panel. **CASE** ▸ *As part of your IT job, you spoke to numerous QST managers to determine which apps employees will use most often for searches. You want to practice customizing search settings using one of the more popular apps.*

STEPS

1. **With the PC settings screen in view, click or tap Search in the left pane**
   The Search category appears, as shown in **FIGURE F-9**, displaying general and app-specific search options.

2. **Point to any of the options in the right pane of the PC settings screen, then scroll down**
   The scroll bar allows you to view all of the options in the Search category.

3. **Under the Use these apps to search category, drag the Bing slider to Off**
   The Bing app is turned off.

QUICK TIP
To display the Search panel, press
⊞+[Q].

4. **Point to the upper-right corner and move down (on a computer) or swipe left from the right edge of the screen (on a mobile device), then click or tap the Search button on the Charm bar**
   The Search panel appears.

5. **Point to the apps on the Search panel to display the scroll bar, then scroll down to view all the apps**
   The Bing app does not appear in the Search panel, as shown in **FIGURE F-10**.

6. **Click or tap the upper-left corner (on a computer) or swipe right from the left side of the screen (on a mobile device)**
   The PC settings screen appears.

7. **Drag the Bing slider to On**
   The Bing app is turned on.

FIGURE F-9: Viewing search settings

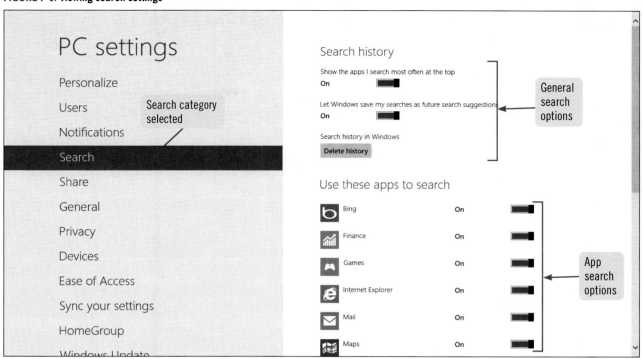

Search category selected

General search options

App search options

FIGURE F-10: Viewing apps on the Search panel

Current apps; Bing app deleted from Search panel

Setting search history options

When you search for files and information in Windows 8 using the Search button on the Charm bar, you can set search options to have Windows 8 keep track of your searches to help you perform custom searches faster in the future. In PC settings under Search, you can set options to show the apps you search most often at the top of the Search panel, let Windows save your searches as future search suggestions in the Search panel, or clear the search history. To set the search options, click or tap the Settings button on the Charm bar, click or tap Change PC settings on the Settings panel, click Search in the left pane, then drag the Show the apps I search most often at the top slider to On or the Let Windows save my searches as future search suggestions slider to On. If the list of suggestions is getting too long or you no longer want Windows to keep track of your search history, you can click or tap the Delete history button.

Change General Settings

Learning Outcomes
• View general PC settings
• Change general PC settings

The General option under PC settings allows you to set an array of options, including the time, app switching, spelling, language, and the Windows operating system. You can specify the time in your area and whether you want to automatically adjust for daylight saving time. For app switching, you can specify whether to allow switching between recent apps and the method you want to use. For example, you can turn on or off a specific option called "When I swipe in from the left edge, switch directly to my most recent app." You can also view available storage information for the apps installed on your system. This is useful when hard drive space is limited and you need to decide which apps to keep and which apps to uninstall. If you're having system problems, you can set options to refresh, remove, or reinstall the Windows 8 operating system. **CASE** *Quest Specialty Travel is located in San Diego, California. As part of your IT job to set up computers and mobile devices for all QST employees, you want to set the time zone to Pacific Time and turn on daylight saving time in PC settings.*

STEPS

1. **With the PC settings screen in view, click or tap General in the left pane**
   The General category appears, as shown in **FIGURE F-11**, displaying general and app-specific options.

2. **Point to any of the options in the right pane of the PC settings screen, then scroll down**
   A scroll bar allows you to view all options in the General category.

3. **Note the current time zone, click or tap the Time list arrow, then click or tap (UTC-8:00) Pacific Time (US & Canada), if necessary**
   The time zone changes to Pacific Time, as reflected in the time displayed above the list arrow box.

4. **Press ⊞+[L]**
   The Lock screen appears, displaying the adjusted time.

5. **Click or tap the Lock screen, enter your password, then click or tap the Submit button**
   The PC settings screen appears, displaying the General category.

6. **Click or tap the Time list arrow, then click or tap the original time zone setting, if necessary**
   The time zone changes back to its original setting.

7. **Scroll down in the right pane, if necessary, until you see the Available storage option, then click or tap View app sizes**
   A menu appears, as shown in **FIGURE F-12**, displaying a list of installed apps and the amount of space each one utilizes. On first use, it will take a few seconds to calculate the app file sizes.

8. **Click or tap off the menu**
   The App sizes menu closes.

FIGURE F-11: Viewing general PC settings

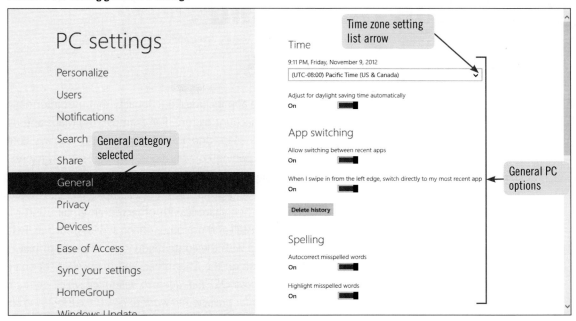

FIGURE F-12: Displaying app sizes

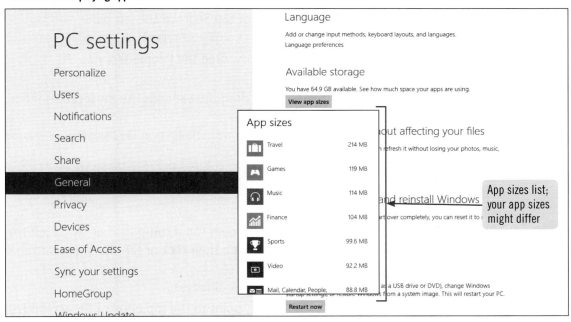

Change Share and Privacy Settings

Learning Outcomes
• Change sharing settings
• Change privacy settings

When you use apps such as Maps or Messaging, the app includes functionality that uses information from Windows, such as my location, and my name and account picture. For example, the Maps app uses your current location (my location) to pinpoint it on a map, and the Messaging app displays your name (my name) and account picture during instant messaging conversations. You can set privacy settings to enable or disable these and other options to specify the level of protection you want. Windows 8 makes it easy to share information, either text or pictures, using other apps. For example, you can select text or pictures on a Web page in Internet Explorer, and then share it with others in an email using Mail. The default sharing app is Mail; however, you can also install and use other online services, such as Twitter and Facebook. The process is pretty simple. Open an app with the content you want to share, display or select the information or item, click or tap the Share button on the Charm bar, and then select the sharing app you want to use. **CASE** *You have met with various QST managers to determine which apps employees use to share information and which options they need for privacy. You want to practice customizing share and privacy settings so that you are comfortable when you set up computer and mobile devices for the company.*

STEPS

1. **With the PC settings screen in view, click or tap Share in the left pane**

   The Share category appears, as shown in **FIGURE F-13**, displaying general and app-specific options.

2. **Under the Use these apps to share category, drag the People slider to Off**

   The People app is turned off for sharing.

3. **Click or tap Privacy in the left pane, then drag the Let apps use my location slider to On, if necessary**

   The Privacy category options are all turned on, as shown in **FIGURE F-14**. The Maps app, for example, is able to use your location to pinpoint it on a map.

4. **Click or tap the lower-left corner to switch to the Start screen, then click or tap the Maps tile on the Start screen**

   The Maps app opens.

5. **Point to the upper-right corner and move down (on a computer) or swipe left from the right edge of the screen (on a mobile device), then click or tap the Share button on the Charm bar**

   The Share panel appears with the People app no longer displayed.

6. **Click or tap off the Share panel to close it, point to the top edge of the screen (cursor changes to a pointing finger), then drag down to the bottom edge of the screen**

   The Settings panel and Maps app close.

7. **Click or tap the upper-left corner (on a computer) or swipe right from the left side of the screen (on a mobile device)**

   The PC settings screen appears.

8. **Drag the Let apps use my location slider back to its original state, if necessary, click or tap Share in the right pane, then drag the People slider to On**

   The options are returned back to their original settings.

9. **Point to the top edge of the screen (cursor changes to a pointing finger), then drag down to the bottom edge of the screen**

   The PC settings screen closes and the Start screen appears.

FIGURE F-13: Viewing Share settings

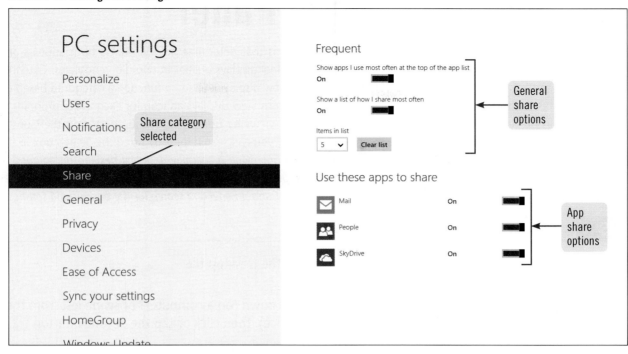

FIGURE F-14: Viewing Privacy settings

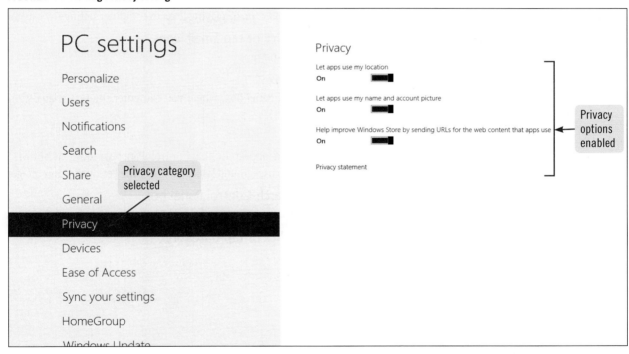

Changing location settings in the Control Panel

You can use the Location Settings icon to set options to let users control how apps use their location. On the Start screen, click or tap All apps on the App bar, click or tap Control Panel, then click or tap the Location Settings icon in Small icons or Large icons view. Select or clear the Turn on the Windows Location platform check box, where you can let users choose their own location settings for apps. If you want to provide information to Microsoft to improve location services, you can select the Help Improve Microsoft location services check box. When you're done, click or tap Apply.

Use the Control Panel

The Control Panel is a collection of utility programs that determine how Windows both appears and works on your PC or mobile device. The Control Panel displays utilities in two different views: Category and Small or Large icons. Control Panel Category view displays utilities in functional categories based on tasks with some direct links, while Small or Large icons view displays an icon for each utility program as in previous versions of Windows. You can change views by using the View by button in the Control Panel. If you're not sure where an option is located, you can search for it by using the Search box in the Control Panel. **CASE** *QST is in the process of approving a specially designed desktop background to accompany the Windows 8 program. Part of your responsibilities will be to add this background to all employee computers and mobile devices. You want to open the Control Panel and search for the background setting so that you know where to make the change.*

STEPS

1. **With the Start screen in view, click or tap the Desktop tile**
   The Desktop opens.

2. **Point to the upper-right corner and move down (on a computer) or swipe left from the right edge of the screen (on a mobile device), then click or tap the Settings button ⚙ on the Charm bar**
   The Settings panel appears.

3. **Click or tap Control Panel on the Settings panel**
   The Control Panel window opens, as shown in **FIGURE F-15**, displaying links to computer settings by category.

4. **Click or tap the View by list arrow, then click or tap Small icons**
   A list of computer settings appears by small icons and type.

5. **Click or tap in the Search Control Panel box**
   The insertion point appears in the Search Control Panel box, where you can enter the text related to the Control Panel options that you want to find.

6. **Type background**
   Control Panel settings that relate to background appear in the Control Panel window, as shown in **FIGURE F-16**. Note that the link to change the desktop background is located under the Personalization category.

7. **Click or tap the Close button ✕ in the Search Control Panel box**
   The search in the Control Panel is canceled and you return to the Control Panel settings in Small icons view.

8. **Click or tap the View by list arrow, then click or tap Category**
   A list of computer settings appears by category.

FIGURE F-15: Viewing the Control Panel

FIGURE F-16: Searching the Control Panel

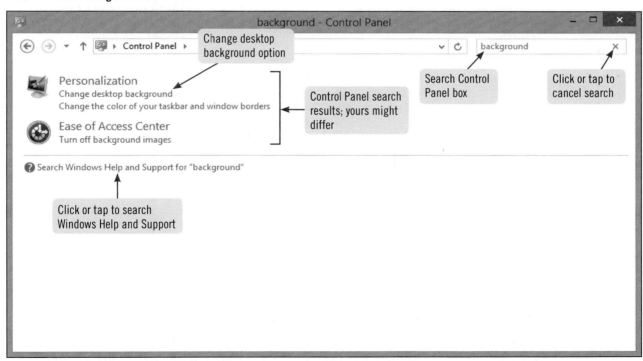

Accessing the Control Panel settings

You can access the Control Panel several different ways. One way is to click or tap the Control Panel tile on the All Apps screen, which you can access on the App bar from the Start screen. Another way is to click or tap the Open Control Panel button on the Computer tab from a File Explorer window in the desktop app. If you're trying to locate a specific Control Panel setting, you can use the Search Control Panel box in the Control Panel window or use the Search panel from the Charm bar.

Personalize the Desktop

Learning Outcomes
• Change the desktop theme
• Change the desktop background

You can change the entire appearance of your current desktop by applying desktop themes. A desktop **theme** is a customized user interface that includes a desktop background, screen saver, pointers, sounds, icons, and fonts based on a set theme, such as baseball, science, travel, or underwater. You can use one of the predefined desktop themes (Windows Default or High Contrast) or create your own. If a preset theme isn't exactly what you want, you can change the appearance of colors, fonts, and sizes used for major window elements, such as title bars, icons, menus, borders, and the desktop itself. The theme options differ depending on the theme type, either Windows or High Contrast. The desktop **background**, or **wallpaper**, is a picture that serves as your desktop's backdrop, the basic surface on which icons and windows appear. You can select one or more background pictures and change how it looks using the Desktop Background dialog box. You can select more than one picture, and set a change picture interval to display them in a specific order or shuffle them. Once you select a background picture, you can display it on the screen five different ways: Fill, Fit, Stretch, Tile, or Center. Instead of selecting a background picture, which can sometimes make icons on the desktop difficult to see, you can also change the background to a color. **CASE** ▶ *As part of the setup for QST company computers and mobile devices, you want to change the desktop theme and background using the Control Panel.*

STEPS

1. **With the Control Panel window in view, click or tap** Appearance and Personalization
    Control Panel settings related to appearance and personalization appear in the window.

2. **Click or tap** Personalization
    Control Panel settings related to personalization appear in the window, as shown in **FIGURE F-17**.

3. **Under Windows Default Themes, note the current theme (Windows by default), then click or tap the** Earth **or** Flowers **theme**
    The theme is applied to the desktop. The desktop background and the window border color adjust to reflect the change.

4. **Click or tap** Desktop Background **at the bottom of the window**
    Desktop Background settings appear in the window, as shown in **FIGURE F-18**. You can select more than one desktop background, which creates a slide show on the desktop, as well as specify the interval when you want a picture to change.

5. **Click or tap the** Change picture every list arrow, **then click or tap** 10 seconds
    The desktop background picture is set to change every 10 seconds.

6. **Click or tap** Save changes
    The Desktop Background options are applied and Control Panel settings related to personalization appear in the window. An unsaved theme appears with the customized options. Every 10 seconds, your desktop background changes to a different picture.

7. **Click or tap the original theme (see Step 3) to restore settings**
    The original theme is restored in the Control Panel.

8. **Click the** Close button ▐ × ▌ **in the Control Panel window, point to the top edge of the screen (cursor changes to a pointing finger), then drag down to the bottom edge of the screen**
    The Control Panel window closes and then the Desktop app closes. The Start screen appears.

FIGURE F-17: Personalization settings in the Control Panel

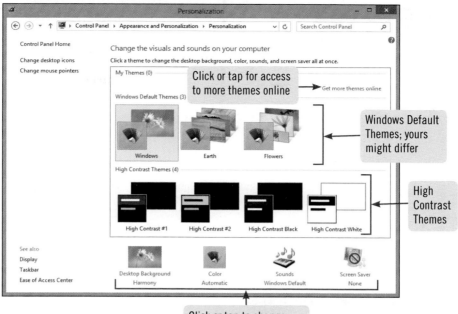

Click or tap for access to more themes online

Windows Default Themes; yours might differ

High Contrast Themes

Click or tap to change individual theme settings

FIGURE F-18: Desktop Background settings in the Control Panel

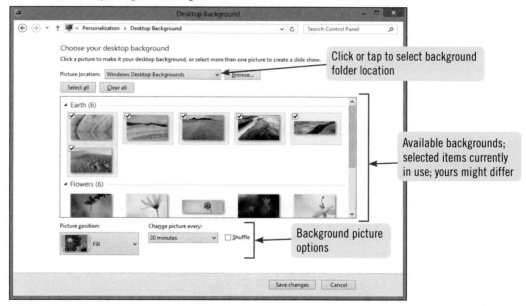

Click or tap to select background folder location

Available backgrounds; selected items currently in use; yours might differ

Background picture options

Customizing desktop icons

The icons on the desktop provide easy access to programs, folders, and system-related shortcuts. If your desktop is getting cluttered, you can quickly show or hide desktop icons. In addition, you can customize the desktop to show or hide the familiar icons: Computer, User's Files, Network, Recycle Bin, or Control Panel. You can also quickly sort, resize, and rearrange desktop icons by right-clicking or tap-holding the desktop, and then using

commands on the View and Sort By submenus. To show or hide desktop icons, right-click or tap-hold a blank area on the desktop, then click or tap Personalize. In the left pane, click or tap Change desktop icons, then select or clear the check boxes to show or hide desktop icons. To change the appearance of an icon, select the icon, click or tap Change Icon, select an icon, then click or tap OK. Click or tap OK, then click or tap the Close button.

Practice

Concepts Review

FIGURE F-19

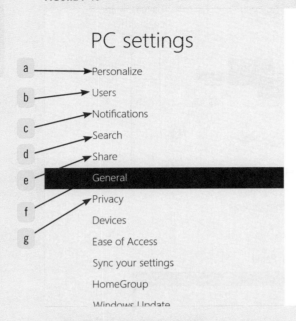
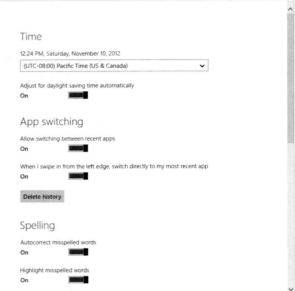

Match the statements below with the elements labeled in the screen shown in FIGURE F-19.

1. Which element lets you change the Start screen?
2. Which element lets you change your password?
3. Which element lets you display status information?
4. Which element lets you delete history?
5. Which element lets you send content to apps?
6. Which element lets you view app sizes?
7. Which element lets apps use my location?

Match each term with the statement that best describes it.

8. Control Panel
9. PC settings
10. Settings panel
11. Theme
12. Wallpaper

    a. A desktop picture
    b. A desktop appearance
    c. A place to customize the desktop
    d. A place to customize windows
    e. A place to access some PC settings

Select the best answers from the following lists of choices.

13. Which of the following is *not* an option on the Settings panel?
    a. Notifications
    b. Search
    c. Keyboard
    d. Power

14. **Which of the following allows you to change the Start screen?**
   a. Personalize
   b. Notifications
   c. General
   d. Users

15. **Which of the following allows you to change the Lock screen?**
   a. Personalize
   b. Notifications
   c. General
   d. Users

16. **Which of the following allows you to change your password?**
   a. Personalize
   b. Notifications
   c. General
   d. Users

17. **Which of the following allows you to get status information?**
   a. Personalize
   b. Notifications
   c. General
   d. Users

18. **Which of the following allows you to set spelling options?**
   a. Personalize
   b. General
   c. Users
   d. Share

19. **Which of the following allows you to access language options?**
   a. Personalize
   b. General
   c. Users
   d. Share

20. **Which of the following allows you to reinstall Windows?**
   a. Personalize
   b. General
   c. Users
   d. Share

21. **Which of the following allows you to change your time zone?**
   a. Personalize
   b. General
   c. Users
   d. Share

22. **Which of the following allows you to access the Control Panel?**
   a. Start screen
   b. Desktop screen
   c. Settings panel
   d. Search panel

23. **Which of the following items is *not* part of a desktop theme?**
   a. Background
   b. Color
   c. Icons
   d. Screen saver

Skills Review

1. **View Windows settings.**
   a. Open the Settings panel from the Charm bar.
   b. Open the PC settings screen.
   c. Scroll through the categories.
   d. Select a category.
   e. Scroll through the options.

2. **Personalize the Start and Lock screen.**
   a. Select the Personalize category in the PC settings screen.
   b. Display Start screen settings.
   c. Note the current background design and color.
   d. Select a background design and background color.
   e. Display Lock screen settings.
   f. Note the current background image.
   g. Select a background image.
   h. Return the background image to its original setting.

3. **Change user account settings.**
   a. Select the Users category in the PC settings screen.
   b. Create a picture password.
   c. Select the QST New Logo file in the Quest Travel folder where you store your Data Files.
   d. Draw three gestures, then confirm.
   e. Lock the screen, then draw the gestures as the password.
   f. Remove the picture password.

Skills Review (continued)

4. Change notification settings.

a. Select the Notifications category in the PC settings screen.

b. Enable Show app notifications on the lock screen, if necessary.

c. Lock the screen to view the notification icons.

d. Sign back in to your account.

e. Select the Notifications button on the Settings panel.

f. Hide notifications for three hours.

g. Enable Show app notifications in the PC settings screen.

5. Change search settings.

a. Select the Search category in the PC settings screen.

b. Turn off Internet Explorer.

c. Open the Search panel from the Charm bar.

d. Confirm that the Internet Explorer app no longer appears.

e. Close the Search panel.

f. Switch back to the PC settings screen.

g. Turn on Internet Explorer.

6. Change general settings.

a. Select the General category in the PC settings screen.

b. Note the current time zone.

c. Change the time zone to Eastern Time (US & Canada), if necessary.

d. Lock the screen to view the adjusted time.

e. Sign back in to your account.

f. Return the time zone back to its original setting.

g. View the app sizes.

7. Change share and privacy settings.

a. Select the Share category in the PC settings screen.

b. Turn off Mail.

c. Select the Privacy category in the PC settings screen.

d. Turn on Let apps use my location, if necessary.

e. Switch to the Start screen, then start the Maps app.

f. Open the Share panel from the Charm bar.

g. Confirm that the Mail app no longer appears.

h. Close the Share panel and the Maps app.

i. Switch back to the PC settings screen.

j. Return the share and privacy options back to their original settings.

k. Close the PC settings screen.

8. Use the Control Panel.

a. Start the desktop.

b. Open the Control Panel from the Settings panel.

c. Change the view to Large icons.

d. Search for background in the Control Panel.

e. Close the search in the Control Panel.

f. Change the view to Category.

9. Personalize the desktop.

a. Display Appearance and Personalization settings.

b. Display Personalization settings.

c. Note the current theme.

d. Select the Earth or Flowers theme.

e. Select Desktop Background.

f. Change the picture to display every 30 seconds.

g. Save changes.

h. Return the theme back to its original setting.

i. Close the Control Panel.

j. Close the Desktop app.

Independent Challenge 1

You are a new student at Expression University, a school specializing in technology and design. Every student at the university is required to use a Windows 8 device to complete course work and interact with other students and professors. You have just purchased your new Windows 8 device, so you want to personalize the Start and Lock screen to customize the look of your system.

a. Open the PC settings screen.

b. Select the Personalize category.

c. Display Start screen settings.

d. Note the current Start screen settings.

e. Change the background design.

f. Change the background color.

g. Display Lock screen settings.

h. Note the current Lock screen settings.

Independent Challenge 1 (continued)

i. Change the lock screen image.

j. Lock the screen to view the change.

k. Sign in and view the Start screen.

l. Switch back to the PC settings screen.

m. Restore the Lock screen back to its original settings.

n. Restore the Start screen back to its original settings.

o. Close the PC settings screen.

Independent Challenge 2

You just started a new job at Express Auto Claims. You have been provided a new tablet device with Windows 8 to work in the office and out in the field. The first task you want to complete is to add more security to your PC to ensure that you are the only one who can access the claim information on your system. You want to open the PC settings screen, then create both a picture password and a PIN password.

a. Open the PC settings screen.

b. Select the Users category.

c. Create a picture password.

d. Create a PIN password.

e. Lock the screen.

f. Sign in using the picture password.

g. Lock the screen, then sign in using the PIN password.

h. Switch back to the PC settings screen.

i. Remove the picture password.

j. Remove the PIN password.

k. Close the PC settings screen.

Independent Challenge 3

With Windows 8, you can change a variety of settings to customize your system to suit your needs. However, it can sometimes be hard to remember the name of every Control Panel setting. Instead of scrolling through the different options, you can perform a search in the Control Panel to find the one you want. You want to change the power options on your device and back up files. When you open the Control Panel in Category view, you don't see any options for power or backup, so you perform a search to find it.

a. Start the Desktop app.

b. Open the Control Panel.

c. Search for power in the Control Panel.

d. Display the Power Options.

e. Search for **backup** in the Control Panel.

f. Display the File History options.

g. Click or tap Control Panel Home.

h. Close the Control Panel and the Desktop app.

Independent Challenge 4: Explore

You are a freelance graphic designer. You want to create a quick and easy portfolio that contains all of your designs. You decide to create a slide show with your designs as backgrounds on the desktop. You'll need to locate a group of pictures and place them in a folder on your system for use as backgrounds.

a. Start the Desktop app.

b. Open File Explorer.

c. Create a folder in the Pictures folder, then copy at least five graphics into the folder.

d. Open the Control Panel.

e. Display the Personalization settings.

f. Display the Desktop Background settings.

g. Use the Browse button to select your graphics.

h. Change the picture every 30 seconds.

i. Save changes.

j. Switch to the desktop and view the graphics.

k. Switch back to the Control Panel.

l. Delete the unsaved theme.

m. Restore the theme back to its original setting.

n. Close the Control Panel and the Desktop app.

Visual Workshop

Re-create the screen shown in **FIGURE F-20**, which displays the Control Panel window with Personalization settings changed.

FIGURE F-20

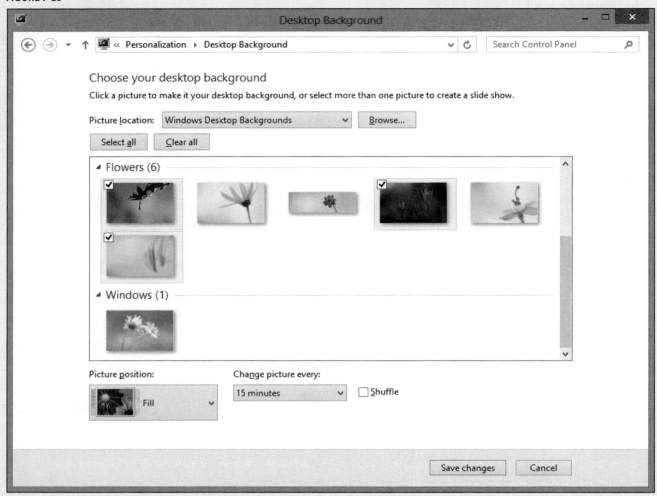

Managing Windows Security

CASE Windows 8 makes communicating with other devices over the Internet more secure and easier than ever. You want to view and customize your settings to make Windows 8 secure from online hackers or malicious software. Important: To perform some of the lessons in this unit, you need to use the administrator password or use an administrator account. See your instructor or technical support person for more information.

Unit Objectives

After completing this unit, you will be able to

- Explore the Action Center
- Manage Windows Firewall
- Manage Automatic Updates
- Defend against malicious software
- Set up Internet security

- Protect your Internet identity
- Protect your Internet privacy
- Delete Internet information
- Set Family Safety controls

Files You Will Need

WIN G-1.cer
WIN G-2.cer

©Itana/Shutterstock

Explore the Action Center

The **Action Center** enables you to manage system security by providing a single place to view alerts and take action about security and maintenance issues with your system. The Action Center makes it easy to find information about the latest virus or security threat, check the status of essential security settings, quickly get support from Microsoft for a security-related issue, and access the Control Panel utilities that allow you to set additional security and privacy settings. The Action Center displays important and recommended alerts to help protect your system and keep Windows running smoothly. As you work, Windows 8 displays security alerts and icons in the notification area on the taskbar to make you aware of potential security risks, such as a new virus, out-of-date antivirus software, if an important security option is turned off, or other security-related issues from Microsoft. To open the Action Center, you can click or tap on an alert, access it from the Control Panel or click or tap the Action Center icon in the notification area on the taskbar. When you click or tap the Action Center icon, a small window with a list of alert messages appears from which you can click or tap to address any issues. In the Action Center, you can also find links to troubleshooters and system restore tools. **CASE** ▸ *As part of your job as the IT specialist at Quest Specialty Travel, you need to make sure company computers are properly protected from outside threats. You want to examine the current security settings on your computer to make sure QST company information is safe.*

STEPS

1. **With the Start screen in view, click or tap the Desktop tile**
   The Desktop app opens, displaying the desktop and taskbar.

2. **If available, click or tap the Action Center icon ▣ in the notification area on the taskbar**
   A message window appears with links to important and recommended alerts. In the window, some options have a security icon 🛡 next to them, as shown in **FIGURE G-1**. When you see a security icon next to any option within Windows 8, it means that you need permission to access the setting, which involves entering an administrator password. This adds an additional level of security to your system.

3. **Click or tap Open Action Center in the message window if available, or click or tap Settings on the Charm bar, click or tap Control Panel, then click or tap Review your computer's status under System and Security**
   The Action Center window opens, displaying the essential security areas and their current status, as shown in **FIGURE G-2**. In this case, there are three recommended issues: one for an untrusted PC in the Security area and two others in the Maintenance area. You can click or tap the Expand button ⌄ or anywhere on the bar to show more information about a specific security area; simply click or tap the Collapse button ⌃ or the bar again to hide detail. You can use the options available to install and update any needed protection software.

4. **Click or tap the Expand button ⌄ for the Security area**
   A list of security information and links to specific security options appear.

5. **In the task pane, click or tap Change Action Center settings**
   The Change Action Center settings dialog box opens, displaying security and maintenance message options under the heading Turn messages on or off.

6. **Click or tap Cancel to dismiss the dialog box without making changes**

7. **In the task pane, click or tap Change User Account Control settings**
   The User Account Control Settings dialog box opens, displaying a notification slider option you can set to help prevent potentially harmful programs from making changes to your system.

8. **Click or tap Cancel to dismiss the dialog box without making changes**

9. **Click or tap System and Security in the Address bar**
   The System and Security window opens, displaying system-, security-, and maintenance-related options.

FIGURE G-1: Alert messages from the Action Center

Alert messages; yours will differ

Security icon; need permission to access

Open Action Center link

Action Center icon

FIGURE G-2: Action Center window

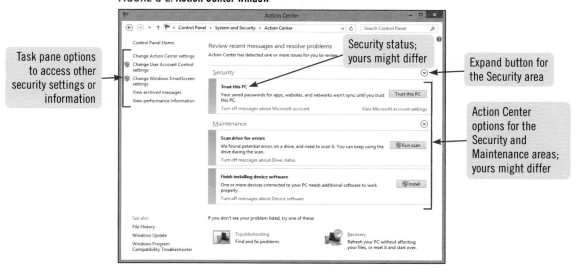

Task pane options to access other security settings or information

Security status; yours might differ

Expand button for the Security area

Action Center options for the Security and Maintenance areas; yours might differ

Protecting against malware

A **computer virus** is a program that attaches itself to a file, reproduces itself, and then spreads to other files. A virus is typically "caught" from programs and files downloaded from the Internet, electronic mail attachments, or shareware disks containing free or inexpensive software or illegally obtained pirated software. When you open a program or file with the computer virus, the computer becomes infected with the virus and can corrupt or destroy data, or disrupt program or Windows functionality. Many viruses stay dormant on a computer before doing any damage, so catching and destroying these viruses before they cause damage can prevent computer disaster. A **worm** is like a virus, but it can spread without human action across networks. For example, a worm might send email copies of itself to everyone in your email

Address Book. A worm can consume memory causing your computer to stop responding or even take it over. A **Trojan horse**, like its mythological counterpart, is a program that appears to be useful and comes from a legitimate source, but actually causes problems, such as gathering personal information or deleting files. **Antivirus software**, or virus detection software, examines the files stored on a disk to determine whether they are infected with a virus, then destroys or disinfects them. Antivirus software provides protection when you start Windows and checks for viruses whenever your computer is on. Popular antivirus software, which needs to be purchased from a software retailer, includes Norton AntiVirus and McAfee VirusScan. New viruses appear all the time, so it is important that your antivirus software be kept up to date.

Manage Windows Firewall

Learning Outcomes
• View firewall status
• View firewall settings

If your computer is directly connected to the Internet, you need a firewall program. A **firewall** is a protective barrier between your computer or network and others on the Internet. **Windows Firewall** protects your computer from unauthorized access from others on the Internet by monitoring communication between your computer and the Internet and preventing unsolicited inbound traffic from the Internet from entering your private computer. Windows Firewall discards all unsolicited communications from reaching your computer unless you specifically allow them to come through. Windows Firewall is enabled by default for all Internet and network connections. However, some computer manufacturers and network administrators might turn it off, so you need to check it before you start using the computer. When Windows Firewall is enabled, you might not be able to use some communication features, such as sending files with a messaging program or playing an Internet game, unless the program is listed in the Allowed Programs window in Windows Firewall. If you use multiple Internet and networking connections, you can enable or disable the specific individual connections or modify firewall settings for each type of network location you use. **CASE** ▶ *Because firewall protection is an essential aspect of computer protection, you want to make sure your Windows Firewall is running so QST company information is safe.*

STEPS

1. **In the System and Security window, click or tap** Windows Firewall
   The Windows Firewall window opens, as shown in **FIGURE G-3**, displaying the current firewall settings. In this case, the settings are for a private network: Windows Firewall is turned on, incoming connections are blocked to apps not on the list of allowed apps, and the notification state is set to display if a new app is blocked.

2. **In the task pane, click or tap** Turn Windows Firewall on or off

3. **If a User Account Control window opens, click or tap** Continue, **or type the administrator password, then click or tap** Yes
   The Customize Settings window opens, as shown in **FIGURE G-4**.

4. **Click or tap the** Turn on Windows Firewall option button **if necessary under Private network settings**
   When Windows Firewall is enabled, hackers or malicious software are prevented from accessing your computer.

5. **Click or tap** Cancel
   The current firewall settings remain the same and the Windows Firewall window opens. Some programs, such as Remote Assistance (a Windows program that allows you to control another computer over the Internet), need to communicate through the firewall, so you can create an exception to allow them to work, yet still maintain a secure computer.

6. **In the task pane, click or tap** Allow an app or feature through Windows Firewall
   The Allowed apps window opens, displaying the current programs or connection ports allowed to communicate through the firewall. A **port** is the actual connection on your computer that links to devices, such as a printer.

7. **Scroll down the list, then click or tap the** Windows Media Player Network Sharing Service (Internet) check box **in the Private column to select it**
   Selecting this option enables the Windows Media Player program to freely communicate over the Internet for network-sharing purposes through the firewall.

8. **Click or tap** OK
   The Windows Firewall window reopens.

9. **Click or tap** System and Security **in the Address bar**
   The System and Security window reopens.

FIGURE G-3: Windows Firewall window

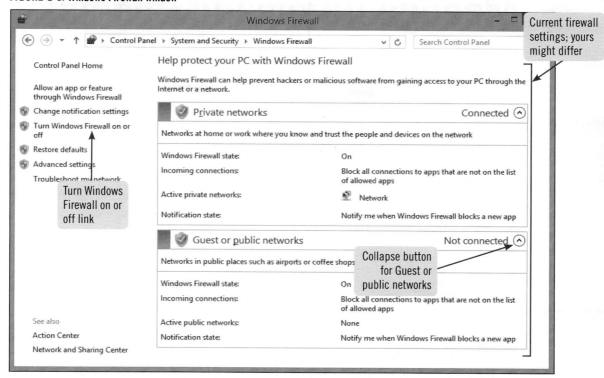

Current firewall settings; yours might differ

Turn Windows Firewall on or off link

Collapse button for Guest or public networks

FIGURE G-4: Customize Settings window

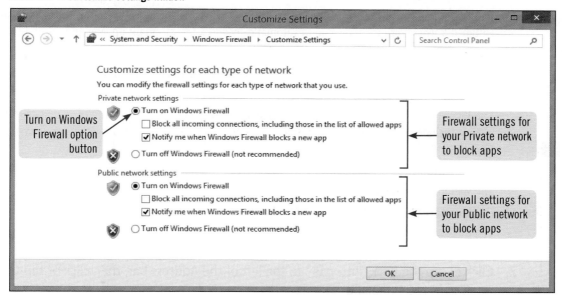

Turn on Windows Firewall option button

Firewall settings for your Private network to block apps

Firewall settings for your Public network to block apps

Adding additional security at start-up

For added security, you can require users to press [Ctrl][Alt] [Delete] before they can select a user account and enter a password when they turn on the computer. This prevents programs, such as spyware or a virus, from stealing your username and password when you enter it on your computer. When you lock your computer or switch users, this security option also requires users to press [Ctrl][Alt][Delete] to log back on. To set the Ctrl+Alt+Delete option, display the Start screen, click or tap the All Apps button on the App bar, click or tap the Run tile, type NetplWiz.exe, then click or tap OK. In the User Accounts dialog box, click or tap the Advanced tab, click or tap the Require users to press Ctrl+Alt+Delete check box to select it, then click or tap OK.

Manage Automatic Updates

Learning Outcomes
- View Windows Update settings
- Check for Windows updates

Microsoft continues to improve Windows 8 with new features or security fixes, known as updates. Windows Update allows you to keep your PC up to date with the latest system software and security updates over the Internet. **Automatic updating** provides protection to make sure your Windows software is up to date and safe. Windows Update provides a central location where you can view currently installed updates and install new updates, and device drivers. Windows Update confidentially and continuously scans your PC for updates that need to be installed and identifies them as important or optional. Important updates are critical to the functionality of your system, whereas optional updates are related to personal preference operations. Windows Update can review device drivers and system software on your computer, compare those findings with a master database on the Web, and then recommend and install updates specifically for your computer. You can also restore a previous device driver or system file using the uninstall option. Because Microsoft provides updates on a regular basis over the Internet, it is important to check for updates. If you want to be notified when updates occur, you can set up Windows 8 to let you know as soon as they happen. The default setting is to have Windows automatically check for them every day. **CASE** *You're not sure how long it's been since your computer at QST has been updated with the latest Windows 8 software. You want to check your computer for updates and current settings.*

STEPS

1. **In the System and Security window, click or tap** Windows Update
   The Windows Update window opens, as shown in **FIGURE G-5**, displaying information and the current settings for Windows Update.

2. **In the task pane, click or tap** Change settings
   The Change settings window opens, displaying the Windows Update notification settings, as shown in **FIGURE G-6**. These settings allow you to automatically check for important updates and install them.

3. **Click or tap** Cancel
   The current Windows Update notification settings remain the same and the Windows Update window reopens.

4. **In the task pane, click or tap** View update history
   The View update history window opens, displaying a list of your computer's complete update history. The history includes the update name, installation status and date, and importance to your system, either Important, Recommended, or Optional.

QUICK TIP
To remove an installed update, click or tap Installed Updates in the task pane in the Windows Update window, select the update, then click or tap Uninstall.

5. **Click or tap** OK
   The Windows Update window reopens.

6. **Click or tap** Installed Updates **at the bottom of the task pane**
   The Installed Updates window opens, displaying a list of the currently installed Windows updates on your computer. Using this window, you can uninstall applications you no longer use or ones causing a problem.

7. **Click or tap the** Back button ⊖ **to the left of the Address bar, then click or tap** Check for updates **in the task pane**
   The Installed Updates window closes and the Windows Update window reopens. Windows Update checks your computer to see if it needs any updates. If it detects that updates are necessary, Windows Update indicates how many updates are available and classifies their importance.

TROUBLE
Important: If you're working on a network run by an administrator, do not install any software without permission.

8. **Click or tap an important or optional update, if available, or skip to the second part of Step 9**
   The Select updates to install window opens. This is where you would choose the updates you want to install. To install an update, you would click or tap the check box(es) next to the update(s), click or tap Install, then click or tap Install updates.

9. **Click or tap** Cancel, **if necessary, then click or tap** System and Security **in the Address bar**
   The System and Security window reopens.

FIGURE G-5: Windows Update window

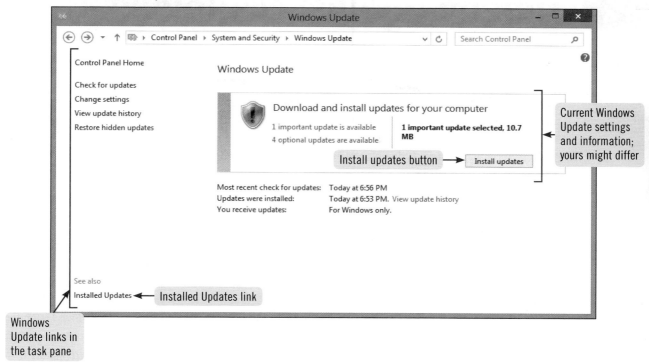

FIGURE G-6: Change settings window

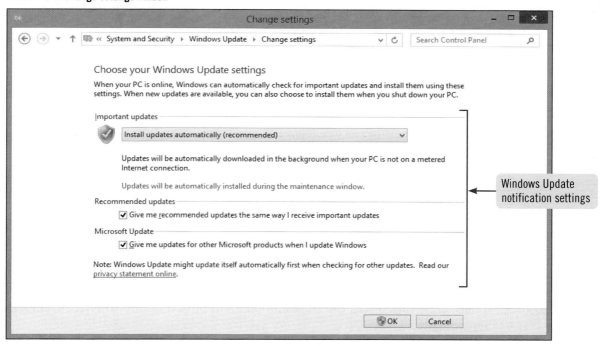

Updating Windows manually in PC settings

You can choose to have Windows regularly check for updates and download them in the background or you can manually select the ones you want to install. You can manually check for updates in the Control Panel or PC settings. To manually set Windows Update settings, display the Start screen, click or tap the Settings button on the Charm bar, click or tap Change PC settings on the Settings panel, click or tap Windows Update under PC settings, then click or tap Check for updates now.

Defend Against Malicious Software

Windows Defender provides information and security against **malware**, which is malicious software, such as viruses and spyware that can delete or corrupt files and steal personal information. **Spyware** is software that attempts to collect your personal information or change computer settings without your consent. Typically, spyware is downloaded without your knowledge and installed on your computer along with free software you willingly accept, such as freeware, games, or music file-sharing programs. Spyware is often associated with adware software that displays advertisements, such as a pop-up ad. Windows Defender uses alerts to protect your computer from malware, spyware, and any other potentially harmful software that attempts to install itself or run on your computer. When you receive an alert of a potential problem, you can use the Microsoft SpyNet community on the Web to help you determine if the software is legitimate to run. Windows Defender determines if there are potential problems by using definitions. A **definition** provides instructions on how to defend against malware software. Because software dangers continually change, it's important to have up-to-date definitions, which you can get online. You can perform a quick scan of essential Windows files or a full scan of your entire computer. If Windows Defender finds a problem, it quarantines the software, which prevents it from running. You can then decide if it is software you indeed want to run. **CASE** ⟩ *You want to continue checking security settings on QST computers to make sure information is safe.*

STEPS

1. **Click or tap in the Search Control Panel box, type** Windows Defender, **then click or tap** Windows Defender **in the System and Security window**
   The Windows Defender window opens, similar to **FIGURE G-7**, displaying status and information about your computer's current protection against malicious and unwanted software.

2. **Click or tap the** Update tab, **then click or tap** Update
   Windows Defender checks for definitions and installs any updates. Upon completion, status information at the bottom of the window is updated with the definition version and date and time.

3. **Click or tap the** Home tab, **click or tap the** Quick option button **under Scan options to select it, if necessary, then click** Scan now
   Windows Defender scans the essential files on your computer, as shown in **FIGURE G-8**. Upon completion, scan statistics appear, including start time, elapsed time, and number of objects scanned. Status information at the bottom of the window is also updated. The status information includes scan schedule, which you can modify.

4. **Click or tap the** History tab
   The History tab information displays options for Quarantined items, Allowed items, and All detected items.

5. **If necessary, click or tap the** Quarantined items option button **to select it, then click** View details
   The Quarantined items option displays any items identified as potential problems.

6. **Click or tap the** All detected items option button, **then click** View details
   The All detected items option displays any items that Windows Defender has detected.

7. **Click or tap the** Settings tab
   The Settings tab information displays options for Windows Defender.

8. **Click or tap the** Close button ⊠ **in the Windows Defender window, then click or tap** ⊠ **in the Search Control Panel box**
   The System and Security window reopens.

FIGURE G-7: Windows Defender window

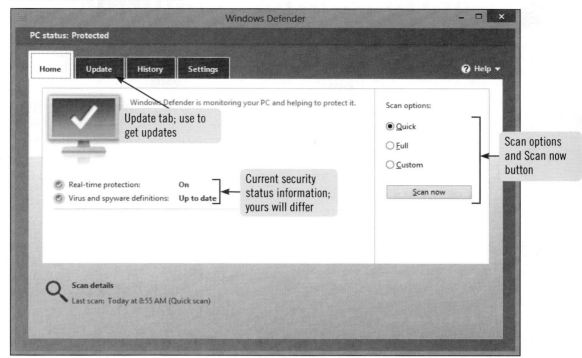

FIGURE G-8: Scanning for malware

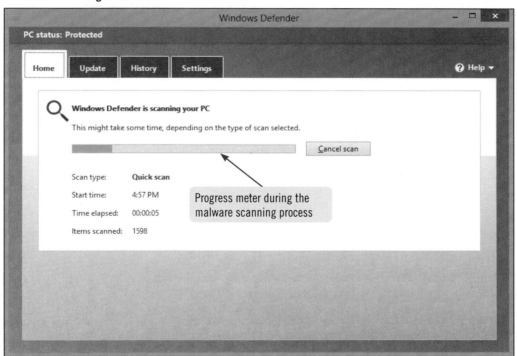

Monitoring and managing programs using Windows Defender

You can use Windows Defender to monitor all the programs on your system or just specific ones. To set monitoring options in the Windows Defender window, click or tap the History tab. To remove or restore quarantined programs, click or tap the Quarantined items option, click or tap the View details button, select a program, then click or tap Remove or Restore. To remove a program from the allowed items (not monitored) list, click or tap the Allowed items option, click or tap the View details button, select a program, then click or tap Remove button.

Set Up Internet Security

Windows provides Internet security options to prevent users on the Internet from gaining access to personal information without your permission, such as credit card information if you shop online. In addition, Windows security options protect your computer from unsafe software downloaded or run from the Internet. Internet security is divided into **zones**, or Web site areas, to which you can assign different levels of security. There are four security zones: Internet, Local intranet, Trusted sites, and Restricted sites. See **TABLE G-1** for a description of each security zone. When you access a Web page or download content from a site, Internet Explorer checks its security settings and determines the Web site's zone, which displays on the right side of the Internet Explorer status bar. All Internet Web sites are by default assigned to the Internet zone until you assign individual Web sites to other zones. **CASE** *You want to check Internet security settings to make sure company computers are secure for Internet use and that the QST Web site is set as a trusted site.*

STEPS

1. **In the task pane, click or tap** Network and Internet, **then click or tap** Internet Options
   The Internet Properties dialog box opens, displaying the General tab.

2. **Click or tap the** Security tab
   The Internet Properties dialog box reopens, displaying the Internet zone and its current security level, as shown in **FIGURE G-9**. The security levels are High, Medium-high, and Medium. You can move the slider up for a higher level of security or down for a lower level of security.

3. **Drag the slider up or down to adjust the security level, then click or tap** Yes **if a Warning message dialog box opens**
   A detailed description appears next to the security level, which changes as you adjust the security level.

4. **Under Select a zone to view or change security settings, click or tap** Trusted sites
   The security-level information for Trusted sites appears, where you can add and remove trusted sites or change the security-level settings. The security levels are Low, Medium-low, Medium, Medium-high, and High.

5. **Click or tap** Sites
   The Trusted sites dialog box opens, where you can add trusted Web sites.

6. **Click or tap in the** Add this website to the zone text box, **then type** https://www.questspecialtytravel.com
   For an Internet site to be accepted as a trusted site, it needs to be a secure site, which is indicated by a "https" in the Web address, as shown in **FIGURE G-10**.

7. **Click or tap** Add
   The site is added as a trusted site.

8. **Click or tap the site in the Websites box, then click or tap** Remove
   The site is removed from the trusted site zone.

9. **Click or tap** Close **in the Trusted sites dialog box, then click or tap** Cancel **in the Internet Properties dialog box**
   The Network and Internet window opens.

FIGURE G-9: Internet Properties dialog box with the Security tab displayed

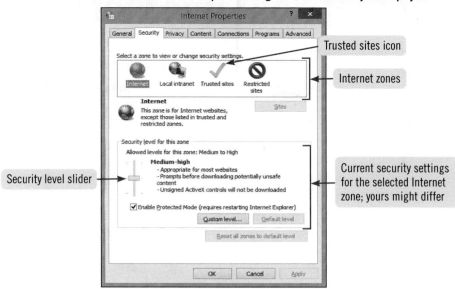

Trusted sites icon

Internet zones

Security level slider

Current security settings for the selected Internet zone; yours might differ

FIGURE G-10: Trusted sites dialog box

"https" indicates a secure site

Web site to add as a trusted site

TABLE G-1: Security zones in Internet Explorer

zone	description	default setting
Internet	Contains all Web sites that are not assigned to any other zone	Medium-high
Local intranet	Contains all Web sites that are on your organization's intranet and don't require a proxy server	Medium-low
Trusted sites	Contains Web sites that you believe will not threaten the security of your computer	Medium
Restricted sites	Contains Web sites that you believe will threaten the security of your computer	High (blocks all cookies)

Protect Your Internet Identity

Learning
Outcomes
• Add a personal
  certificate
• View a personal
  certificate

To further protect your privacy, you can use certificates to verify your identity and protect important information, such as your credit card number, on the Internet. A **certificate** is a digitally signed statement verifying the identity of a person or the security of a Web site. A certificate is also known as a **Digital ID** in other programs, such as Microsoft Outlook. For normal transactions over the Internet in which you provide personal information, you won't have to think about certificates. When you visit a secure Web site (one whose address often starts with "https" instead of "http"), it automatically sends you its certificate. When Internet Explorer receives the certificate, it displays a lock icon on the status bar, which you can click or tap to view a report, and validates the certificate information, which includes the Web site address, expiration date, and certifying authority. If any of the information in the certificate is invalid, Internet Explorer blocks access to the site. If you need to provide a certificate by request of a Web site, you can obtain a personal security certification from an independent Certification Authority (CA). There are two types of certificates: personal and Web site. A **personal certificate** verifies your identity to a secure Web site that requires a certificate, whereas a **Web site certificate** verifies its security to you before you send them information. **CASE** ▶ *Because you're going to be transferring QST information and files over the Internet, you want to learn more about using certificates. You decide to import a certificate issued by John Casey, a coworker at QST, to see how it works.*

STEPS

1. **In the Network and Internet window, click or tap Internet Options**
   The Internet Properties dialog box opens, displaying the General tab.

2. **Click or tap the Content tab, then under Certificates, click or tap Certificates**
   The Certificates dialog box opens, displaying the Personal tab information. The Personal tab stores your individual ("personal") certificates, while the other tabs in this dialog box, such as Other People, store certificates based on the purpose described by the tab name. The subsequent tabs are identified as trusted or untrusted, which indicates whether you should use them or not. Because the certificate example is not yours and not issued by a CA, you want to import and store it under the Other People tab.

3. **Click or tap the Other People tab, click or tap Import to start the Certificate Import Wizard, then click or tap Next**
   A Certificate Import Wizard dialog box opens, asking you to specify the certificate file you want to import.

QUICK TIP
To obtain a personal certificate, find a certification authority on the Trusted Root Certification Authorities tab in the Certificates dialog box or search for one on the Internet. The certification authority works with you to create the certificate file and import it to your computer.

4. **Click or tap Browse to display the Open dialog box, navigate to the location where you store your Data Files, double-click or tap the file WIN G-1.cer, then click or tap Next**
   The next Certificate Import Wizard dialog box opens, asking you to specify the location in which you want to place the certificate. Other People appears in the Certificate store text box.

5. **Click or tap Next to display a summary of your choices in the wizard, click or tap Finish, then click or tap OK in the Certification Import Wizard dialog box to confirm**
   The John Casey certificate appears in the Certificates dialog box, as shown in **FIGURE G-11**.

6. **Double-click or double-tap the John Casey certificate**
   The Certificate dialog box opens, as shown in **FIGURE G-12**, displaying information about the specific certificate, including its trustworthiness and the dates between which it's valid.

TROUBLE
If the Remove button is not available, press [Delete] instead. See your network administrator for permission, if necessary.

7. **Click or tap OK to close the Certificate dialog box, click or tap the John Casey certificate to select it, if necessary, click or tap Remove, then click or tap Yes in the message box to confirm the deletion**

8. **Click or tap Close to close the Certificates dialog box, then click or tap Cancel**
   The Internet Properties dialog box closes without any changes saved, and the Network and Internet window reopens.

FIGURE G-11: Certificates dialog box with a personal certificate

Certificate issued by John Casey

FIGURE G-12: General tab in the Certificate dialog box

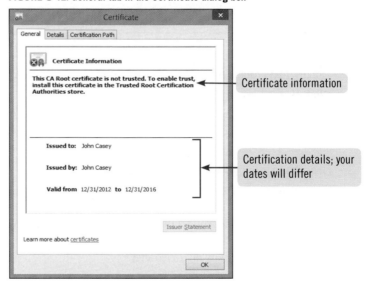

Certificate information

Certification details; your dates will differ

Providing security with the Information Bar

The Information Bar in Internet Explorer makes it easy for you to make informed decisions about potentially harmful content entering your computer. By default, Internet Explorer blocks pop-ups, certain programs, downloads, security risks, and other harmful threats. If the default settings in Internet Explorer are turned on, the Information Bar appears under the Address bar when a Web site tries to open a pop-up window, install an add-on, such as an ActiveX control, or download a file to your system, or if it encounters a certificate error. Pop-up windows typically display annoying ads; click or tap the Turn on Pop-up Blocker check box on the Privacy tab in the Internet Properties dialog box to enable it. ActiveX controls provide added functionality to Internet Explorer, which makes using the Internet more enjoyable. However, it also opens the door for spyware and adware to invade your computer and privacy. When the Information Bar appears, you can click or tap it to display options for dealing with the program or pop-up or to get more information. You can also ignore the Information Bar and continue viewing the Web site, although all the features on the site might not function properly if you choose not to allow the blocked content or program.

Protect Your Internet Privacy

Learning
Outcomes
• Adjust the Internet
  privacy level
• View a privacy
  report

When you browse the Internet, you can access and gather information from Web sites, but Web sites can also gather information about you without your knowledge. You can set Internet privacy options to protect your personal identity from unauthorized access. When you visit a Web site, the site creates a **cookie** file, known as a **first-party cookie**, which stores information on your computer, such as your Web site preferences or personal identifiable information, including your name and email address. The next time you visit that site, it can access the cookie to collect this information. Not all cookies are harmful; many first-party cookies save you time reentering information on a return visit to a Web site. However, there are also **third-party cookies**, which are created by Web sites using advertising banners, for example, you are not currently viewing. Once a cookie is saved on your computer, only the Web site that created it can read it. Windows privacy options allow you to block or permit cookies for Web sites in the Internet zone; however, when you block cookies, you might not be able to access all the features of a Web site. When a Web site that you have blocked tries to place a cookie, a red icon appears on the status bar. To find out if the Web site you are viewing in Internet Explorer contains third-party cookies or if any cookies have been restricted, you can get a privacy report from the site. The privacy report lists all the Web sites with content on the current Web page and shows how each site handles cookies. **CASE** *As you continue to check the current security settings on your computer, you want to check the privacy settings and get a privacy report for a Web page.*

STEPS

1. **Click Internet Options**
   The Internet Properties dialog box opens, displaying the General tab information.

2. **Click the Privacy tab**
   The Privacy tab dialog box opens, as shown in **FIGURE G-13**, displaying a slider, which you use to select a privacy setting to block cookies for the Internet zone. You move the slider up for a higher level of privacy or down for a lower level of privacy.

3. **Drag the slider to adjust the privacy setting**
   When you change your privacy settings, a detailed description appears next to the level. When you apply the privacy changes, they might not affect cookies that are already on your computer, but they will affect any new ones. Whether you set the privacy level to a high setting, which blocks most or all cookies, or a low setting, which blocks only a few or no cookies, you can click or tap Sites in the section below to override cookie handling for individual Web sites.

TROUBLE
If a blank page appears in Internet Explorer, see "Browse the Web with Internet Explorer" in Unit C for information to visit a Web site.

4. **Click Cancel**
   The Internet Properties dialog box closes without making any changes and the Network and Internet window reopens.

5. **Click the Internet Explorer button 🄴 on the taskbar**
   Internet Explorer opens, displaying your home page.

QUICK TIP
To view a Web site's privacy policy summary, select a Web site in the Privacy Report dialog box, then click or tap Summary.

6. **Click the Tools button ⚙ on the toolbar, point to Safety, then click or tap Webpage privacy policy**
   The Privacy Report dialog box opens, as shown in **FIGURE G-14**, displaying all the Web sites associated with the current Web page and how your computer handled their cookies.

7. **Click Close to close the Privacy Report dialog box, then click or tap the Close button ✕ in the Internet Explorer window**
   Internet Explorer closes and the Network and Internet window reopens.

FIGURE G-13: Internet Properties dialog box with the Privacy tab displayed

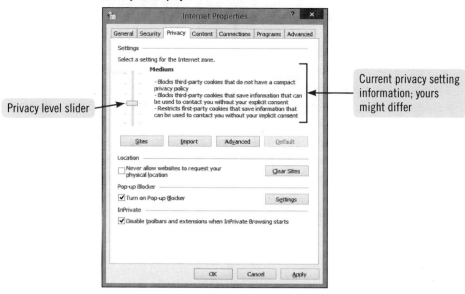

Privacy level slider

Current privacy setting information; yours might differ

FIGURE G-14: Privacy Report dialog box

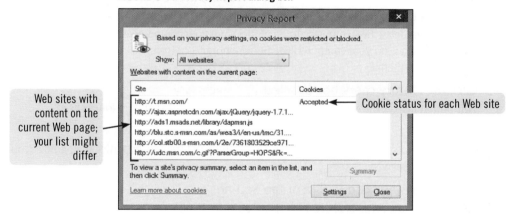

Web sites with content on the current Web page; your list might differ

Cookie status for each Web site

Blocking content with InPrivate filtering

Many Web sites display and use content—such as maps and advertisements—supplied from other third-party Web sites. These content providers can gather and track information about you and your browsing habits without your knowledge. With InPrivate filtering, you can block this from happening. InPrivate filtering analyzes the Web sites you visit looking for third-party content trying to track your movements, and then gives you the option to allow or block the content. You can also have InPrivate filtering automatically block any invasive content from a third party that it detects. InPrivate filtering is off by default and needs to be turned on each time you use Internet Explorer. When you close Internet

Explorer, InPrivate filtering is turned off. In Internet Explorer (desktop), click or tap the Tools button on the toolbar, point to Safety, and then click or tap InPrivate Filtering to enable or disable InPrivate filtering. On first use, click or tap Block for me to block web sites automatically or Let me choose which providers receive my information. You can disable toolbars and extensions for InPrivate browsing. In the Internet Options dialog box, click or tap the Privacy tab, select or clear the Disable toolbars and extensions when InPrivate Browsing starts check box, and then click or tap OK.

Delete Internet Information

Learning Outcomes
- Delete unwanted Internet files
- Set browsing history settings

As you browse the Web, Internet Explorer stores information about your activities, including the information you have provided to Web sites when you log on (passwords) or fill out a form, the location of Web sites you have visited (history), and preference information used by Web sites (cookies). Internet Explorer also saves Web pages, images, and media (temporary Internet files) for faster viewing in the future. If you frequently browse the Web, Internet Explorer can gather and store a large amount of Internet-related data (including normal and InPrivate browsing), which can fill up your hard drive and slow down your computer. To help prevent computer performance problems, you need to periodically delete the Internet files and information; yet you can still preserve the files and information for your trusted sites in your Favorites. You can delete the Internet files and information individually or all at once. **CASE** ▶ *Your computer at QST seems to be slowing down, so you decide to clean up the temporary Internet files on the computer and check related settings to reduce the amount stored in the future.*

STEPS

1. **Click Internet Options**
   The Internet Properties dialog box opens, displaying the General tab.

2. **Under Browsing history, click or tap Delete**
   The Delete Browsing History dialog box opens, as shown in **FIGURE G-15**, displaying the different types of files and data stored when you browse the Web.

3. **Click the Temporary Internet files and website files check box to select it, if necessary, then click or tap the Preserve Favorites website data check box to select it, if necessary**
   These options delete the temporary Internet files from your computer, except for the ones in your Favorites, freeing disk space on your computer. The files are not placed in the Recycle Bin, so you need to be sure you want to delete them.

4. **Click the History check box to select it, if necessary**
   This option deletes the list of Web sites you have recently visited and no longer need.

5. **Click Delete**
   The Delete Browsing History dialog box closes and the Internet Properties dialog box reopens with the General tab displayed.

6. **Under Browsing history, click or tap Settings**
   The Website Data Settings dialog box opens with the Temporary Internet Files tab displayed, as shown in **FIGURE G-16**. You can view or change settings to customize the way temporary Internet files and history items are deleted.

7. **In the Disk space to use (8 – 1024MB) box, click or tap the Down arrow until it displays 40 MB**
   Changing this decreases the space allocated to store temporary Internet files.

8. **Click the History tab, then in the Days to keep pages in history box, click or tap the Up arrow until it displays 25**
   Changing this increases the number of days Internet Explorer builds the History list.

9. **Click Cancel, then click or tap OK**
   The Temporary Internet Files and History Settings and Internet Properties dialog boxes close without saving changes, and the Network and Internet window reopens.

FIGURE G-15: Delete Browsing History dialog box

Preserve Favorites website data check box

Temporary Internet files and website files check box

Delete Browsing History options

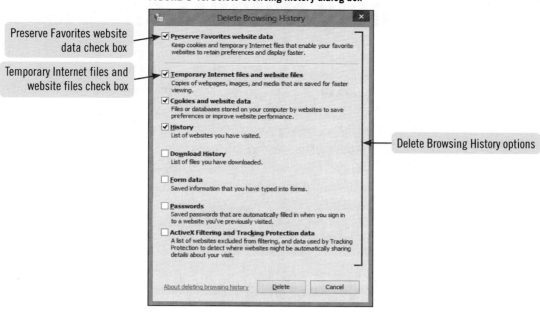

FIGURE G-16: Website Data Settings dialog box

Disk space to use Up/Down arrows

Encrypting files using BitLocker

If you have an internal or external hard drive, or removable drive, you can use BitLocker to encrypt the entire system drive, including the Windows system files needed to start up and log on to Windows 8. A **partition** is a section of a disk drive that behaves like a separate drive. Partitioning is particularly useful if you run more than one operating system. BitLocker helps protect your system and blocks hackers from accessing sensitive information. When you add files to your computer, BitLocker automatically encrypts them. When you copy files to another location, the files

are decrypted. After you turn on BitLocker, it's critical that you create a recovery password, because BitLocker locks up the entire drive if it detects a problem during start-up. To use BitLocker, open the Control Panel, click or tap System and Security, click or tap BitLocker Drive Encryption, click or tap Turn On BitLocker for the drive you want to encrypt, follow the BitLocker setup wizard, then click or tap the Close button. If the Turn On BitLocker button is not available, your drive configuration is not suitable for BitLocker.

Set Family Safety Controls

Family Safety helps you manage your child's access to the Internet, programs, and files on your computer. Family Safety allows you to set limits on Web access, the amount of time spent logged on the computer, and which games and apps can be used. Family Safety allows you to set options based on material you deem inappropriate, due to elements such as language or violence. You can specify different settings for each user account on your computer, so the level of access you want for each individual can be set accordingly. You can also review activity reports on a periodic basis to check what your children are specifically doing during their time on the computer. In addition to the basic parental controls, you can download and install additional online Web site filters and activity reports. With the Family Safety Web site from Microsoft, you can limit searches, monitor and block or allow Web sites, and limit communication in Windows Live Spaces, Messenger, or Hotmail. **CASE** ▶ *During a visit to the office, your child wants to use your computer, so you want to set up Family Safety settings.*

STEPS

Important: Before you complete the steps in this lesson, you need to have access to a standard user account on your system. See your instructor or technical support person.

1. **In the task pane, click or tap** User Accounts and Family Safety, **then click or tap** Family Safety

   If a standard user is attached to this account, then skip to Step 3. If not, a Family Safety window opens, asking you for permission to make changes to the security or personal settings.

2. **If prompted, click or tap** Continue, **or type the administrator password, then click or tap** Yes

   The Family Safety window opens. See **TABLE G-2** for a description of the different type of controls you can set.

3. **Under Choose a user and set up Family Safety, click the standard user account specified by your instructor or administrator**

   The User Settings window opens.

4. **Under Family Safety, click or tap the** On, enforce current settings option button **to select it, if necessary**

   Selecting this option enables Family Safety settings and collects information about computer usage by the user, as shown in **FIGURE G-17**.

5. **Under Windows settings, click or tap** App restrictions

   The App Restrictions window opens, displaying options to allow all programs or only the ones you want to allow the user to have access to.

6. **If necessary, click the** <account name> can only use the apps I allow option button **to select it**

   The App Restrictions window opens, as shown in **FIGURE G-18**, displaying options to block specific programs.

7. **Click or tap the** <account name> can use all apps option button **to select it, then click or tap the** Back button ⊖

   The App Restrictions window closes and the User Settings window opens.

8. **Under Family Safety, click or tap the** Off option button

   The original settings are restored.

9. **Click or tap the** Close button ⊠ **in the User Settings window**

   The User Settings window closes without making any changes.

FIGURE G-17: User Settings window

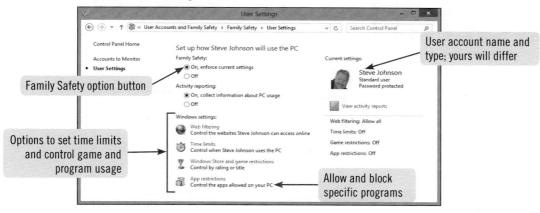

Family Safety option button

Options to set time limits and control game and program usage

User account name and type; yours will differ

Allow and block specific programs

FIGURE G-18: App Restrictions window

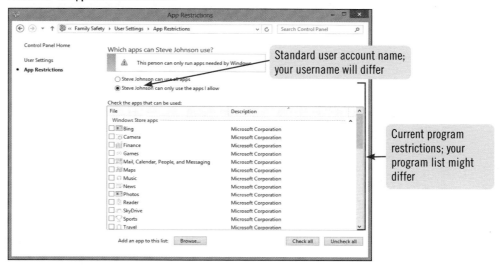

Standard user account name; your username will differ

Current program restrictions; your program list might differ

TABLE G-2: Family Safety settings

settings	description
Web filtering	Select options to block or allow Web sites based on ratings or content
Time limits	Click and drag the usage hours you want to block or allow
Windows Store and game restrictions	Select options to block or allow games and Windows Store apps based on ratings or content
App restrictions	Select an option to use all apps or only approved apps
Windows Live Family Safety	Select options to block or allow Web sites or communications with contacts and get reports for online activity; available when Family Safety is downloaded and installed from Windows Live Essentials

© 2014 Cengage Learning

Changing a user account

There are two main types of user accounts: administrator and standard. The **administrator** account is for the person who needs to make changes to anything on the computer as well as manage user accounts. A **standard** account is for people who need to manage personal files and run programs. If you have an administrator account, you can create a new user account or delete an existing one. When you add a new user to your computer, Windows creates a separate identity, allowing the user to keep files completely private and customize the operating system with personal preferences. The name you assign to the user appears on the Welcome screen and on the Start menu when the user is logged on. The steps to change and delete user accounts differ, depending on whether your computer is part of a company or personal network. To change a user account on a personal network, open the Control Panel, click or tap the Change account type link, click or tap the user account you want to change, click or tap the Change the account type link, select an account type, click or tap Change Account Type, then click or tap Close.

Practice

Concepts Review

Label each component of the desktop personal computer shown in FIGURE G-19.

FIGURE G-19

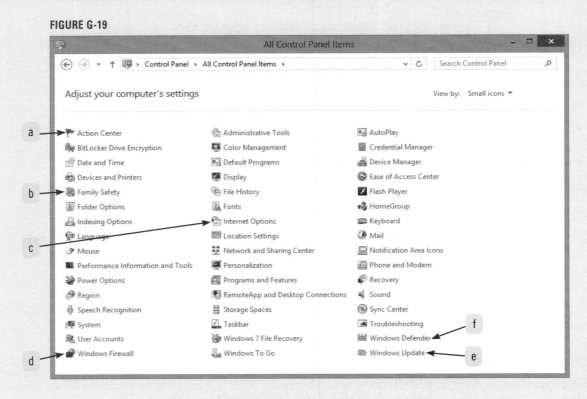

1. Which element allows you to view essential protection settings?
2. Which element allows you to limit computer time?
3. Which element protects your privacy?
4. Which element prevents access to your computer?
5. Which element provides malware protection?
6. Which element allows you to install Windows updates?

Match each term with the statement that best describes it.

7. **Spyware**   **a.** A program that tries to collect information about you
8. **Virus**   **b.** A security system that creates a protective barrier between your computer and others on the Internet
9. **Worm**   **c.** A program you open that infects your computer
10. **Certificate**   **d.** A program you don't need to open for it to infect your computer
11. **Firewall**   **e.** A statement that verifies the identity of a person or the security of a Web site

Select the best answer from the list of choices.

12. **Which of the following is *not* considered malware?**
    - **a.** Virus
    - **b.** SpyNet
    - **c.** Worm
    - **d.** Trojan horse

13. **Which of the following programs protects you from viruses?**
    - **a.** Antivirus
    - **b.** SpyNet
    - **c.** Windows Defender
    - **d.** Windows Update

14. **Which of the following creates a protective barrier between your computer and the Internet?**
    - **a.** Definition
    - **b.** Firewall
    - **c.** Content Advisor
    - **d.** Digital ID

15. **Which of the following is *not* a security zone?**
    - **a.** Internet
    - **b.** Intranet
    - **c.** Trusted sites
    - **d.** Restricted sites

16. **Which of the following are types of certificates?**
    - **a.** Personal and Web site
    - **b.** Trusted and approved
    - **c.** Trusted and personal
    - **d.** Personal and approved

17. **Which of the following is also known as a certificate?**
    - **a.** Definition
    - **b.** Digital ID
    - **c.** Cookie
    - **d.** Port

18. **Which of the following is *not* an Internet file cleanup operation?**
    - **a.** Cookies
    - **b.** History
    - **c.** Favorites
    - **d.** Passwords

19. **Which of the following is *not* a Family Safety option?**
    - **a.** Web restrictions
    - **b.** Windows Store and game restrictions
    - **c.** Time limits
    - **d.** App restrictions

Skills Review

1. **Explore the Action Center.**
   - **a.** Open the Control Panel.
   - **b.** Open the System and Security window.
   - **c.** Open the Action Center window.
   - **d.** Expand each of the Action Center areas.
   - **e.** Go back to the System and Security window.

2. **Manage Windows Firewall.**
   - **a.** Open the Windows Firewall window.
   - **b.** Open the Allowed apps dialog box.
   - **c.** Change program exceptions to deselect Windows Media Player Network Sharing Service (Internet).
   - **d.** Go back to the System and Security window.

3. **Manage Automatic Updates.**
   - **a.** Open the Windows Update window.
   - **b.** View the update history.
   - **c.** Open the Change settings window.
   - **d.** Check for updates. (*Stop*: Don't install any updates without permission.)
   - **e.** Go back to the System and Security window.

Skills Review (continued)

4. Defend against malicious software.

  a. Open the Windows Defender window. (*Hint*: Use the Search Control Panel box.)

  b. Check for new definitions if necessary.

  c. If prompted, grant permission to make security changes.

  d. Perform a full scan.

  e. Display Windows Defender history.

  f. View Allowed items and options.

  g. Close the Windows Defender window.

5. Set up Internet security.

  a. Open the Network and Internet window.

  b. Open the Internet Properties dialog box, then display security settings.

  c. Change the security level.

  d. Display trusted sites.

  e. Add a site to the trusted sites zone.

  f. Remove the added site.

  g. Close the Trusted sites dialog box.

6. Protect your Internet identity.

  a. Display content settings in the Internet Properties dialog box.

  b. Open the Certificates dialog box.

  c. Import the file **WIN G-1.cer** from the location where you store your Data Files into the Other People tab.

  d. Remove the certificate.

  e. Close the Certificates dialog box.

7. Protect your Internet privacy.

  a. Display privacy settings in the Internet Properties dialog box.

  b. Change the privacy level to Low.

  c. Close the Internet Properties dialog box without accepting any changes.

  d. Start Internet Explorer.

  e. Visit a Web page other than your home page and access a Web page privacy report.

  f. Close the report and Internet Explorer.

8. Delete Internet information.

  a. Open the Internet Properties dialog box, then display the Delete Browsing History dialog box.

  b. Delete temporary Internet files, yet retain Preserve Favorites website data.

  c. Delete cookies.

  d. Close the Delete Browsing History dialog box.

  e. Open the Settings dialog box for Browsing history, review the settings, then close it without making any changes.

  f. Close the Internet Properties dialog box.

9. Set Family Safety controls.

  a. Open the Family Safety window.

  b. If prompted, grant permission to make security changes.

  c. Select a user account to change parental controls.

  d. Set time restrictions.

  e. View the App Restrictions window, then close it without making any changes.

  f. Close the Family Safety window.

Independent Challenge 1

You work at a small pet shop supply company called PetStop. Because you have experience with computers and the Internet, your manager asks you to set Internet security and privacy settings for the company computers.

    a. Open the Internet Properties dialog box from the Control Panel.
    b. Display the security settings, then change the security level for the Internet to High.
    c. Display privacy settings, then change the privacy level to High.
    d. Delete cookies and temporary Internet files, yet preserve Favorites.
    e. Close the Internet Properties dialog box and the Control Panel without accepting any changes.

Independent Challenge 2

You are the network administrator at Robotz, Inc., a toy company that specializes in the production and distribution of robots. You want employees to update their computer systems with the latest Windows 8 system updates. You access Windows Update and determine which components you want the employees to install.

    a. Open the Windows Update window from the Control Panel.
    b. Check for updates.
    c. View Installed Updates.
    d. View the update history.
    e. Check Windows Update settings for your computer.
    f. Close the Windows Update window.

Independent Challenge 3

You manage an international computer security company called Secure-One International. You want to test your security system with noncertified certificates. Gary O'Neal, an employee, was asked to create his own certificate and try to pass it off as an authorized certificate from a trusted Certification Authority.

    a. Open the Internet Properties dialog box from the Control Panel.
    b. Display the content settings, then open the Certificates dialog box.
    c. Import the file **WIN G-2.cer** from the location where you store your Data Files into the Other People tab.
    d. Remove the Gary O'Neal certificate, then close the Certificates dialog box.
    e. Close the Internet Properties dialog box and the Control Panel without accepting any changes.

Independent Challenge 4: Explore

Even if you don't have children of your own, you might have visitors one day with children who want to play games on your computer. Rather than just letting children have access to your entire system, you want to set up a standard user account with Parental Controls.

    a. Open the User Accounts and Family Safety window from the Control Panel.
    b. Set up Family Safety for a standard user.
    c. Turn on Family Safety.
    d. Open the App Restrictions window, select the wordpad.exe check box, then close the window.
    e. With permission from your network administrator, switch to the standard user, if necessary, open the WordPad and Hearts programs to view the parental controls in place, then switch back to the administrator.
    f. Restore the Family Safety controls for the standard user.
    g. Turn off Family Safety.
    h. Close the Family Safety window.

Visual Workshop

Re-create the screen shown in **FIGURE G-20**, which shows an App Restrictions window for a user account; your specific result will differ.

FIGURE G-20

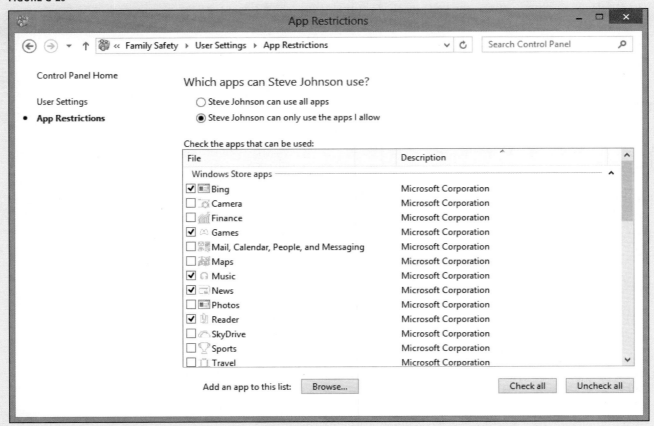

Managing Windows Devices

CASE ▶ Windows 8 allows you to install, remove, and work with devices attached to your system. As a computer specialist at Quest Specialty Travel, you often need to install, manage, and remove various hardware devices, such as printers, to keep company computers up to date.

Important: If you are concerned about changing the aspects of Windows 8 and do not wish to customize, simply read through this unit without completing the steps.

Unit Objectives

After completing this unit, you will be able to

- View Windows devices
- Install a printer
- View printer properties
- Share a printer
- Manage printers and print jobs
- Install hardware devices
- Remove hardware devices
- Use devices with apps
- Sync with other devices

Files You Will Need

Quest Travel (folder)	Hosanna (folder)
Business (folder)	June Donor.rtf
QST Focus.rtf	June State.rtf
QST Press Release.rtf	

©Itana/Shutterstock

View Windows Devices

Learning Outcomes
• View devices in PC settings
• View devices in the Control Panel

A **device** is any physical hardware that you plug into and that is controlled by your system. An example of a hardware device is a network or sound card that you install internally, or a printer or digital camera that you plug in externally. Windows 8 uses plug-and-play technology for hardware, making it easy to install and uninstall devices quickly. With **plug-and-play** support, you simply plug the device in, and Windows configures the device to work with your existing hardware and resolves any system conflicts. When you install a hardware device, Windows installs related software, known as a **driver**, which allows the hardware to communicate with Windows and other software applications. Plug and play matches up physical hardware devices with the software device drivers that operate them and establishes channels of communication between each component. With plug and play, you can be confident that any new device will work properly with your computer and that Windows will restart correctly after you install or uninstall hardware. Windows automatically notifies all other devices of any new device so there are no conflicts and manages the power requirements of your hardware and peripherals by shutting them down or conserving power when you are not using them. In addition, if you are working in another program when you install or uninstall a device, plug and play lets you know that it is about to change your configuration and prompts you to save your work. **CASE** ▶ *As the Computer Specialist at Quest Specialty Travel, part of your responsibilities is to install any new hardware devices and make sure they work properly. The Marketing Department just purchased a new printer. Before you install it, you want to check to see what devices are currently installed.*

STEPS

1. **With the Start screen in view, point to the upper-right corner and move down (on a computer) or swipe left from the right edge of the screen (on a mobile device)**

   The Charm bar opens, displaying Windows options.

2. **Click or tap the Settings button 🔧 on the Charm bar**

   The Settings panel opens, displaying settings for the Start screen at the top and Windows PC settings at the bottom.

3. **Click or tap Change PC settings on the Settings panel**

   The PC settings screen opens. The Personalize category at the top is selected in the left pane and options for that category are displayed along the top of the right pane. The Personalize category includes three options: Lock screen, Start screen, and Account picture.

4. **Click or tap Devices in the task pane of the PC settings screen**

   The Devices category is selected in the left pane and the currently installed devices appear in the right pane, as shown in **FIGURE H-1**, along with the Add a device button at the top.

5. **Point to the top edge of the screen (cursor changes to a pointing finger), then drag down to the bottom edge of the screen**

   The PC settings screen closes and the Start screen appears.

6. **With the Start screen in view, click or tap the Desktop tile**

   The Desktop opens.

7. **Point to the upper-right corner and move down (on a computer) or swipe left from the right edge of the screen (on a mobile device), click or tap the Settings button 🔧 on the Charm bar, then click or tap Control Panel on the Settings panel**

   The Control Panel window opens, displaying links to computer settings by category.

8. **Under the Hardware and Sound category, click or tap View devices and printers**

   The Devices and Printers window in the Control Panel appears, as shown in **FIGURE H-2**, displaying the currently installed devices and printers on your system.

FIGURE H-1: Viewing devices in PC settings

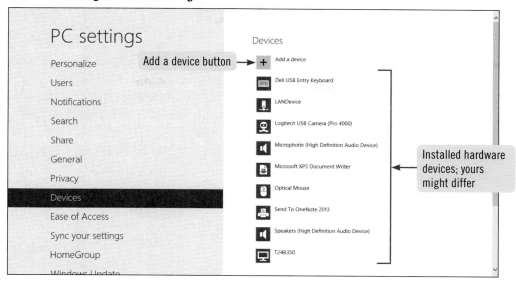

FIGURE H-2: Viewing devices in the Control Panel

Installing a plug-and-play device

To install a plug-and-play device, you need to do the following: (1) Gather your original Windows 8 installation disc(s), the hardware device that you want to install, and the program download or discs that came with the device, if available. (2) Turn off your computer before you install an internal hardware device, such as a network card or a sound card, into your computer. For some external hardware devices, such as a USB flash drive, you don't need to turn off your computer; check your device for details. (3) Follow the manufacturer's instructions to plug in or attach the new device to your computer. (4) Turn on your computer if necessary. Windows tries to detect the new device and install the device drivers. If the device driver is not available on your computer, you are prompted to insert the Windows 8 installation DVD or the manufacturer discs that come with the device to the appropriate drive. If Windows still doesn't recognize the new hardware device, it might be an older hardware device, known as a **legacy device**, which is no longer compatible. Else, the device might not be plug-and-play compatible or it might not have installed correctly. To manually install the hardware device, you can use the Add a device Wizard in the Devices and Printers window, and then follow the wizard instructions.

Install a Printer

**Learning
Outcomes**
• Install a printer
• View printers in
  the Control Panel

To install a printer, you do not need to shut down your computer. Simply attach the printer cable to the appropriate connector on your computer, according to the manufacturer's instructions, and plug in the power cord. If you connect your printer to your computer through a USB port, Windows should automatically detect the new hardware device and install the printer. If Windows doesn't detect your printer, you can also use the Add Printer Wizard to manually perform the task. The Add Printer Wizard asks you a series of questions to help you install either a network or local printer, establish a connection, and print a test page. A **local printer** is a printer that is directly connected to your computer, whereas a **network, wireless**, or **Bluetooth printer** is one that is connected to either a wired or wireless network to which you have access. **Bluetooth** is a wireless short-range radio connection aimed at simplifying communications among Internet devices and between devices and the Internet. **CASE** ▸ *The Marketing Department at Quest Specialty Travel is trying out a new HP Color LaserJet 9500 printer. You want to install the driver for the new printer so they can evaluate its performance in relation to their color printing needs.*

STEPS

1. **With the Devices and Printers window still in view, click or tap** Add a printer **on the toolbar**
   The Add Printer Wizard dialog box opens, then searches for any existing local or network printers.

2. **Click or tap** The printer that I want isn't listed
   The Add Printer Wizard dialog box opens, as shown in **FIGURE H-3**, asking you to select one of four options to find a printer: shared, TCP/IP address-based, Bluetooth or wireless network, or local printer.

3. **Click or tap the** Add a local printer or network printer with manual settings option button**, if necessary, then click or tap** Next
   The next wizard dialog box appears, asking which port you want to use with this printer. A **port** is the physical location on your computer where you connect the printer cable. You can connect the cable to either a printer port, which is labeled LPT1 or LPT2, to a communications port, which is labeled COM1 or COM2, or to a Universal Serial Bus port, which is labeled USB. A printer port is called a **parallel port**, as it can send more than 1 byte simultaneously. A communications port is called a **serial port** because it can send information only 1 byte at a time. A **USB port** is an external hardware interface that enables you to connect a USB device as a plug-and-play device. A single USB port can be used to connect up to 127 peripheral devices, such as mice, and keyboards, and supports data transfer rates of 480 Mbps (480 million bits per second).

4. **Click or tap the** Use an existing port option button **if necessary, make sure the recommended port (typically LPT1) is selected in the list box, then click or tap** Next
   The next wizard dialog box appears, asking you to select a printer.

5. **Scroll down the Manufacturer list, click or tap** HP**, click or tap** HP Color LaserJet 9500 PCL6 Class Driver **or another similar available printer in the Printers list, then click or tap** Next
   The next wizard dialog box appears; HP Color LaserJet 9500 PCL6 Class Driver appears as the printer name.

6. **In the Printer name text box, click or tap** Next **to accept the name, click or tap the** Do not share this printer option button**, then click or tap** Next
   The next wizard dialog box appears, asking if you want to set the printer as the default and print a test page. When you start a print job without specifying a particular printer, the job is sent to the **default printer**. The default printer is indicated in the Printers folder with a green circle containing a check mark. Printing a test page is an important final step to make sure the printer is working properly. However, in this example, the printer is not connected, so you do not print a test page.

TROUBLE
If a dialog box opens informing you that Windows 8 needs to install a printer driver, insert the Windows 8 installation disc in the appropriate drive, click or tap OK. Otherwise, click or tap Cancel, then click or tap OK.

7. **Click or tap the** Set as the default printer **check box to deselect it, if available, then click or tap** Finish
   The Devices and Printers window reopens with the new printer, as shown in **FIGURE H-4**.

FIGURE H-3: Add Printer Wizard dialog box

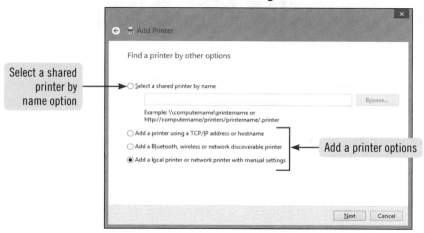

Select a shared printer by name option

Add a printer options

FIGURE H-4: Devices and Printers window with the new printer

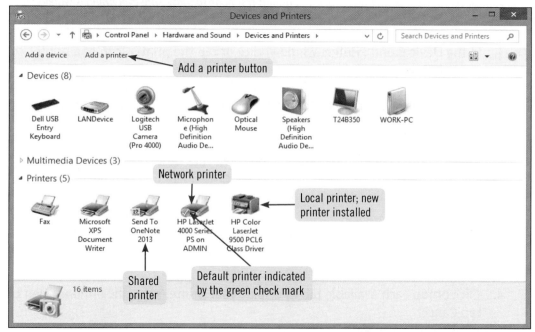

Add a printer button

Network printer

Local printer; new printer installed

Shared printer

Default printer indicated by the green check mark

Understanding printers

Although there are many different kinds of printers, there are two main categories: ink- or bubble-jet, and laser. An **ink-jet printer** works by spraying ionized ink at a sheet of paper. Ink-jet printers are less expensive and considerably slower than laser ones, but still produce a good quality output. A **laser printer** utilizes a laser beam to produce an image on a drum, which is rolled through a reservoir of toner and transferred to the paper through a combination of heat and pressure. Laser printers are faster and produce a higher-quality output than ink-jets, but are also more expensive. Printers are classified by two main characteristics: resolution and speed. Printer resolution refers to the sharpness and clarity of a printed page and is measured by the number of dots per inch (dpi). For example, a 300-dpi printer is one that is capable of printing 300 distinct dots in a line one-inch long, or 90,000 dots per square inch. The higher the dpi, the sharper the print quality. Printer speed is measured in pages per minute (ppm); the higher the ppm, the faster the print speed. In general terms, ink-jet printers range from about 4 to 10 ppm, while laser printers range from about 10 to 30 ppm. The speed depends on the page's contents; text and/or one-color pages will print faster than those containing graphics and/or using multiple colors.

View Printer Properties

Learning Outcomes
• View printer status
• View printer properties

Once you install a printer, it appears in the Devices and Printers window and is accessible in the Print dialog box for all of the programs installed on the computer. You can view printer properties to get information about a printer's computer connection or network location, sharing options, related software drivers, color management options, graphics settings, installed fonts, and other advanced settings, such as spooling. **Spooling**, also known as **background printing**, is the process of storing a temporary copy of a file on the hard disk and then sending the file to the print device. Spooling allows you to continue working with the file as soon as it is stored on the disk instead of having to wait until the file is finished printing. In addition to printer properties, you can also view and change personal printer preferences, such as orientation, page order, pages per sheet, paper size, paper tray selection, copy count, and print quality and color. When you change personal printing preferences from the Devices and Printers window, the default settings are changed for all documents you print to that printer. You can also change personal printing preferences from the Print or Page Setup dialog boxes within a program. In this case, the settings are changed only for the individual document you are printing. **CASE** ▶ *After installing the new printer, you decide to check printer properties and print a test page to make sure everything is working properly.*

STEPS

TROUBLE
If a connected printer is not available, click or tap the icon for the HP Color LaserJet 9500 PCL6 Class Driver.

1. **In the Devices and Printers window, click or tap the printer icon of a printer connected to your system**

   When you select a printer icon, status information for that printer appears in the Details pane at the bottom of the window, as shown in **FIGURE H-5**, and, if the window is in Tiles view, status information appears under the icon. The status information includes the number of documents to be printed and whether the printer is ready to print.

2. **Right-click or tap-hold the printer icon, then click or tap Printer properties**

   The Properties dialog box opens displaying the General tab, similar to the one shown in **FIGURE H-6**. **TABLE H-1** describes the printer Properties tabs in the dialog box; your tabs might differ.

3. **Click or tap Preferences**

   The Printing Preferences dialog box opens, displaying your printer's specific options. Tabs and options vary from printer to printer. When you change these printing preferences, the default settings are changed for all documents you print to this printer.

4. **Click or tap each available tab to display your printer's specific options, then click or tap Cancel**

   The Properties dialog box opens, displaying the General tab.

TROUBLE
If you do not have a printer connected to your computer, skip to Step 5.

5. **Click or tap Print Test Page**

   The page prints, and then a dialog box opens, asking if the test page printed correctly.

6. **Click or tap Close in the dialog box, then click or tap the Ports tab in the Properties dialog box**

   The Ports tab displays a list of ports available on the computer. A check mark appears in the check box next to the port to which the printer is connected.

7. **Click or tap the Advanced tab**

   The Advanced tab displays the printer's current driver and indicates your specific printing choices, including print spooling options.

8. **Click or tap Cancel**

   The printer Properties dialog box closes and the Devices and Printers window reopens.

FIGURE H-5: Devices and Printers window with a selected printer

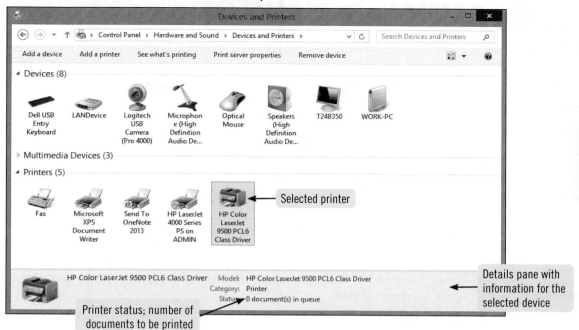

Selected printer

Details pane with information for the selected device

Printer status; number of documents to be printed

FIGURE H-6: HP Color LaserJet 9500 PCL6 Class Driver Properties dialog box with the General tab displayed

Title of the Properties dialog box reflects the name of the printer

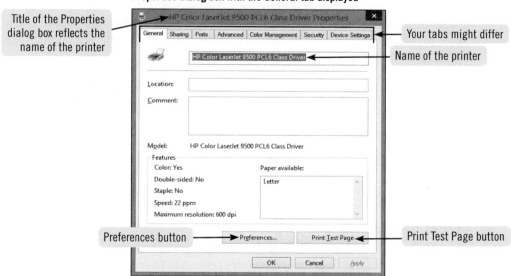

Your tabs might differ

Name of the printer

Preferences button

Print Test Page button

TABLE H-1: Printer options tabs in the printer Properties dialog box

tab	description
General	Lists general information about the printer and allows you to print a test page
Sharing	Allows you to share the printer over a network
Ports	Lists the printer's connection port and software drivers
Advanced	Lists software drivers and allows you to change printer options
Color Management	Allows you to adjust color settings and select color profiles to correctly print colors for a specific printer
Security	Allows you to set permissions to print and manage printers and documents
Device Settings	Allows you to change printer device and related settings

Share a Printer

If you have a printer connected to your computer and your computer is connected to a network, you can share your printer with other network users. This type of printer is called a **shared printer**. Before you can share a printer, you need to turn on printer sharing in the Network and Sharing Center window, which you can accomplish by using the Sharing tab in the printer Properties dialog box. A shared printer is indicated by an icon of two heads attached to the printer icon in the Devices and Printers window. For security purposes, if Windows Firewall is enabled (the default setting) on the computer with the shared printer, you need to select the File and Printer Sharing check box in Allowed apps in Windows Firewall for others to use the shared printer. **CASE** ▶ *Because all of the employees in the Marketing Department need to use the new printer, you want to set it up for sharing over the network.*

STEPS

1. **In the Devices and Printers window, right-click or tap-hold the** HP Color LaserJet 9500 PCL6 Class Driver icon, **click or tap** Printer properties, **then click or tap the** Sharing tab

   The HP Color LaserJet 9500 PCL6 Class Driver Properties dialog box opens displaying the Sharing tab options, as shown in **FIGURE H-7**.

2. **Click or tap** Network and Sharing Center

   The Network and Sharing Center window opens, displaying network and sharing options.

3. **Click or tap** Change advanced sharing settings **in the task pane**

   The Advanced sharing settings window displays the current settings for the printer, as shown in **FIGURE H-8**. To share your printer with other network users, you need to enable the Turn on file and printer sharing option. If you want to password protect the use of your shared printer, you need to enable the Turn on password protected sharing option (scroll down the Advanced sharing settings window to locate this option, then expand All Networks to view it).

4. **Click or tap the** Close button ▨×▨ **in the Advanced sharing settings window**

   The Advanced sharing settings window closes and the printer Properties dialog box reopens without any changes to the current printer settings.

5. **Click or tap the** Share this printer check box **to select it, if available**

   The additional print sharing options now available are listed in the printer Properties dialog box, as shown in **FIGURE H-9**. The name of the printer appears as the share name for the printer in the Share name text box and the Render print jobs on client computers check box is selected by default. This option spools print jobs on the user's computer instead of the computer with the shared printer.

6. **Click or tap** Additional Drivers, **if available**

   The Additional Drivers dialog box opens, displaying the drivers available for installation if your printer is going to be used by other users running different versions of Windows.

7. **Click or tap** Cancel, **if available, or skip to Step 8**

   The printer Properties dialog box reopens.

8. **Click or tap** OK **to close the HP Color LaserJet 9500 PCL6 Class Driver Properties dialog box**

   The Devices and Printers window reopens. Two heads appear ▨ in the lower-left corner of the HP Color LaserJet 9500 PCL6 Class Driver printer icon, indicating that the printer is a shared printer.

FIGURE H-7: HP Color LaserJet 9500 PCL6 Class Driver
Properties dialog box with the Sharing tab displayed

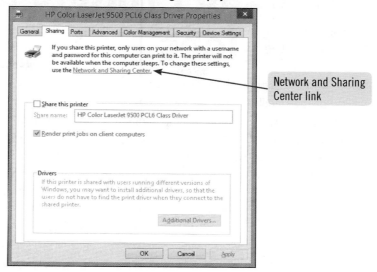

Network and Sharing
Center link

FIGURE H-8: Advanced sharing settings window

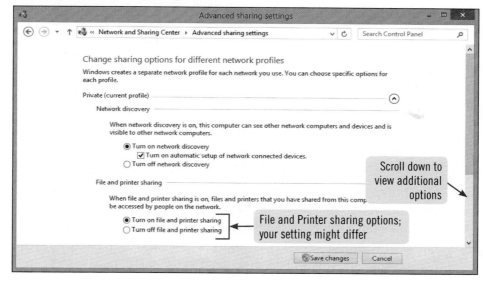

Scroll down to
view additional
options

File and Printer sharing options;
your setting might differ

FIGURE H-9: Printer sharing options

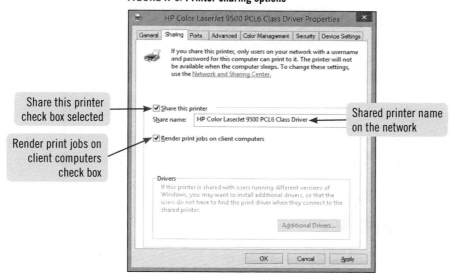

Share this printer
check box selected

Render print jobs on
client computers
check box

Shared printer name
on the network

Windows 8

**Learning
Outcomes**
• Pause a printer
• Pause and cancel a
  print job

Manage Printers and
Print Jobs

After you send a print job to the printer, you can check the status. To get quick status, you can display Tiles view or the Details pane with a selected device in the Devices and Printers window. To manage one or more print jobs, you can open the appropriate printer icon in the Devices and Printers window or on the taskbar in the notification area. A window opens showing the **print queue**, which is the list of files to be printed. You can use this window to cancel print jobs, temporarily pause print jobs, view printer properties, and so on. If you are having problems with a printer or print job, you can **defer**, or halt, the printing process to avoid receiving error messages. With deferred printing, you can send a job to be printed even if your computer is not connected to a printer. To do this, you pause printing, and the file remains in the print queue until you turn off pause printing. **CASE** > *Because multiple employees in the Marketing Department are using the shared printer, you want to show them how to manage their individual print jobs, including how to pause a printer and cancel print jobs. Because you are not actually printing to an existing printer, you will use deferred printing in this lesson.*

STEPS

QUICK TIP
To print a document
in an Explorer
window, right-click
or tap-hold the
document icon, then
click or tap Print.

1. **In the Devices and Printers window, click or tap the** HP Color LaserJet 9500 PCL6 Class Driver icon **if necessary, click or tap** See what's printing **on the toolbar, click or tap** Printer **on the menu bar, then click or tap** Pause Printing

    The HP Color LaserJet 9500 PCL6 Class Driver window opens with Paused listed after the printer name in the title bar. The Pause printing command prevents the computer from attempting to send a print job to the printer.

2. **Point to the upper-right corner and move down (on a computer) or swipe left from the right edge of the screen (on a mobile device), click or tap the** Search button 🔎 **on the Charm bar, type** WordPad, **then click or tap the** WordPad tile **to open the program**

3. **Click or tap the** File tab button `File`, **click or tap** Open, **navigate to the location where you store your Data Files, double-click or double-tap the** Quest Travel folder, **double-click or double-tap the** Business folder, **then double-click or double-tap** QST Focus.rtf **to open it**

QUICK TIP
To get printer status,
point to the printer
icon 🖶 in the noti-
fication area of the
taskbar.

4. **Click or tap** `File`, **click or tap** Print, **click or tap the** HP Color LaserJet 9500 PCL6 Class Driver icon **in the Print dialog box, as shown in** FIGURE H-10, **if necessary, then click or tap** Print

    A pop-up notification briefly appears on the screen telling you that the file was sent to the paused printer, and a printer icon appears in the notification area on the taskbar, indicating that print jobs are pending. Because you paused the printer, nothing prints; the job simply remains in the print queue until you either delete the job or unpause the printer.

QUICK TIP
To print the paused
file, right-click or
tap-hold the file,
then click or tap
Resume.

5. **Click or tap the** Close button ⊠ **in WordPad to exit the program**

    The HP Color LaserJet 9500 PCL6 Class Driver – Paused window opens, as shown in **FIGURE H-11**. The window displays the printer status in the title bar and the print job currently in the queue.

QUICK TIP
To delete a single file
from the print queue,
select the file, click or
tap Document on the
menu bar, click or
tap Cancel, then click
or tap Yes to confirm.

6. **In the HP Color LaserJet 9500 PCL6 Class Driver – Paused window, right-click or tap-hold** QST Focus.rtf, **then click or tap** Pause **to change the printing status for the file**

7. **Click or tap** Printer **on the menu bar, click or tap** Cancel All Documents, **then click or tap** Yes **to confirm the cancellation of all print jobs from the queue**

8. **Click or tap** ⊠ **in the HP Color LaserJet 9500 PCL6 Class Driver window**

    The printer window is closed and the Devices and Printers window appears.

FIGURE H-10: Printing a file to a paused printer

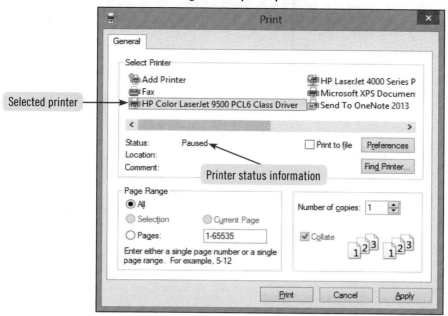

Selected printer →

Printer status information

FIGURE H-11: HP Color LaserJet 9500 PCL6 Class Driver window with paused print jobs

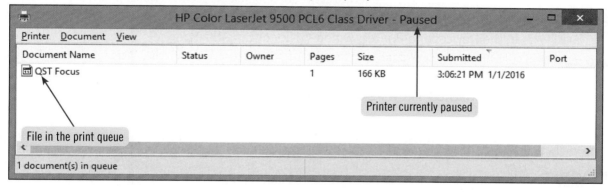

Printer currently paused

File in the print queue

Creating and viewing an XPS document

If you ever used Adobe Reader to view a document or create a PDF document, you can accomplish the same type of tasks with Microsoft's XPS (XML Paper Specification). With XPS, you can share files with others even if your software programs are different. In addition, you can set permissions and add digital signatures to protect a document from unauthorized viewing and printing. You create an XPS document by printing a file using the Microsoft XPS Document Writer printer. The XPS Viewer—available in Windows 8—allows you to open any XPS document. When you open an XPS document, it looks the same on the destination as it would on the source computer. To create and view an XPS document, open the program and document you want to create as an XPS document, click or tap File on the menu bar, click or tap Print, select Microsoft XPS Document Writer as your printer, click or tap Print, specify a location, name the XPS document, then click or tap Save. Return to the start screen, type xps, click or tap XPS Viewer, click or tap File on the menu bar, click or tap Open, navigate to and select the XPS document you want to view, click or tap Open, then use the buttons on the toolbar to set and remove security permissions, add a **digital signature** (an electronic stamp like a written signature), print the document, or change the view percentage. When you're done, click or tap the Close button.

Install Hardware Devices

Before you install a new hardware device, be sure to carefully read the product documentation and installation guide provided by the manufacturer. If the hardware device comes with an installation disc, it is recommended that you do not use the Add a device Wizard provided by Windows 8. Instead, you should use the manufacturer's disc and related instruction to install the hardware. If the product documentation instructs you to perform a typical plug-and-play installation, you need to physically connect your hardware to the computer. In most cases, Windows automatically detects your new hardware device and installs its related device driver software. If Windows doesn't detect the new hardware, you can start the Add a device Wizard in the Devices and Printers window and select the new hardware device to install it. The wizard detects the hardware attached to your computer and asks you a series of questions to help you set up the necessary software for the new hardware device to work properly on your computer. **CASE** ▶ *The Marketing Department just received a new digital camera for an upcoming project. In order to test it, you want to connect and install the hardware device to your computer. If Windows 8 doesn't automatically install the device, you use the Add a device Wizard to search for and install it.*

STEPS

 If you do not have a hardware device, simply read through the rest of the unit without completing the steps.

1. **Attach a hardware device to your computer, then wait for Windows to detect and install it**

   Windows 8 automatically tries to detect and install the hardware device, in this case a Canon PowerShot A595 IS digital camera, and its related device driver software, as shown in **FIGURE H-12**. If the hardware device is automatically installed by Windows 8, skip to the next lesson; otherwise, continue with the next step.

2. **In the Devices and Printers window, click or tap Add a device on the toolbar**

   The Add a device Wizard opens and starts to search for any attached hardware devices, as shown in **FIGURE H-13**.

   TROUBLE
   If the hardware device doesn't appear in the Add a device Wizard, click or tap Cancel.

3. **If the attached hardware device appears in the list, select the device icon, then click or tap Next**

4. **Follow the Add a device Wizard instructions to complete the installation; steps vary depending on the hardware device**

   TROUBLE
   If the Windows 8 installation disc is not available, skip Step 5, click or tap OK, then click or tap Cancel.

5. **If necessary, insert the Windows 8 installation DVD in the appropriate drive, click or tap OK, then click or tap the Close button ⊠ in the Windows 8 DVD window**

   Windows installs the appropriate driver to complete the installation. The newly installed hardware device appears in the Devices and Printers window.

FIGURE H-12: Windows 8 detects and installs a hardware device

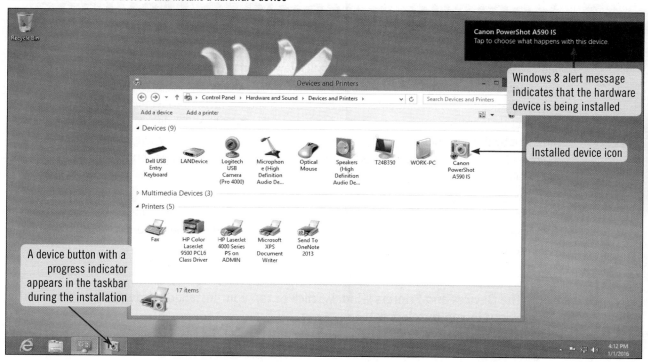

Windows 8 alert message indicates that the hardware device is being installed

Installed device icon

A device button with a progress indicator appears in the taskbar during the installation

FIGURE H-13: Add a device Wizard

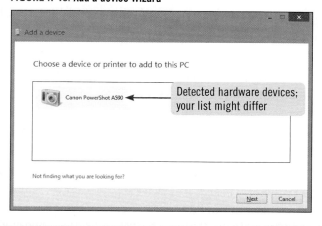

Detected hardware devices; your list might differ

Managing devices

When you install a new operating system, such as Windows 8, it is important to make sure that you are using the latest software drivers with your system hardware. If not, your hardware devices might not work properly. You can view your system hardware using a Windows utility called Device Manager. **Device Manager** organizes all the hardware devices attached to your computer by hardware types, also known as **hardware classes**. If an exclamation point within a yellow triangle icon appears next to a specific device, it indicates a conflict with some other device. To fix it, you can try to uninstall and reinstall the device or seek technical support from the device manufacturer. With Device Manager, you can determine the software driver versions being used with your system hardware, update the software driver with a newer version, roll back to a previous driver version if the device fails with the new one, or uninstall a driver. After viewing your software driver version numbers, you can contact the manufacturer or visit their Web site to determine the latest versions. Most manufacturers allow you to download drivers from their Web sites for free. To display device properties and view device drivers, open the Control Panel in the Desktop app, click or tap the Hardware and Sound link, click or tap the Device Manager link under Devices and Printers, then click or tap Yes to grant permission to make changes, if necessary. Select the device that you want to view; click or tap the Expand indicator, if necessary, to display the device. To view device properties, click or tap the Properties button on the toolbar. To update software drivers, click or tap the Update Driver Software button on the toolbar. To remove a device, click or tap the Uninstall button on the toolbar.

Remove Hardware Devices

Learning Outcomes
• Remove a device in the Control Panel
• Remove a device in PC settings

If you no longer use a hardware device, or you have an older hardware device that you want to upgrade, you can easily remove it from your computer. Before you remove the physical hardware device from your computer, however, you need to remove the hardware device drivers and related software. If the documentation for the hardware device recommends a specific method to remove a device, then use the manufacturer's instructions to remove it. For example, if you have a USB device, in many cases, you can remove it by simply unplugging it when the device is not actively in use. To ensure a hardware device is not in use and properly removed, Windows recommends using the Remove device button in the Devices category in PC settings or Devices and Printers window in the Control Panel. If you're familiar with the Device Manager, you can also remove hardware devices and any related device drivers. **CASE** *The marketing manager decides that the new printer and digital camera would be best suited to the needs of the Advertising Department. You want to delete the printer and digital camera and the related hardware device drivers that you installed.*

STEPS

1. **In the Devices and Printers window, click or tap your installed hardware device from the previous lesson to select it**

   The hardware device, in this case the Canon PowerShot A590 IS digital camera, is selected in the Devices and Printers window, as shown in **FIGURE H-14**.

2. **Click or tap the Remove device button on the toolbar**

   The Remove Device dialog box opens, asking if you want to delete the hardware device.

3. **Click or tap Yes to confirm the deletion**

   The Devices and Printers window reopens without your hardware device listed.

4. **Point to the top edge of the screen (cursor changes to a pointing finger), then drag down to the bottom edge of the screen**

   The Desktop app closes and the Start screen appears.

5. **With the Start screen in view, point to the upper-right corner and move down (on a computer) or swipe left from the right edge of the screen (on a mobile device), click or tap the Settings button ⚙ on the Charm bar, then click or tap Change PC settings on the Settings panel**

   The PC settings screen opens. The Personalize category at the top is selected in the task pane and options for that category are displayed along the top of the right pane. The Personalize category includes three options: Lock screen, Start screen, and Account picture.

6. **Click or tap Devices in the task pane of the PC settings screen, then click or tap the HP Color LaserJet 9500 PCL6 Class Driver icon**

   The Devices category is selected in the task pane and the currently installed devices appear in the right pane, as shown in **FIGURE H-15**, along with the Add a device button at the top.

7. **Click or tap the Remove device button, then click or tap Remove to confirm**

   The PC settings screen removes the printer device. If a printer contains a print job, the Delete command will not work. You need to purge all print jobs before you can delete a printer.

8. **Point to the top edge of the screen (cursor changes to a pointing finger), then drag down to the bottom edge of the screen**

   The PC settings screen closes and the Start screen appears.

FIGURE H-14: Deleting a device in the Devices and Printers window

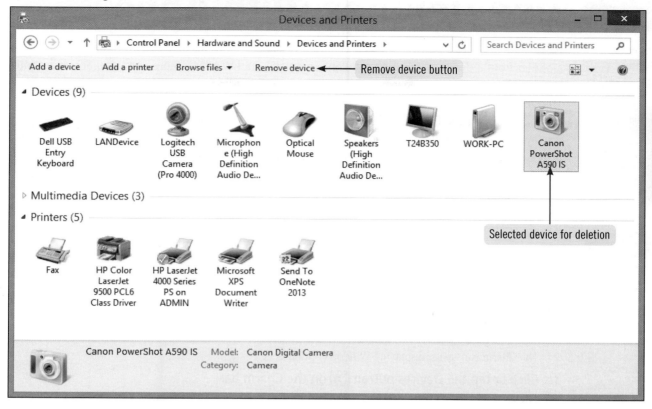

FIGURE H-15: Deleting a device in PC settings

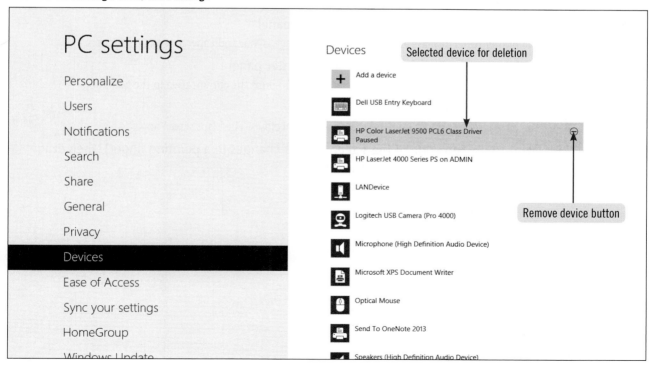

Use Devices with Apps

Learning Outcomes
• Display devices for use in apps
• Print a document in an app

Windows 8 provides different ways to access your devices. In an earlier lesson, you learned how to access a printer from a desktop app using the Print command. In a Windows Store apps, you access a printer using the Devices panel. You can access the Devices panel by using the Devices button on the Charm bar, The Devices panel allows you to work with devices attached to your system when you work with Windows Store apps. Using the Devices panel, you can print from a Windows Store app, configure a secondary display, use Play To for displaying device-based media on a compatible television, or send files to portable devices using technologies such as NFC (Near Field Communications). For example, you can print directions in the Maps app or set options to use a second screen to display more information or have more screen space to play a game. **CASE** ▶ *The Advertising Department often needs to provide hard copy directions to local suppliers. You want to print a map from the Maps app using the Devices panel to make sure it works properly.*

STEPS

1. **With the Start screen in view, click or tap the Maps tile**
   The Map app opens, displaying your current location.

2. **Point to the upper-right corner and move down (on a computer) or swipe left from the right edge of the screen (on a mobile device)**
   The Charm bar opens, displaying Windows options.

3. **Click or tap the Devices button 🖵 on the Charm bar**
   The Devices panel opens, as shown in **FIGURE H-16**, displaying a list of available devices that you can use with the app.

TROUBLE
If a printer is not available, read but do not perform Steps 4 through 7.

4. **Click or tap an available printer from the Devices panel**
   The Devices panel displays a printer panel with minimal settings to print the current page in the Maps app, as shown in **FIGURE H-17**. In this case, the options are set to print one copy of the one page.

5. **Click or tap More settings on the Devices panel**
   The printer panel displays additional options for Page layout and Paper and quality options.

6. **Click or tap the Back button ⊙ on the printer panel**
   The printer panel reappears with minimal settings to print the current page in the Maps app.

7. **Click or tap Print**
   The page is sent to the printer and the printer panel closes. The Maps screen appears.

8. **Point to the top edge of the screen (cursor changes to a pointing finger), then drag down to the bottom edge of the screen**
   The Maps app closes and the Start screen appears.

FIGURE H-16: Devices panel with available devices

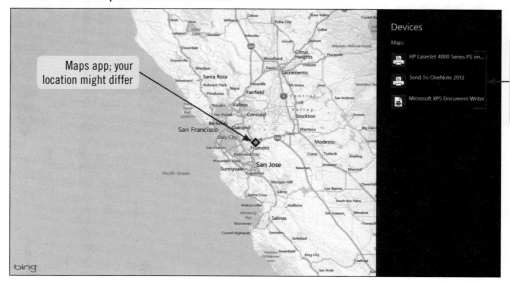

Maps app; your location might differ

Available devices for use in the Maps app; your list might differ

FIGURE H-17: Printing with the Devices panel

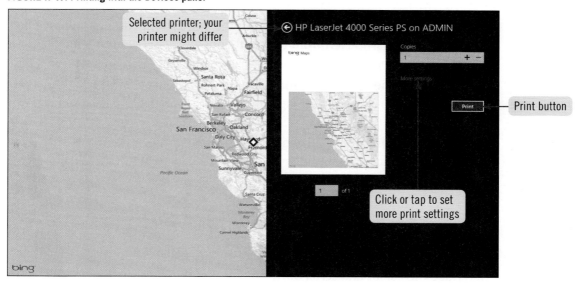

Selected printer; your printer might differ

Print button

Click or tap to set more print settings

Using a second screen

If you need more space on your desktop to work, you can add a secondary monitor to your system. This allows you to view and work with more than one full size window on the screen at the same time. For example, you can work on a document in WordPad on one monitor and search for Web content in your Web browser on the other monitor. One monitor serves as the primary display while the other serves as the secondary display. You can set the multiple displays to duplicate the displays on both monitors, extend the displays over two monitors, and show the desktop only on one or the other. In addition, you can set different screen resolutions and different orientation settings for each monitor. You can connect multiple monitors to individual video cards or to a single card that supports multiple video ports. After you connect the secondary monitor, Windows automatically detects the new device and applies the video settings best suited to the display. You can set display options on the Devices panel or in the Control Panel. In the Start screen or app, click or tap the Devices button on the Charm bar, click or tap Second screen, then select an option: PC screen only, Duplicate, Extend, or Second screen only. In the Screen Resolution dialog box, you can also set options for using multiple monitors. In the desktop, right-click or tap-hold a blank area on the desktop, click or tap Screen resolution, click or tap Detect to discover the new monitor, click or tap a monitor icon, select options for the selected monitor, click or tap OK, and then click or tap Keep changes. To arrange multiple monitors, click or tap a monitor icon and drag it in the preview to the positions you want. You can set different screen resolutions and color settings for each monitor.

Sync with Other Devices

Learning Outcomes
• View Windows 8 sync settings
• Change sync settings

If you have multiple devices, such as a desktop computer and tablet, both running Windows, you can **sync** (short for synchronize) system and app settings so they are always the same. When you sign in to Windows 8 with a Microsoft account, you can enable the system to automatically sync your system and some app settings with other devices that also sign in with the same Microsoft account. For example, if you have a desktop computer and tablet both running Windows 8 and you enable sync settings, the specified information based on the settings will automatically sync to be the same on both systems by using your Microsoft account on the cloud. In PC settings, you can enable or disable sync settings for the entire device or enable or disable individual settings. You can sync your settings on this device for personalized settings (Start screen, Lock screen, and Account picture), desktop personalization, passwords (only when trusted), Ease of Access, language preferences, app settings, browser settings, and other Windows settings, including File Explorer, mouse, and more. If your device is connected over a metered Internet connection (one based on minutes), you can specify whether to sync settings or not. **CASE** *QST recently purchased a tablet for the IT Department. You want to enable sync settings on your PC and tablet so your settings on both devices will always be the same.*

STEPS

1. **With the Start screen in view, point to the upper-right corner and move down (on a computer) or swipe left from the right edge of the screen (on a mobile device)**

   The Charm bar opens, displaying Windows options.

2. **Click or tap the Settings button ⚙ on the Charm bar**

   The Settings panel opens, displaying settings for the Start screen at the top and Windows PC settings at the bottom.

3. **Click or tap Change PC settings on the Settings panel**

   The PC settings screen opens. The Personalize category at the top is selected in the task pane and options for that category are displayed along the top of the right pane. The Personalize category includes three options: Lock screen, Start screen, and Account picture.

4. **Click or tap Sync your settings in the task pane**

   The Sync your settings category is selected in the task pane and the sync settings appear in the right pane, as shown in **FIGURE H-18**. In this case, the sync settings for the PC are enabled.

5. **Move the cursor and scroll down (on a computer) or swipe down (on a mobile device) to display all the sync options, as needed**

6. **Drag the Sync settings on this PC slider to Off, if necessary**

   Sync settings for this PC are disabled. All the sync options below it in the right pane are now unavailable, as noted by their grayed appearance. See **FIGURE H-19**.

7. **Drag the Sync settings on this PC slider to On, if the option was already enabled in Step 4**

   Sync settings for this PC are enabled again. All the sync options below it in the right pane are now available.

8. **Point to the top edge of the screen (cursor changes to a pointing finger), then drag down to the bottom edge of the screen**

   The PC settings screen closes and the Start screen appears.

FIGURE H-18: Enabled sync settings

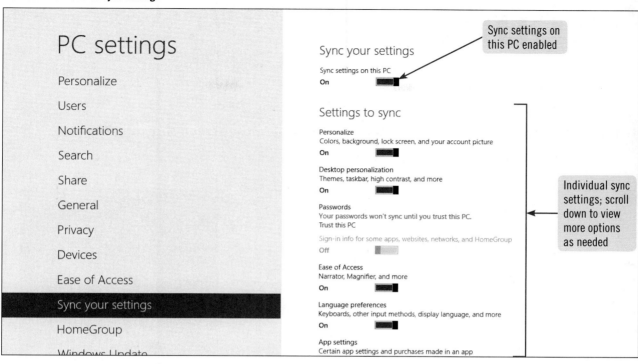

FIGURE H-19: Disabled sync settings

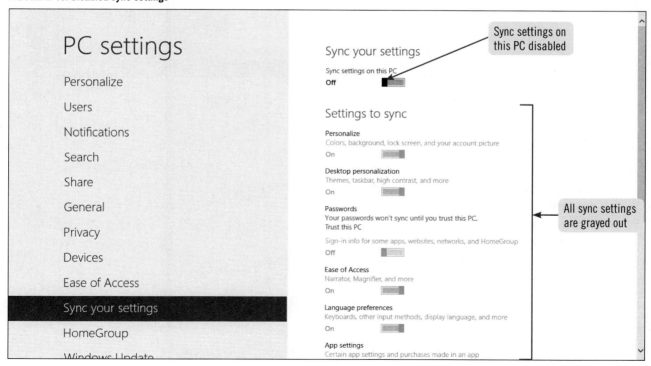

Practice

Concepts Review

Match the statements below with the elements labeled in the screen shown in FIGURE H-20.

FIGURE H-20

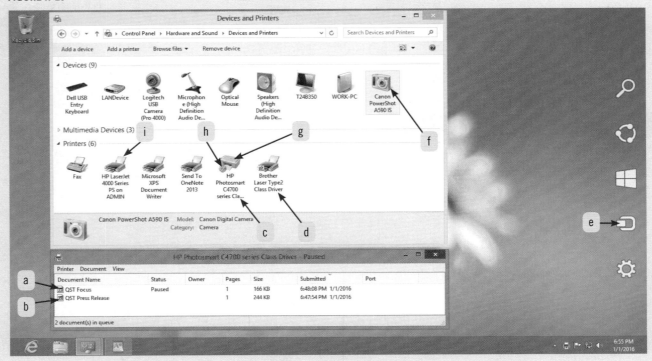

1. Which element points to a local printer?
2. Which element points to a shared printer?
3. Which element points to a network printer?
4. Which element indicates the default printer?
5. Which element points to a hardware device?
6. Which element displays hardware devices?
7. Which element points to a paused printer?
8. Which element points to a paused file?
9. Which element points to an unpaused file?

Match each term with the statement that best describes it.

10. Driver
11. Port
12. Device Manager
13. Hardware device
14. Hardware classes

a. Location on a computer where you connect a cable
b. Location where you work with device drivers
c. The way hardware communicates with Windows and other software
d. Hardware types attached to a computer
e. Any physical device you connect to a computer

Select the best answer from the list of choices.

15. When you install a hardware device, what is the related software that Windows installs called?
    - **a.** Wizard.
    - **b.** Driver.
    - **c.** Port.
    - **d.** None of the above

16. Which of the following printers is *not* connected directly to your computer?
    - **a.** Local printer
    - **b.** Shared printer
    - **c.** Network printer
    - **d.** None of the above

17. What kind of printer is indicated by an icon containing a green circle with a check mark?
    - **a.** Shared.
    - **b.** Default.
    - **c.** Local.
    - **d.** Networked.

18. What kind of printer is indicated by an icon containing two heads?
    - **a.** Shared.
    - **b.** Default.
    - **c.** Local.
    - **d.** Networked.

19. What is the physical location on the back of your computer where you connect a hardware device called?
    - **a.** Wizard.
    - **b.** Driver.
    - **c.** Port.
    - **d.** None of the above

20. Which of the following is a port name?
    - **a.** LPT1
    - **b.** COM1
    - **c.** USB
    - **d.** All of the above

21. Which of the following device connections sends information 1 byte at a time?
    - **a.** Parallel
    - **b.** Serial
    - **c.** USB
    - **d.** None of the above

22. Which of the following steps is a way to print a document?
    - **a.** Select the Print command from a program.
    - **b.** Select the printer from the Devices panel.
    - **c.** Drag a document to the printer icon.
    - **d.** All of the above

23. What is the name for an arrangement of files to be printed?
    - **a.** Print queue.
    - **b.** Print window.
    - **c.** Print spool.
    - **d.** Print list.

24. What is the process of storing a temporary copy of a file on the hard disk before sending it to be printed called?
    - **a.** Management.
    - **b.** Spooling.
    - **c.** Sharing.
    - **d.** Deferring.

25. What is the list of hardware types which are attached to your computer that Device Manager provides you with called?
    - **a.** Hardware adapters.
    - **b.** Hardware resources.
    - **c.** Hardware drivers.
    - **d.** hardware classes.

26. Which of the following locations do you enable device syncing from?
    - **a.** Control Panel
    - **b.** PC settings
    - **c.** Devices panel
    - **d.** All of the above

Skills Review

1. **View Windows devices.**
   - **a.** Open the PC settings screen, then select Devices.
   - **b.** View the installed devices, then close the PC settings screen.
   - **c.** Open the Devices and Printers window, then view the installed devices.
   - **d.** View the installed devices.

Skills Review (continued)

2. Install a printer.

    a. In the Devices and Printers window, use the Add Printer Wizard to add a local printer.

    b. Select an existing port.

    c. Choose EPSON as the manufacturer, then Epson ESC/P Standard 1 V4 Class Driver as the model. (If that model is already installed on your computer, select another printer or keep the existing driver.)

    d. Use the default printer name (do not set the printer as the default, however), then click Finish.

3. View printer properties.

    a. Select the printer icon in the Devices and Printers window for a printer connected to your computer.

    b. View the various printer properties, then view the printer preferences.

    c. Print a test page, then close the printer Properties dialog box.

4. Share a printer.

    a. Open the printer Properties dialog box for the Epson ESC/P Standard 1 V4 Class Driver printer.

    b. Open the Network and Sharing Center.

    c. Make sure file and printer sharing is turned on, then close the dialog box.

    d. Share the printer.

    e. View the additional drivers, if available, then cancel the dialog box.

    f. Close the Epson ESC/P Standard 1 V4 Class Driver Properties dialog box.

5. Manage printers and print jobs.

    a. In the Devices and Printers window, open the Epson ESC/P Standard 1 V4 Class Driver printer.

    b. Pause the printing for the Epson ESC/P Standard 1 V4 Class Driver printer.

    c. Open WordPad, navigate to the location where you store your Data Files, open the Quest Travel folder, open the Business folder, then open the QST Press Release.rtf file.

    d. Print to the Epson ESC/P Standard 1 V4 Class Driver printer, then exit WordPad.

    e. Pause the printing for the **QST Press Release.rtf** file.

    f. Cancel all documents, then confirm the cancellation.

    g. Close the Epson ESC/P Standard 1 V4 Class Driver printer window.

6. Install hardware devices.

    a. Attach a hardware device to your computer, then wait for Windows to detect and install it.

    b. In the Devices and Printers window, start the Add a device Wizard.

    c. Choose to install hardware from a list. If no choices are available, click or tap Cancel.

7. Remove hardware devices.

    a. In the Devices and Printers window, select the device installed in Step 6a.

    b. Remove the device, then close the Desktop app.

    c. Open the PC settings screen, then select Devices.

    d. Select the Epson ESC/P Standard 1 V4 Class Driver printer, then remove the device.

    e. Close the PC settings screen.

8. Use devices with apps.

    a. Open the Maps app, then display the Devices panel.

    b. Select an available printer, then print the Maps page.

    c. Close the Maps app.

9. Sync with other devices.

    a. Open the PC settings screen, then select Sync your settings.

    b. Turn off Sync settings on this PC, if necessary.

    c. Turn on Sync settings on this PC, if the option was already enabled in Step 9b.

    d. Close the PC settings screen.

Independent Challenge 1

You are an administrator at the U.S. Geological Survey and are in charge of creating earthquake reports on seismic activity in California. Your manager recently approved the purchase of a new color laser printer to help you create better reports. You want to install this printer on your computer.

a. Install a printer using the Add Printer Wizard.

b. Assume the following about the installation: The printer is local, use an open port (LPT or COM), the manufacturer is HP, and the printer model is Lexmark 6500e Series Class Driver.

c. Do not set the printer as default and do not print a test page.

d. Open the Lexmark 6500e Series Class Driver Properties dialog box, then verify that the port and printer assignments are correct.

e. Delete the printer you just added.

f. Check the properties for an existing printer connected to your computer, then print a test page.

g. Close all open windows.

Independent Challenge 2

You are the director of a youth center called Hosanna Homes for troubled teens. Half of your funding comes from the state, and the other half comes from private donations. At the end of the month, you need to send a financial report to the state indicating the status of each teen at the home. You also send a report to donors to let them know how the funds were allocated each month. You want to print the documents from WordPad to a printer attached to your computer.

a. Pause printing on an existing printer connected to your computer.

b. Using WordPad, open the file named **June State.rtf** in the Hosanna folder in the location where you store your Data Files.

c. Print the document.

d. Open the file named **June Donor.rtf** in the Hosanna folder in the location where you store your Data Files.

e. Print the document.

f. Open the printer window, then cancel the print job **June State**.

g. Click or tap Printer on the menu bar, click or tap Pause Printing to turn off Pause Printing, then print the job June Donor.

h. Check the status of the printer, then close all open windows.

Independent Challenge 3

You are the owner of Always in Focus Photography, a photography studio that specializes in wedding and location photography. As a photographer and businessperson, you want to provide the best products for your clients in the most efficient and effective way. As such, you are constantly on the lookout for new cameras and other technologies. You recently bought a new digital camera, and you need to install it.

a. Attach the hardware device to your computer.

b. If the device didn't install, start the Add a device Wizard.

c. Use the wizard to install an imaging device.

d. Display the properties for this device.

e. Remove the installed device, then close all open windows.

Independent Challenge 4: Explore

Many people have more than one computer or tablet in their homes. It is helpful to set up networks so that users can share information as well as devices such as printers. You just purchased a new photo printer and you want to share it with the other users on your network.

    a. Install a photo printer using the Add Printer Wizard.
    b. Assume the following about the installation: The printer is local, use an open port (LPT or COM), the manufacturer is HP, and the printer model is HP Photosmart C4700 series Class Driver.
    c. Do not set the printer as default and do not print a test page.
    d. Share the printer, pause the printer, then send two print jobs of your own to the printer.
    e. Delete the print jobs, delete the printer you added, then close all open windows.

Visual Workshop

Display the Devices and Printers window with the HP Photosmart C4700 series Class Driver and Brother Laser Type2 Class Driver selected, as shown in **FIGURE H-21**. Your other devices and printers will vary.

FIGURE H-21

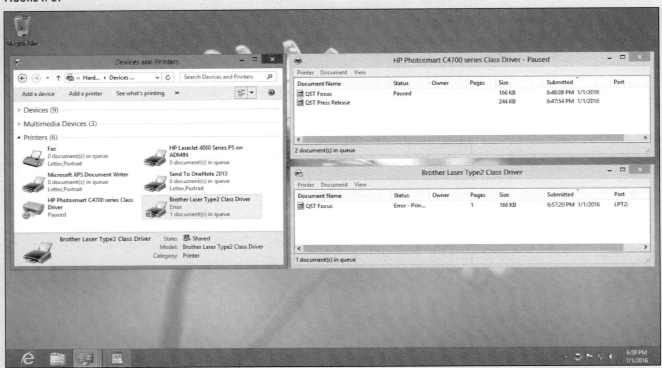

Glossary

Action Center A dedicated place in Windows that enables you to manage system security. Within this location you can view alerts and take action about security and maintenance issues with your system.

Active Refers to the window you are currently using.

Address bar Displays the address of the current Web page or the contents of a folder or local or network computer drive.

Administrator A specialized account for the person who needs to make changes to anything on the computer as well as manage user accounts.

Antivirus software A program that examines the files stored on a disk to determine whether they are infected with a virus, then destroys or disinfects them.

Applications (Apps) *See* programs.

AutoComplete A feature that suggests possible matches with previous filename entries or Web addresses.

Automatic Updating A feature that provides protection when you update your Windows software to make sure it's safe.

Background A picture that serves as your desktop's backdrop, the basic surface on which icons and windows appear; you can customize its appearance using the Desktop Background dialog box.

Background printing The process of storing a temporary copy of a file on the hard disk and then sending the file to a print device. *See* Spooling.

Blind carbon copy (Bcc) An e-mail option to send a copy of your e-mail message to another person whose name will not appear in the e-mail message.

Bluetooth A wireless short-range radio connection aimed at simplifying communications among Internet devices and between devices and the Internet.

Bluetooth printer A type of printer that is connected to either a wired or wireless network to which you have access.

Broadband High speed connections to the Internet that are continually connected and use a network setup.

Buffer A temporary memory storage area that transmits streaming media to play continuously.

Burn The process of copying files and folders to a compact disc. Also known as burning.

Cable modems Cable television lines that provide a completely digital path from one computer to another.

Calendar An app that allows you to update the appearance and organization of events and to schedule time for completing specific tasks, meetings, vacations, holidays, or for any other activity.

Carbon copy (Cc) An e-mail option to send a copy of your e-mail message.

Cascading The display of open windows in which they are presented stacked side by side and overlapping.

Case sensitive When a program makes a distinction between uppercase and lowercase letters and nonalphabetical characters (numbers and symbols).

CD or CD-ROM *See* Compact Disc-Read-Only Memory.

CD-R *See* Compact Disc-Recordable.

CD-RW *See* Compact Disc-Rewritable.

Certificate A digitally signed statement verifying the identity of a person or the security of a Web site.

Charm bar A vertical toolbar that when visible displays Search, Share, Start, Devices, and Settings options on the right-side of the screen.

ClearType A feature that smoothes out the edges of fonts on portable computers or flat screen monitors to look the same as fonts on the printed page.

Clicking (Single-clicking) The act of pressing a mouse button once and releasing it.

Clip A video, audio, or mixed media segment.

Compact Disc (CD) *See* Compact Disc-Read-Only Memory.

Compact Disc-Read-Only Memory (CD-ROM) An optical disk on which you can stamp, or burn, up to 1 GB (typical size is 650 MB) of data in only one session. The read-only disc cannot be erased or burned again with additional new data.

Compact Disc-Recordable (CD-R) A type of read-only CD on which you can burn up to 1 GB of data in multiple sessions. The disc can be burned again with additional new data, but cannot be erased.

Compact Disc-Rewritable (CD-RW) A type of CD on which you can read, write, and erase data, just like a removable or hard disk.

Computer virus A program that attaches itself to a file, reproduces itself, and spreads to other files, usually meant to cause harm to the infected computers.

Contact A person or company with whom you communicate.

Control Panel A collection of utility programs that that determine how Windows both appears and performs on your computer or device.

Conversation thread Consists of the original message on a particular topic along with any responses that include the original message.

Cookie A file created by a Web site that stores information on your computer, such as your Web site preferences or personal identifiable information, including your name and email address, when visiting that site. Also known as a first-party cookie.

Default printer The printer that a print job is automatically sent to if a particular printer is not specified.

Defer To halt the printing process to avoid receiving error messages.

Definition Instructions that determine how to defend against malicious software.

Delete To remove a file or folder from a disk.

Desktop A graphical background on screen that represents a desk.

Device Any physical hardware that you plug into and that is controlled by your system.

Device Manager A Windows utility that organizes all the hardware devices attached to your computer by hardware types.

Digital ID Another name for a certificate in some programs. *See* Certificate.

Digital signature An electronic stamp like a written signature.

Digital Subscriber Lines (DSL) Wires that provide a completely digital path from one computer to another using telephone lines.

Digital Video Disc (DVD) A type of read-only optical disc that holds a minimum of 4.7 GB (gigabytes), enough for a full-length movie.

Digital Video Recordable (DVD-R) A type of read-only DVD on which you can burn up to 4.7 GB of data in multiple sessions. The disc can be burned again with additional new data, but cannot be erased.

Digital Video Rewritable (DVD-RW) A type of DVD on which you can read, write, and erase data, just like a removable or hard disk.

Double-clicking Clicking the left mouse button twice in a row to open a window, file, or program.

Double-tapping The act of touching and removing your finger twice in a row on an item, such as a tile or icon, to select it.

Dragging The act of holding down the left mouse button or your finger and moving it in order to relocate items or text on a page.

Driver Related software that Windows installs when you install a hardware device in order for the hardware to communicate with Windows and other software applications.

DVD *See* Digital Video Disc.

DVD-R *See* Digital Video Disc-Recordable.

DVD-RW *See* Digital Video Disc-Rewritable.

Edit The process of changing the contents of a file.

Electronic mail A system used to send and receive messages electronically. Also known as e-mail.

E-mail *See* Electronic mail.

Emoticons Graphical symbols which help communicate your emotions electronically.

Events Activities that you schedule using the Calendar app for organizational purposes.

Favorites list Located in the Navigation pane, it provides links to commonly used folders and saved searches to reduce the number of clicks or taps it takes to locate a file or folder.

File An electronic collection of information that has a unique name, distinguishing it from other files.

File extension A three letter extension at the end of a filename that refers to the program Windows uses to distinguish, create, and open files of that type.

File hierarchy A logical structure for files and folders that mimics how you would organize files and folders in a filing cabinet.

File management The process of organizing and keeping track of files and folders.

Firewall A protective barrier between a computer or network and others on the Internet.

First-party cookie *See* Cookie.

Folders list A file hierarchy in the Navigation pane of a file management window that displays all drives and folders on the computer and connected networks.

Graphical user interface (GUI) Pronounced "gooey." The use of tiles, icons, thumbnails, and windows in which you can control the basic operation of a device and the programs that run on it through the use of graphics.

Gadget A mini-program that resides on the desktop.

Gesture The movement of one or more fingers on a computer touch screen or mobile device that accesses the computer's functions and "tells" it what you want it to do.

Grouping A way to display a sequential list of all of the files by heading type.

Hardware classes Hardware types that Device Manager utilizes when organizing all the hardware devices attached to your computer.

Help and Support A book stored on your computer with additional links to the Internet, complete with a search feature, an index, and a table of contents to make finding Windows-related information easier.

Hits A menu list of matched results from an Internet search.

Home page The main Web page around which a Web site is built that opens every time you start Internet Explorer.

Hyperlinks (links) Highlighted text or graphics in a Web page that open other Web pages when you click or tap them.

Icons Graphical representations or meaningful symbols on the Windows 8 Start screen intended to provide information for the items they represent, such as files and programs.

Ink-jet printer A less expensive, slower but good quality device which utilizes sprayed ionized ink.

InPrivate browsing A way browse the Web without of keeping track of browsing history, searches, temporary Internet files, form data, cookies, and user names and passwords.

Instant message(IM) An online typewritten conversation in real time between two or more contacts

Internet A global collection of millions of computers linked together to share information.

Internet account A set of connection information provided by an Internet Service Provider (ISP) or Local Area Network (LAN) administrator that allows you to access the Internet, and send and receive e-mail.

Internet Service Provider (ISP) A company that provides Internet access.

Keyword A word or phrase you submit to a search engine to find various Web sites on the Internet. *See also* Search engine.

Laser printer A print device that utilizes a laser beam in combination with heat and pressure to produce a fast, high-quality, but expensive printout.

Legacy device Older hardware devices which Windows doesn't recognize due to lack of compatibility.

Libraries Special folders that catalog specific files and folders in a central location, regardless of where the items are actually stored on your hard drive.

Linking Connecting an object created in one program to a document created in another program so that changes made will be reflected in both.

Links *See* Hyperlinks.

Live icons Thumbnails that display the first page of documents, the image of a photo, or album art for songs, making it easier to find exactly what you are looking for.

Load The process of displaying a Web page in a browser from a server.

Local printer A printer that is directly connected to your computer.

Lock screen A full screen image that appears when you first start Windows 8 consisting of time, date, and notification icons (with app status).

Loop An option that repeatedly plays a media clip until you stop it.

Malware Malicious software, such as viruses and spyware, that can delete or corrupt files and gather personal information.

Maximize A button located in the upper-right corner of the window that enlarges a window so it fills the entire screen.

Microsoft Internet Explorer A program that helps you access the World Wide Web.

Minimize A button located in the upper-right corner of the window that reduces the size of a window.

Mouse A hand-held pointing device that you roll across a flat surface (such as a desk or a mouse pad) to correspondingly move the pointer on the screen.

Multitasking Working with more than one Windows program at the same time.

Network printer A type of printer that is connected to either a wired or wireless network to which you have access.

Newsgroups Electronic discussion groups where users share information about a particular topic.

Operating system Software that controls the operation of your computer or mobile device and the applications you run on it. Windows 8 is an example of an operating system.

Outbox An email storage folder where an outgoing e-mail message is placed temporarily before it is sent automatically to the recipient.

Pane Refers to a part of a window that is divided into two or more sections.

Parallel port A printer port that can send more than 1 byte simultaneously.

Partition A section of a disk drive that behaves like a separate drive.

Path A location to a file from the drive to the folder.

Personal certificate A type of certificate that verifies your identity to a secure Web site; *see* Certificate.

Pinch in Moving your thumb and finger close together or spaced apart to correspondingly make a screen element appear smaller or larger.

Pinned Item Located at the left end of the taskbar, refers to items that are can be easily accessed to quickly start desktop apps or files.

Plug and play Technology that Windows 8 uses for hardware that makes it easy to install and uninstall devices quickly.

Pointer A small symbol on the screen that indicates current position.

Pointing Positioning the mouse pointer over an icon or over any specific item on the screen.

Pointing device Hardware connected to or built into the computer you use to position the pointer on the screen that indicates its position.

Port The physical location on your computer where you connect the printer cable.

Printing A process to create a printout.

Print queue The list of files to be printed in a print job

Program Task-oriented software you use to accomplish specific tasks, such as sending and receiving electronic mail, browsing the Internet, and managing files. Also known as applications.

Properties Information that Windows automatically adds to a file when it is created, such as the filename, creation date, modified date, and size.

Random Access Memory (RAM) A type of device memory; temporary storage space whose contents are erased when you turn off the device.

Recycle Bin A temporary storage area for deleted files that is located on your desktop.

Restore Down A button located in the upper-right corner of the window that returns a window to its previous size. Appears only when a window is maximized.

Ribbon A tab-based toolbar for easy access to commands.

Rich Text Format (RTF) A standard text format that includes formatting information and provides flexibility when working with other programs.

Right-clicking Clicking the right mouse button on an item to display a menu that lists task-specific commands.

Rip To copy individual music tracks or entire CDs to your computer and create your own jukebox or playlist of media.

ScreenTip A description of an item or relevant status information that Windows displays on your screen when you position the mouse pointer over the item.

Scroll bar A bar that appears at the bottom and/or right edge of a window whose contents are not entirely visible. Each scroll bar contains a scroll box and two scroll arrows. A scroll bar allows you to display more window content by dragging or swiping left or right or up and down.

Scroll box A box located in the vertical and horizontal scroll bars that indicates your relative position in a window. *See also* Scroll bar.

Search box A text box that searches to find installed programs and other Windows items.

Search engine A program you access through a Web site to search through a collection of information found on the Internet.

Search provider A company that provides a search engine directly from Internet Explorer to look for information found on the Internet.

Select To click an item, such as an icon, indicating that you want to perform some future operation on it.

Serial port A communications port that can send only 1 byte of information at a time.

Separation bar The vertical line that splits the screen using the snap feature.

Shared printer A type of print device that can be used with other network computers.

Shortcut A link that you can place in any location that gives you instant access to a particular file, folder, or program on your hard disk or on a network.

Shut down The action you perform when you are finished working with Windows to make it safe to turn off your computer or device.

Sign-in screen A security screen that opens when you first start Windows 8 that requires you to identify yourself on the computer or device.

Skin The Windows Media Player's appearance.

Snap A Windows 8 feature that enables you to display two apps side by side.

Sorting A way to display files and folders in alphabetical order, either A to Z or Z to A.

Sound scheme A collection of sounds associated with events.

Spam Unsolicited mass email messages.

Spooling. *See* background printing.

Spyware Software that tries to collect personal information or change computer settings without your consent.

Standard A type of computer account for people who need to manage personal files and run programs.

Start bar Contains thumbnails of currently opened apps which allow you to switch between an open app or the Start screen.

Start screen The screen that appears after you sign in to Windows 8 containing application tiles in groups with information. The Start screen provides a central place to access apps, utilities, and device settings.

Status bar Used in a program to display information about the program or currently selected item.

Streaming media A technique for transferring media so that it can be processed as a steady and continuous stream. The Windows Media Player delivers streaming video, live broadcasts, sound, and music playback over the Internet.

Swiping A type of gesture that involves dragging your finger with a flicking motion at the end of a movement.

Tags User-defined file properties.

Tapping The act of touching and removing your finger on an item, such as a tile or icon, to select it.

Taskbar A horizontal bar located at the bottom of the desktop, which allows you to start apps and switch among currently running apps.

Theme A customized user interface that includes a desktop background, screen saver, pointers, sounds, icons, and fonts based on a set subject area such as baseball, science, travel, or underwater.

Third-party cookie A file created by a Web site you are not currently viewing, such as a banner ad on the current Web site you are viewing, that stores information on your computer, such as your preferences and history.

Thumbnails *See* Icons.

Thread An instant message conversation that consists of text exchanges.

Tiles Small pictures on the Windows 8 Start screen intended to provide information for the items they represent.

Title bar The name of the document and program at the top of a window.

Toolbar Used in a program to display buttons for easy access to the most commonly used commands.

Touch Pad A pointing device for laptop or notebook computers.

Trojan Horse A program that appears to be useful and comes from a legitimate source, but actually causes problems, such as gathering personal information or deleting files.

USB port An external hardware interface that enables you to connect to a USB device as a plug and play device.

Undo A command that reverses the last change made.

Uniform Resource Locator (URL) A Web page's address.

Unpin Removing a pinned item from the taskbar.

Wallpaper *See* Background.

Winks Graphical animations that help convey your emotions electronically.

Web Part of the Internet that consists of Web sites located on computers around the world connected through the Internet.

Web address A unique address on the Internet where a Web page resides. *See also* URL.

Web browsers Software applications that you use to "surf the Web," or navigate and display Web pages.

Web pages Specially formatted documents that contain highlighted words, phrases, and graphics that open other Web pages when you click or tap them.

Web site A location on the World Wide Web that contains Web pages linked together.

Web site certificate A type of certificate that verifies its security with a Web site before you send it information. *See* Certificate.

Window Rectangular frame on your screen that can contain several icons, the contents of a file, or other usable data.

Windows Firewall A Windows feature that monitors all communication between your computer and the Internet and prevents unsolicited inbound traffic from the Internet from entering your computer.

Windows Media Player A Windows program that allows you to play video, sound, and mixed-media files.

Windows program Software designed to run on computers and devices using the Windows operating system.

Wireless connection A type of Internet connection that uses radio waves or microwaves to maintain communications.

Wireless printer A type of printer that is connected to either awired or wireless network to which you have access.

WordPad A Windows word-processing program that comes as a built-in accessory.

World Wide Web (WWW) *See* Web.

Worm A computer virus that can spread without human action across networks.

XML Paper Specification (XPS) A secure fixed-layout format—similar to an Adobe PDF file—developed by Microsoft that retains the format you intended on a monitor or printer.

Zoom button A button that appears on the Start screen when you move the pointer that allows you to change the screen size to display items smaller or larger for better viewing.

Zone Internet security areas (Internet, Local intranet, Trusted sites, and Restricted sites) where you can assign different levels of security.

Index